MINOR CREATURES

ANIMAL LIVES
Jane C. Desmond, Series Editor; Barbara J. King, Associate Editor
for Science; Kim Marra, Associate Editor

BOOKS IN THE SERIES

*Displaying Death and Animating Life: Human-Animal
Relations in Art, Science, and Everyday Life*
by Jane C. Desmond

*Voracious Science and Vulnerable Animals:
A Primate Scientist's Ethical Journey*
by John P. Gluck

*The Great Cat and Dog Massacre: The Real Story
of World War Two's Unknown Tragedy*
by Hilda Kean

*Animal Intimacies: Interspecies Relatedness
in India's Central Himalayas*
by Radhika Govindrajan

MINOR CREATURES

Persons, Animals, and
the Victorian Novel

IVAN KREILKAMP

THE UNIVERSITY OF CHICAGO PRESS

CHICAGO AND LONDON

The University of Chicago Press, Chicago 60637
The University of Chicago Press, Ltd., London
© 2018 by The University of Chicago
All rights reserved. No part of this book may be used or reproduced in any
manner whatsoever without written permission, except in the case of brief
quotations in critical articles and reviews. For more information, contact the
University of Chicago Press, 1427 E. 60th St., Chicago, IL 60637.
Published 2018
Printed in the United States of America

27 26 25 24 23 22 21 20 19 18   1 2 3 4 5

ISBN-13: 978-0-226-57623-7 (cloth)
ISBN-13: 978-0-226-57637-4 (paper)
ISBN-13: 978-0-226-57640-4 (e-book)
DOI: https://doi.org/10.7208/chicago/9780226576404.001.0001

Library of Congress Cataloging-in-Publication Data

Names: Kreilkamp, Ivan, author.
Title: Minor creatures : persons, animals, and the Victorian novel /
  Ivan Kreilkamp.
Other titles: Animal lives.
Description: Chicago ; London : The University of Chicago Press, 2018. |
  Series: Animal lives | Includes bibliographical references and index.
Identifiers: LCCN 2018016687 | ISBN 9780226576237 (cloth : alk. paper) |
  ISBN 9780226576374 (pbk. : alk. paper) | ISBN 9780226576404 (e-book)
Subjects: LCSH: Animals in literature. | English fiction—19th century—History
  and criticism. | Pets in literature. | Human-animal relationships in literature.
Classification: LCC PR468.A56 K73 2018 | DDC 823/.809362—dc23
LC record available at https://lccn.loc.gov/2018016687

♾ This paper meets the requirements of ANSI/NISO Z39.48-1992 (Permanence
of Paper).

TO CELESTE, IRIS, AND SARAH

Animals whom we have made our slaves
we do not like to consider our equals.
—Charles Darwin, Notebook B

CONTENTS

Figure 1 *Grasper, from Life,* 1834. Pencil on paper. Drawing by Emily Brontë. Brontë Parsonage Museum, Haworth, Yorkshire, UK/Bridgeman Images.

CHAPTER ONE

Home, Animal, Novel

W hat invention of eighteenth-century England develops, during the nineteenth century, into a major instance of and vehicle for the culture's high valuation of sympathy and domestic life and becomes known worldwide as a quintessential embodiment of English identity and a national self-image founded on an idealized vision of home? If the genre of the realist novel comes to mind, the modern domestic animal or pet also fits the bill. As England became known as a nation of shopkeepers, it was also preeminently associated with long novels and beloved domesticated animals, two cultural forms that, I argue in this book, developed not just in parallel but in tandem. Indeed, the history of English domestic fiction is deeply bound up with that of the domestic animal.

This book aims to offer a corrective to the fundamental anthropocentrism of our understanding of the British Victorian novel, while also arguing that a kind of anthropocentrism is in many ways inextricable from the form of the realist novel. I argue that anthropocentrically reading the genre of the novel distorts and blinds us to other forms of relation, models of personhood, and distinctions that a less purely human-focused approach would allow us to see within novels. Animals proliferate and matter in Victorian fiction in interesting and surprising ways, and their presence has shaped the genre of the novel in ways we have not yet fully recognized. The approach I am suggesting can help us understand not only (more obviously) the ways the novel depicts and thinks about animals but also (less obviously) the ways the *human* is defined and conceptualized in fiction. Peter Stallybrass and Allon White argue that "[w]hat is socially peripheral is often symbolically central" (20). One of my claims is that, in the Victorian period, the three major normative categories of the *human*, the *home*, and the *novel* are all conceptualized in relation to an animal existence that is at once marginal or excluded but symbolically central and always a shaping influence. This explains why my primary focus is on domestic or domesticated animals—cats, sheep, cattle, birds, and especially dogs. The Victorian novel serves, among other things, as a cultural form of domestication, a means of bringing animals symbolically away from pure nature into culture. Of course, human beings have been domesticating animals for many centuries. But my claim is that, beyond any simple mimetic representation of domestication and pet keeping, the Victorian novel came to depend importantly, for its repertoire of significations, on pets and pet keeping as demonstrations and proofs of the constitution of the home as a sentimentally charged space.

To view the form of the novel as anthropocentric or human-centered is by no means entirely wrong. Human beings are certainly in most obvious ways at the center of the novel as a genre. Where do we find animals, animality, or nonhuman creatures in Victorian novels? In realist novels, at least—it's a different story in children's and fantasy literature[1]—they tend to exist away from the center, at the margins: in forms, embodiments, and characterizations that are minor, ephemeral, precarious, short-lived, and disadvantaged. We might say they are in various ways thin rather than fully developed. Animals in realist texts tend to be not just quintessentially "minor" characters, as defined by Alex Woloch, but doubly so, minor even in relation to the minorness of a human minor character. If minor characters are, in Woloch's phrase, "the proletariat of the novel" (27), the animals we find in the pages of canonical Victorian fiction may be the proletariat of the proletariat, the residuum existing in a space at the threshold of representability. They are typically so minor that they often fail to register as characters or within the field of the characterological. One of this book's goals is to bring to the evolving field of literary animal studies a sharper attention than is typical within this approach to questions of literary form. For and in all of their minorness and marginality, animals do inhabit and even shape Victorian fiction in ways that have not been fully accounted for.[2]

Minor Creatures makes the case that, in the Victorian period, the genre of the realist novel became a key institution of both humanization and animalization, a procedure by which the two categories of the human and the animal could be established, maintained, and separated. The novel participates in a process of dividing up the world into humans (individuals capable, ideally or supposedly, of becoming protagonists or full-fledged characters) and nonhumans (things and animals that fall below the threshold of the characterological). The category of what Fredric Jameson has recently, in *The Antinomies of Realism*, dubbed "protagonicity" is significantly shaped in the Victorian realist novel by the marginal yet fundamental role of the animal, that being who defines the outer limit of who or what can count as a protagonist or even as a character.[3] (In this light, children's and fantasy literature of the period can be read as a generic space in which a latent desire, within the realist novel, for non-human protagonicity can be freely indulged.)

Jacques Derrida characterizes Defoe's *Robinson Crusoe*, by most accounts the inaugural text of English fictional realism, as "a long discussion between Robinson and so many beasts" that chronicles "the assertion of mastery . . . of self, over slaves, over savages and over beasts," but that in so doing also turns itself into "an immense zoology" (*Beast* 2: 28, 49). I agree with Derrida that, even from the early origins of the genre, novelists obsessively returned to the question of human-animal distinction and did so in a thoroughly anthropocentric manner, with the human/nonhuman division almost invariably redounding to the detriment or at least the minoritizing of the latter. To fall on the wrong side of this divide in a novel is to become dispensable, impermanent, precarious, only fleetingly representable, and potentially consumable as food or otherwise used as material. The capacity to be rendered as a novelistic character becomes part of what it means to be human—as Nancy Armstrong puts it, "the history of the novel and the history of the modern subject are virtually the same" (3); the novel gains power as a cultural force of meaning making and humanizing. Throughout the development of the nineteenth-century novel, we see greater and greater awareness of these dynamics—and also the beginnings of resistance to them; such resistance is especially pronounced in the later nineteenth-century fiction of Thomas Hardy and Olive Schreiner, whose work implicitly (and sometimes explicitly) questions fiction's role in humanizing and marking human/nonhuman distinctions. In this sense, then, my goal is less to deny the novel's own anthropocentrism than to call for greater awareness of this anthropocentrism as a contested and constructed status—and as an inconsistent and shifting one—and thereby to call for a less anthropocentric critical practice. Jane Bennett has recently suggested, in regard to a so-called nonhuman turn in recent critical practice, that its major goal "is to find new techniques, in speech and art and mood, to disclose the participation of nonhumans in 'our' world" ("Systems" 225). In this spirit, *Minor Creatures* aims to disclose the participation and presence of nonhumans in the human world of the nineteenth-century novel.

Novelists had, to greater and lesser degrees (but until perhaps Schreiner and Hardy, none to a *very* great degree), some inkling that novels had become crucial tools of anthropocentric humanizing, and to greater or lesser degrees they sometimes tried to resist and think around this process. Even in the most resolutely anthropocentric or human-centered novels, one can often find traces of persistent or resistant animality and reminders that consciousness, will, intentionality, signification, and the like may not be the sole province of the human.

The form of the realist novel, with its emphasis on well-developed integrated or round characters—defined against its many flat characters—took shape in such a way that the genre was almost incapable of recognizing animal or nonhuman existence. Any such recognition was visible only in the margins of canonical midcentury texts; by the later nineteenth-century novel, and in the wake of *On the Origin of Species* and then *The Descent of Man*, we begin to see new attempts to represent the animal not only with sympathy but as a kind of agency-bearing person or novelistic character—at the risk (as in Schreiner) of almost ceasing to be realist novels.

Susan Fraiman comments that, "[o]nce an obscure and idiosyncratic subfield, by 2009 . . . animal studies had been remade as a newly legitimate, high-profile area of humanities research, its status evinced by burgeoning numbers of special issues, conferences, and publications at top presses" (91). Kari Weil in her 2012 book asks, "Why animal studies now? It has become clear that the idea of 'the animal'—the instinctive being with presumably no access to language, texts, or abstract thinking—has functioned as an unexamined foundation on which the idea of the human and hence the humanities have been built" (23).[4] I first began working on the earliest pieces of this project over a decade ago, before the flourishing of animal studies, inspired primarily by three strands of scholarship. The first was the historical research of Harriet Ritvo—especially her 1987 book *The Animal Estate*—and that of other scholars that her work led me to (James Turner, Keith Thomas, Coral Lansbury, among others). Focused on the underexamined history of human-animal relations in the nineteenth century, this scholarship opened my eyes to the importance of the animal-welfare and antivivisection movements and led me to the conclusion that, of all the various reform movements in this period, the push for greater protection for animal welfare seemed to be the one given the least rigorous or sustained attention by literary and cultural critics. Animal-welfare or animal-rights politics were so often condescended to or dismissed as eccentric or marginal in the late twentieth century that I suspected the significance of these movements to nineteenth-century thought had also been underestimated. Indeed, in both centuries scholars found it difficult to recognize animal-welfare politics as something other than trivial or minor or a distraction from a more properly human set of concerns.

The second strand of scholarship that energized my initial thinking on these topics (and continues to do so) was a very different theoretical/ philosophical discourse dedicated to questions of animality, human-animal relations, and the representation of animals within Western thought. My first introduction to this discourse was Jacques Derrida's 2002 essay "The Animal That Therefore I Am (More to Follow)" (later incorporated into a book). And in the work of Cary Wolfe and others, I soon encountered a lively new scholarly conversation—now a major subfield—dedicated to analyzing the figure of the animal both in Derrida's work and in a range of other Western theorists and philosophers.[5] Among other things, this present book turned into an extended conversation with Derrida's late writings on animals and an attempt to put them to use as an interpretive resource. "Politics supposes livestock," Derrida states in a reading of Kant's *Anthropology*. "There is therefore neither socialization, political constitution, nor politics itself, without the principle of domestication of the wild animal" (*Animal* 96). I extend these claims in this book to suggest that there is no realist novel without the presence, albeit often marginal or occluded, of the animal as a potential subject of domestication or friendship.

A third crucial influence on this project has been scholarship that considers the interrelations between Darwin and Darwinian thought and Victorian literature. The two most foundational texts in this tradition are Gillian Beer's *Darwin's Plots* and George Levine's *Darwin and the Novelists*, both of which cleared the way for later work that followed their efforts to consider Darwinian subtexts, influences, and resonances in Victorian literature, especially Victorian fiction. As I began this project, even as I drew from this tradition of Darwinian scholarship, I also began to wonder if its influence had blocked certain alternative ways of conceptualizing human-animal relationships. Could our failure to pay sufficient attention to the ethical, political, and aesthetic role played by animals in Victorian culture, and in fiction specifically, be somewhat paradoxically explained by the overwhelming influence within Victorian studies of scholarship devoted to Darwin's work and legacy? The extraordinarily fruitful scholarship devoted to Darwin's work and influence, examining the links between Victorian culture and natural history, placed the 1859 publication of *On the Origin of Species* as the primary turning point in the narrative we tell about animals in the period—a narrative that tends to conceptu-

alize the "animal" as primarily "natural" rather than fully a part of the
cultural realm. But this focus may in some sense have led to the neglect of
another, related history focused more on *domesticated* and pet animals—a
history whose key dates would include 1824, the year of the founding of
the Society for the Prevention of Cruelty to Animals, and 1876, the year
of the Cruelty to Animals Act, and in which problems of ethics are as
crucial as those of science or natural history. Attention to "the Victorian
animal" has for so long been routed through *On the Origin of Species* that
we have exhaustively considered certain questions—regarding evolution,
natural section, and human-animal distinction, for example—while neglecting others no less important, especially those involving *domesticated*
animals, who may seem to belong less to nature than to culture in our
accounting. Such questions include: how should the history of Victorian
domestication and pet keeping bear upon our understanding of the Victorian home and its fictions? How are Victorian practices of sympathy and
kindness, on the one hand, and cruelty or mistreatment, on the other, defined in relation to animals? How are the categories of the individual, the
self, the character, or the protagonist defined through human-animal distinction? How does protagonicity operate in the Victorian novel through
continual worrying over the boundary between the human being (always
a potential protagonist) and the animal (always ineligible for that status)?

As I continued to work on the project, however, it became clear to me
that even if certain aspects of Darwin's work—and of his legacy—may
have blocked recognition of the animal as a figure within culture (rather
than "nature"), a rereading of certain of Darwin's texts from a slightly
different perspective offers a crucial resource for such a consideration. As
Cannon Schmitt puts it, Darwin defined "a new and enduring human subject in the nineteenth century. . . . The human in question was decisively
modern because thoroughly biological and 'natural': an animal among animals, a product of inexorable laws working themselves out over the course
of profane, sublunary time no less than beetles or monkeys" (3). But if Darwin's human was "thoroughly biological and 'natural'" (and animal), then
the converse could also be said to be true: Darwin's *animal* was, surprisingly often, domesticated and "cultural." We may think of Darwin primarily as arguing for a wildness or animality within the human, but he was
also fascinated by a domestication or human influence within the animal.
His less read *The Variation of Animals and Plants under Domestication*,
in which he writes about Victorian practices of animal breeding, such as
pigeon fancying, grapples throughout with the question of what it means
for an animal to become "domesticated," to fall under the influence of,

and conceptually to approach, the human. Darwin himself kept and bred pigeons, and he wrote extensively on domestication as a natural-historical force. He seems to view certain animals such as dogs and monkeys as, in Claude Lévi-Strauss's evocative phrase, "metonymical human beings" (207), possessing something like a *partial* personhood in the degree to which they come close to human society. Many of Darwin's arguments depend on comparisons at once analogical and metaphorical (these animals behave in ways that are similar to human behavior) and metonymic (these animals share common heritage, as mammals, with humans). Such comparisons always raise the unsettling potential that the nonhuman might in fact be barely distinguishable from the human. We are accustomed to think about this potential primarily diachronically, in terms of heritage and family resemblance over time: Darwin, of course, persuaded much of the literate world for the first time that mankind evolved from and thus shared many qualities with animal progenitors. But even as he kept his eye on the very *longue durée* of species evolution, Darwin was also interested in more synchronic questions regarding the overlaps between nineteenth-century humans and nonhumans in relations of proximity, closeness, contact, and domestication.

So it turned out that I did not need to bracket Darwin's work altogether to pursue the questions that interested me—but only to shift attention to slightly different texts and concepts within his corpus. As John R. Durant points out, the parallel that Darwin first observed on his visit to Tierra del Fuego in 1832 "between wild and domesticated animals, on the one hand, and savage and civilized man, on the other," became central to his ideas about human evolution as "a passage from barbarity to civility" (286). The question of "domestication" and what it means for nonhuman animals to "approach" (literally and metaphorically), or to be in effect befriended by, the human recurs throughout much of Darwin's work. What does it mean, he often seems to ask, for animals to live near or with human beings and to share their space, to resemble them, to behave in comparable ways to them, to forge metonymical ties with them? What brings an animal under the sign of culture and the human? As Durant puts it, Darwin's "anthropomorphic zoology combined with zoomorphic anthropology in effecting the unification of animals and man" (292)—he moved animals closer to the human, and humans closer to the animal, than previous thinkers had done, and this two-way shift is especially visible in human domestication of animals. Darwin often seems to be trying to determine where precisely the lines should be drawn between the "animal" and the "human," the "natural" and the "cultural." And he is fascinated by *domestication* as a force that is, itself, at once metaphorically and metonymically related to natural selection: human domestication of animals at once resembles, as if in miniature, the forces of natural selection that occur in much larger timescales and also operates, in effect *within* natural selection, as an interior version of the processes occurring more broadly.

Domestication operates in Darwin's work as a fundamentally unnatural or even *perverse* force, in the sense that domestication is, by definition, an imitative and partially deforming "artificial" supplement to natural selection. Domestication marks the boundary between a natural animal, subject to the normal laws of natural selection, and one that has been brought under the influence of human culture, turned into something "made" (in that sense almost resembling an artwork): a friend, or servant, or food source for man. In the opening pages of *The Variation of Animals and Plants under Domestication*, Darwin defines domestication as harnessing the "natural" force of natural selection to serve mankind's own "wants and pleasures," which he defines as definitionally "abnormal" because unnatural: "As the will of man thus comes into play, we can understand how it is that domesticated breeds show adaptation to his wants and pleasures. We can further understand how it is that domestic races of animals and cultivated races of plants often exhibit an abnormal character, as compared with natural species; for they have been modified not for their own benefit, but for that of man" (4). By domesticating and "breeding" animals, humans torque an animal species or breed's development away from a natural state, in which it always operates "for the benefit" of its own kind, into an artificially modified one in which its modifications benefit man.

As Harriet Ritvo points out, within nineteenth-century biology and natural history, "[m]onsters were tautologically defined as deviations from established norms," but, in practice, "[m]onstrosity had to be determined . . . according to a sliding scale of deviation" (*Platypus* 148). For Darwin, domestication was always, in a sense, "deviation" from the norm of natural selection as it would operate without man's agency and interference—even if, in practice, it is generally impossible to distinguish clearly between norm and deviation. Darwin's work undermines the distinction of mankind within nature, but he does allow for human distinction in the capacity to produce the deviation that is domestication—in the human drive to deform the natural in accordance with (often unconscious) human "wants and pleasures." Human beings are unique in having engaged in large-scale intentional domestication of other species. One of the stories

Darwin tells in *The Variation of Animals and Plants under Domestication* is of a human propensity for the domestication of animals, which he begins by assuming must be a mostly modern phenomenon but which he eventually understands may be ancient and indeed fundamental to the human: "Savages in all parts of the world easily succeed in taming wild animals" (2: 405); "we are quite unable to disentangle the effects of the direct action of the conditions of life,—of use or habit—of natural selection—and of that kind of selection which we have seen is occasionally and unconsciously followed by man even during the rudest periods of history" (2: 210–11). Human culture as such may be unimaginable, he suggests, without the drive to domesticate the nonhuman.

All domestication and breeding is to a degree artificial and abnormal, then, even as it is also basic to the human. In more radical or extreme forms, such domestication produces monsters. In modern sheep breeding, for example, "In some few instances new breeds have suddenly originated; thus, in 1791, a ram-lamb was born in Massachusetts, having short crooked legs and a long back, like a turnspit-dog. From this one lamb the *otter* or *ancon* semi-monstrous breed was raised" (1: 104). Darwin notes what could almost be considered a polymorphously perverse human lust for artificial breeding and adaptation, which operates with no apparent limits and according to a logic of fashion and caprice: "[I]t is not surprising that . . . our highly-bred pigeons have undergone an astonishing amount of change; for in regard to them there is no defined limit to the wish of the fancier, and there is no known limit to the variability of their characters. What is there to stop the fancier desiring to give to his Carrier a longer and longer beak, or to his Tumbler a shorter and shorter beak? nor has the extreme limit of variability in the beak, if there be any such limit, as yet been reached" (1: 233). Darwin compares animal domestication to high fashion in its extreme variability and its tendency to drive toward radical extremes:

> It is an important principle that in the process of selection man almost invariably wishes to go to an extreme point. Thus, there is no limit to his desire to breed certain kinds of horses and dogs as fleet as possible, and others as strong as possible; certain kinds of sheep for extreme fineness, and others for extreme length of wool; and he wishes to produce fruit, grain, tubers, and other useful parts of plants, as large and excellent as possible. With animals bred for amusement, the same

principle is even more powerful; for fashion, as we see in our dress, always runs to extremes. (1: 226)

Darwin's domestication book is governed by a paradox: it aims to tell the history of the human domestication of animals and plants but discovers that such a history is very difficult to narrate because it may be inextricable from the history of human culture more generally. "[N]o record has been preserved of the origin of our chief domestic breeds" (2: 424). The human itself is inseparable from the drive to breed, to artificially domesticate, to turn the "natural" into culture in the form of domesticated animals.[6]

My brief discussion here of *The Variation of Animals and Plants under Domestication* has focused on what I've described as an artificial—or even perverse—domestication that Darwin sees as produced by the unchecked desires and will of man as an agent of selection. The much more famous book he published a few years later, *The Descent of Man*, suggests another aspect of Darwin's approach to the topic: what we might name *sentimental domestication*. In this book, Darwin sometimes treats both wild and domesticated animals as sentimentally endowed "characters," or at least as something approaching that privileged status. A series of anecdotes regarding sociable and apparently sympathetic behavior on the part of wild animals leads, for example, to an extended discussion of a particular "heroic monkey" whose status in the text raises the possibility of an animal possessing, if not precisely protagonicity, then at least an individual, and persistent, (textual) character. After several previous anecdotes about animal behavior, Darwin writes,

> I will give only one other instance of sympathetic and heroic conduct, in the case of a little American monkey. Several years ago a keeper at the Zoological Gardens shewed me some deep and scarcely healed wounds on the nape of his own neck, inflicted on him, whilst kneeling on the floor, by a fierce baboon. The little American monkey, who was a warm friend of this keeper, lived in the same large compartment, and was dreadfully afraid of the great baboon. Nevertheless, as soon as he saw his friend in peril, he rushed to the rescue, and by screams and bites so distracted the baboon that the man was able to escape, after, as the surgeon thought, running great risk of his life. (103)

This "little American monkey" is a "warm friend of the keeper," on the near side of a line dividing the social-cultural (and sympathetic) realm of human beings from the more wild and instinctive world of wild animals like the baboon. This division is unstable, since Darwin's point in this section of the book is that one can find numerous examples of animals, from cattle and cows to eagles and macaws, who behave in apparently "sympathetic," sociable, and other-directed ways, thereby blurring the conventional opposition between the wild-natural and the human-cultural-domesticated. But this particular little monkey has been, precisely, particularized by Darwin's description, characterized and granted something approaching a more human characterological status and textual personhood.

Darwin's monkey is—and of course such a definition threatens to become circular—character-like because he is particularized and sympathetic. In the course of this passage, he even receives an article promotion: from "a" to "the" heroic monkey. He approaches humanness and the human being; he overcomes his instinctive fears to perform selflessly and thereby becomes a "friend" to the keeper. But his character-bearing quality is also a matter of recurrence and of textual persistence. Most other animals in the text are not textual individuals or are only very briefly so; they cannot really recur in the text because their status as simply *a* rather than *the* means that, once mentioned, they slip back into the undifferentiated anonymity of large categories: species, herds, and so on—types rather than individuals.

But Darwin soon returns to *the* monkey who may have saved the keeper's life: "[M]any a civilized man, or even boy, who never before risked his life for another, but full of courage and sympathy, has disregarded the instinct of self-preservation, and plunged at once into a torrent to save a drowning man, though a stranger. In this case man is impelled by the same instinctive motive, which made the heroic little American monkey, formerly described, save his keeper, by attacking the great and dreaded baboon" (110). Part of the force of this reference lies in the way the monkey, in his second appearance in the text, has become *more particularized* than the human beings in the anecdote, who are a generalized group of "many" men and boys. "Formerly described," he is now textually revived and granted a kind of permanence. Asked to remember this monkey, we imbue him with a new textual solidity or persistence.

We soon lose sight of the monkey over the next five hundred-odd pages, but he makes a triumphant return in one of the most famous and controversial passages in all of Darwin's work, in the final pages of *The Descent of Man*: as the more sympathetic, perhaps even more "humane" alternative to a group of "savages" whose kinship Darwin partially and illogically disavows even as he acknowledges it.

"[T]here can hardly be a doubt that we are descended from barbarians," Darwin concludes.

> The astonishment which I felt on first seeing a party of Feugians [*sic*] on a wild and broken shore will never be forgotten by me, for the reflection at once rushed into my mind—such were our ancestors. These men were absolutely naked and bedaubed with paint, their long hair was tangled, their mouths frothed with excitement, and their expression was wild, startled, and distrustful. They possessed hardly any arts, and like wild animals lived on what they could catch; they had no government, and were merciless to every one not of their own small tribe. He who has seen a savage in his native land will not feel much shame, if forced to acknowledge that the blood of some more humble creature flows in his veins. For my own part I would as soon be descended from that heroic little monkey, who braved his dreaded enemy in order to save the life of his keeper, or from that old baboon, who descending from the mountains, carried away in triumph his young comrade from a crowd of astonished dogs—as from a savage who delights to torture his enemies, offers up bloody sacrifices, practises infanticide without remorse, treats his wives like slaves, knows no decency, and is haunted by the grossest superstitions. (618)

Even if we are persuaded (as influentially argued by Adrian Desmond and James Moore, for example) that the larger logic of Darwin's arguments is fundamentally antiracist, this passage—a touchstone for any scholar interested in the racial subtexts of Darwin's writing—is troubling in its unapologetic recoiling from these "savage[s]" who live with "no government," "like wild animals." But what is usually overlooked here is the return of "that heroic little monkey," who, in this third and culminating appearance in the book, lays final claim to character status. Darwin in effect promotes both the heroic monkey and the old baboon (who also appeared in the earlier passage in which we first met the monkey; he is not the "fierce baboon" whom the monkey scared off in the zoo) at the expense of the Fuegians, who are described as "more savage" and even as more like "wild animals" than the primates. Where the savages are cruel and antisocial, the monkey and baboon are friends and "comrade[s]," sentimental actors.

Darwin's closing suggestion here in *The Descent of Man* is that kinship with a small subset of individuated nonhuman animals is more palatable than alliance with "savage" non-Western human beings. This is a logic of sentimental domestication in which certain animals are redefined as "the" rather than "a," as individual beings, as potential "friends" or "comrades"—even as other certain human beings are, almost in consequence, as in a zero-sum equation, marked as more "like wild animals." As Cannon Schmitt argues, Darwin recurs to the heroic monkey and the old baboon "in order to push 'civilized' and 'savage' humans further apart by grouping the former with animals against the latter, who now stand outside any community whatsoever" (50). Animality and wildness and domestication become fungible, potentially shifting markers of nearness to, or distance from, personhood. The monkey in Darwin's anecdotes is in fact technically domesticated—a zoo inhabitant—while the baboon was a wild animal, but both are conceptually domesticated, given a temporary pride of place as metonymic human beings, as "more humble creature[s]" who are nevertheless kin or "friend."

Something like this very process—by which some creatures become animalized and distanced from the human, while others are domesticated or granted partial personhood and brought close to humanity—also operates throughout the novels of the Victorian period, in which sympathetic personhood often depends on the capacity to grant some limited version of that status to nonhuman animals. Or, more simply, in Victorian novels, sympathetic people must love and individuate certain domestic animals or pets (even as they consign others to the great mass of other unprivileged animals). Deidre Lynch argues that, in the late eighteenth century, literature, "something to be taken personally by definition" began to "deman[d] love" (8), that a newly "subjectivity-saturated language of involvement and affection" (10) began to inflect readers' relationship to literature. I suggest that the love of literature and the love of pets, both situated in a sacralized space of domesticity, emerge historically in similar and interconnected ways. It began to seem, in the Victorian period, that to be a good, humane person, it was necessary to care deeply (though not *too* deeply) for both (some) animals and novels.

Elaine Freedgood has influentially carried insights from so-called thing theory to Victorian novel criticism, arguing that our criticism has tended prematurely to limit the range of significant or interpretable entities within realist novels to human beings, neglecting or misreading the crucial narratives in which things, rather than people, take center stage. So, she argues, for example, *Jane Eyre* starts to read very differently if we take seriously its representation of mahogany wood as something other than background or a material substratum for the action of the (living) human characters who sit on (lifeless) mahogany furniture (30–44). Along somewhat parallel lines, I am interested in what happens when one reads a Victorian novel as a representation of multiple life-forms and organisms in their interaction and interrelation, as opposed to focusing on human beings alone. To draw on a phrase from Miguel Tamen, the question is: what counts as an "interpretable object," as mattering (rather than mere matter), as significant or signifying? Tamen asserts that "there are no interpretable objects or intentional objects, only what counts as an interpretable object or, better, groups of people for whom certain objects count as interpretable" (3). One of my goals is to render the nonhuman creatures of Victorian fiction more "interpretable." I hope in so doing to bring to criticism of the Victorian novel some of the spirit of Jane Bennett's Latourian admonitions: "Give up the futile attempt to disentangle the human from the nonhuman. Seek instead to engage more civilly, strategically, and subtly with the nonhumans in the assemblages in which you, too, participate" (*Vibrant* 116).

Even anti- or posthumanist novel criticism and theory can often be quite anthropocentric in its unexamined assumption that agency and identity within narratives—or even the lack or absence of those categories—belong exclusively to human beings, whether whole subjects or not.[7] And although the rise of posthumanism or of the "nonhuman turn" in recent criticism has begun to change this, these insights have only begun to filter into Victorian studies.[8] No doubt, in just about any canonical Victorian novel, the human plots are insistent and most apparent. Yet we can read between the lines for alternate plots, histories, and images of an organic world filled with a multitude of heterogeneous "species-being"— stories in which the human may occupy a more marginal position.

To read Victorian novels non- (or at least less) anthropocentrically is not, then, irrationally to deny the genre's obvious human focus but rather to consider more flexibly and with greater nuance the line normally taken to mark the distinction between characters and noncharacters; to consider the genre's normative partial exclusion or marginalization of the animal not simply as a given but as crucial to the form. (That is, it is not simply that animals are marginalized or marginal in Victorian novels but that animals *must* be marginalized, albeit not always successfully so.) My approach thus shares with thing theory, or with Latourian actor-network theory, the desire to refuse normative assumptions about who or what "counts" or "matters" or "acts" within a literary text.

Why the "creature" in my title, *Minor Creatures*? The "creaturely" is

a category that has been generative for a number of recent critics, including Julia Lupton, Eric Santner, Tobias Menely, and Heather Keenleyside,
all of them drawing on what Santner defines as a tradition of "German-
Jewish" (xix) thought on the topic going back to the work of Walter Benjamin and Franz Rosenzweig, among others. For Santner, the creaturely
"names the threshold where life becomes a matter of politics and politics
comes to inform the very matter and materiality of life" (12); he defines
"creaturely life" as life "utterly exposed, utterly abandoned to the state
of exception" (180). Lupton writes in "Creature Caliban," a brilliant essay
on *The Tempest*, that "[a]t various points in the theological imagination
of the West, creatureliness has served to localize a moment of passionate passivity, of an abjected, thinglike (non)being, a being of subjected becoming, that precipitates out of the divine Logos as its material remnant"
(2); Caliban as "creature" becomes "an emblem of what Giorgio Agamben
calls 'bare life,' pure vitality drained of its symbolic significance and political capacity and then sequestered within the domain of civilization as
its disavowed core" (Lupton 2). Menely draws on Lupton, Santner, and Benjamin to define "the creaturely" as "[r]eferring to one who is determined,
a being whose first cause is external to it and whose interests exceed its
capacities of realization"; "'creature' fissures the border, otherwise so as-
siduously guarded, that divides the human and the animal" (14). And for
Keenleyside, the term *creature* is in Defoe's *Robinson Crusoe* "the novel's
word for an ontological determination effected by exposure to external
force" (66).

For my part, the concept of the (minor) creature designates the way the
nonhuman animal becomes defined and represented in Victorian fiction
(and culture) as at once "within the domain of civilization" (in Lupton's
words) and yet disavowed; as enculturated and at least partially or conceptually domesticated, allowed within our homes but still not human; as
deserving certain protections but perhaps not quite full rights; as capable
of significations of a kind but not of true voice or speech; as textually represented and sometimes with a persistence or extension over narrative but
also always minor and marginal, never (within realism) attaining full protagonicity. The nonhuman animal is creaturely, or a creature, in the way
it occupies these indeterminate zones as a kind of necessary but partially
disavowed supplement to the human, its status—like Darwin's monkey—
in flux and definitionally up for grabs. Just about any animal—although
certainly some kinds of animals more than others—may potentially be
labeled and treated as a friend, as a part of the world and the texts of the
human; but any animal may also be turned out, expelled or killed, and

redefined as purely animal and fully exterior to the human and its categories. The domesticated animal is creaturely precisely because domestication is always incomplete and provisional: no animal, however loved, fully enters the realm of the human and of culture, fully escapes its animal status. (And, of course, this also implies the complementary Darwinian insight: it's also worryingly the case that no *human* fully escapes its animal status.)

Derrida's remarks on sovereignty and the home can help to suggest what is at stake in the question of which animals are allowed access, either literally or metaphorically, to the home and to the spaces of culture. The "host" or "the one who receives" those into the home bears the right and responsibility "of choosing, electing, filtering, selecting their invitees, visitors, or guests, those to whom they decide to grant asylum, the right of visiting, or hospitality. No hospitality, in the classic sense, without sovereignty of oneself over one's home, but since there is also no hospitality without finitude, sovereignty can only be exercised by filtering, choosing, and thus by excluding and doing violence" (*Of Hospitality* 55). These observations can also be applied to the scene of "domestication" and the question of which animals are consigned to a purely wild and inhuman status (and thus deemed killable with virtually no limitation) and those that are befriended or allowed "in" to human culture and given certain protections. Yet no matter in which category an animal falls—domesticated or not, tame or wild—it is always creaturely in its ambiguous status in relation to the categories and spaces of the human.

The Victorians are like others in human history in that they think to be a person is not to be an animal—but they are *unlike* them in that they make domestic animals central to an image of sentimental domesticity and humanity. And, in this respect, we today are inheritors of the Victorian conception of the animal. Animals must be marginalized in most Victorian fiction, one might say, but they cannot be entirely excluded, precisely because the love of domestic animals had become fundamental to the conception of the Victorian home, family, and perhaps even the very human self. This originary tension is crucial to the specific form of the Victorian novel. The animal is newly included within it, but within carefully proscribed limits. Once that inclusion has occurred, however, space is opened for those limits to be constantly pressured. The construction of the human in the Victorian novel proceeds, I therefore argue, via an explicit or implicit engagement with the animal, often in a relationship of domination or subordination.

To what degree could animals count as characters within nineteenth-century British culture or literature? Animals in the Victorian period, I suggest, are often treated as *semi*human in the realm of culture and as *semi*characters in the realm of literature. What I mean by this is that animals, or certain privileged domesticated animals, are given names and invested with personality and individual identity but that this status is unreliable and subject to sudden abrogation.[9] As Erica Fudge suggests, "[i]n one area—pet ownership—the animal is identified, given a name and a status, whereas in the others—food and clothing—the individual animal disappears" (27). One of the primary signs of the precariousness of pets' status as humanlike characters is their troubled relationship to memory and memorializing, particularly in the form of writing or print. It is typical for a Victorian pet to be treated in certain respects like a person but also typical for an animal to be forgotten or replaced and allowed to disappear without recognition in a manner that would seem troubling in the case of a human being. Animal characters are fundamentally minor, in the sense defined by Woloch in his discussion of the narrative function of the minor character: they are represented but only in passing; given nicknames rather than true markers of identity; they possess no solid claim to recognition or memory on the part of the narrator or any other character. Even the minor human characters Woloch examines possess an enviable robustness of identity and agency by comparison with nearly any represented animal, at least within realist fiction.[10]

On the one hand, as Keith Thomas and others have documented, pets in eighteenth- and nineteenth-century Britain became increasingly invested with qualities of personality and individual identity, so much so that they were not only given names but frequently memorialized in written forms: "When cherished pets died, the bereaved owners might be deeply upset. They would commemorate their passing in epitaphs and elegies. . . . In the eighteenth century the remains of pets might be covered with an obelisk or sculptured tomb. If the owner preceded them to the grave they might attend the funeral; and, from the late seventeenth century onward, they could even hope to receive a legacy for their maintenance" (118). Yet on the other hand, it would seem that such privileged, near-human relationships to memorialization—allowing a pet to be granted a future in memory and history beyond death in the form of writing or inscription or even a financial legacy—remained a relatively rare occurrence. Thomas cites a Dorset farmer who wrote in 1698 that "my old dog Quon was killed, and baked for his grease, of which he yielded 11 lbs" (102). By the nineteenth century, pets—especially dogs—were increasingly given names and in other ways treated as beings possessing individual characteristics and personality. But even so, the fate of that farmer's old dog, killed and baked for grease, would still seem to hover as an implicit threat over any animal. To be a dog is to risk such absolute disintegration, a reduction to material substance that puts the lie to any former claim to subjectivity.[11] If certain very unusual and privileged animals—like Darwin's "heroic little monkey"—are plucked out of the herd or the mass, given a name and a persistent textual identity, this exception always proves the general merciless rule of animality: to be nonhuman is to possess a creaturely, precarious identity.

Pets in Victorian literature embody minorness in various and complex ways—one of which relates to genre. When pets and especially dogs feature as characters in Victorian narratives, those narratives tend to fall into the orbit of one of two minor generic categories, either children's literature or the anecdote. "Whereas earlier dog literature seemed simply a specialized branch of natural history," Harriet Ritvo writes, the new early nineteenth-century genre of "sentimental books about dogs . . . included not only descriptions of the dogs' physical and moral characteristics, but a selection of heartwarming and enlightening anecdotes" (*Animal* 86). By midcentury, British newspapers and periodicals were filled with anecdotes and vignettes about loyal and brave dogs; indeed, to be confined to the sphere of the anecdote would seem to define the Victorian dog's ambiguous position. Within the strictly delimited, bounded form of the anecdote, even acts of bravery, devotion, or heroism cannot guarantee any lasting recognition; an animal "protagonist" of this particular genre possesses an individuality that may be marked as at once exceptional and admirable, and also anonymous and short-lived. Consider this typical notice from *Chambers's Edinburgh Journal*: "Dogs soon become aware of any misfortune in the family to which they belong, and show their sympathy in a variety of ways. . . . A female in Lincolnshire died, who had two favorite dogs. . . . When the deceased was carried to the churchyard, one of the dogs followed the corpse, and neither threats nor entreaties could drive it away" ("Jesse's Scenes" 300). Identified only as "one of the dogs," the creature who is the center of interest in this brief narrative fails to break away from the "group" (of two) in which she is embedded and remains grammatically and conceptually subordinated to that collectivity. This breakdown in individuality, or failure truly to achieve it, suggests a potential tension that may arise when a dog escapes the form of the anecdote and enters a more extended narrative. Generally denied protagonicity or the status of a developed character in such longer narratives, animals, when they are so represented, can embody alternative, nonnovelistic temporalities—anecdotal, minor, interrupted. An animal character is, perhaps by definition, an incomplete or fragile character, one whose continuity over a long span of time or pages cannot be guaranteed or anticipated and whose presence in a realist novel may implicitly challenge that very form's presumption that individual identity can be maintained over long duration. When an animal becomes a character in a realist novel and *recurs* over a longer narrative—like Darwin's monkey—this persistence always contains an element of provisionality and exceptionality, given the normal state of the animal as only fleetingly represented. "The" heroic monkey is defined against the far larger number of those that are not so individuated. And so animal characters often seem to operate as emblems of provisionality, as reminders that those beings whom we individuate or name can very easily slip back below the level of representability. (The dog who rescues Fanny in Hardy's *Far from the Madding Crowd* and is subsequently "stoned away" [328] exemplifies this possibility.)

Because the animal is defined as subject to the whims and desires of human beings, the animal in Victorian fiction is definitionally *precarious* and vulnerable. The laws of what Jacques Derrida dubs "carno-phallogocentrism" ("Eating Well" 280) at once forbid murder but allow "a place left open, in the very structure of these discourses . . . for a non-criminal putting to death." This place is occupied by the animal who *may* be lavished with the special privileges of a pet or domestic animal—including individuality, a name, a right to future memory, some limited protection against violence or being eaten as meat—but may much more likely be subject to a large range of violent acts. Colin Dayan, in a consideration of the role of dogs in Anglo-American legal history, asserts that "[w]hat both dogs and slaves have in common . . . is their standing outside the concerns of civil life" (214). Dogs and other domestic animals stand, as it were, half in and half out of civil life and personhood. Animals in fiction are literally precarious in that their lives often end violently. Especially after the founding of the Society for the Prevention of Cruelty to Animals, representations of the beating of an animal emerge as an increasingly familiar and legible stock scene, an occasion for the demonstration of cruelty (on the part of those beating the animal) and of sympathy (on the part of those observing). As I argue in chapter 2 on the Brontës, such scenes of violence against precarious, vulnerable animals prove important as occasions for the proof of sympathy and a more ethical stance (than that of ordinary, cruel Britons) on the part of both the novels' protagonists and their readers. Animals' role as meat is, of course, central to their precarity, as suggested by Derrida's term *carno-phallogocentrism*.[12]

Certain animals are so fundamental to meat production as to introduce the possibility of slippage between their meat and nonmeat nomenclature, as in *cow* and *beef*. (Claude Lévi-Strauss is very interesting on the ways the names we give to animals signal our willingness to eat them.)[13] But I suggest—in chapter 3 (on Dickens) as well as elsewhere—that *any* animal was marked as proximate to the category of meat, even for species, such as dogs, who are nominally considered to be safe from the fate of being eaten. In chapter 4, "*Middlemarch*'s Brute Life," I argue that a major focus for Eliot in this novel is a kind of repeated primal scene of devouring or "absorption," in which one stronger being absorbs and assimilates a weaker or more precarious being. This strain of imagery in the novel draws on G. H. Lewes's consideration of crabs and crustaceans in his *Sea-Side Studies* but also connects to anthropological concepts of sacrifice and to a submerged but important theme in the novel regarding pet keeping.

For the authors I consider, the precariousness of animals not only could embody powerlessness, lack of agency, and vulnerability to harm but also could at times offer a template for an ethics modeled against prevailing norms of cultural value and identity. For Hardy and Schreiner, the vulnerability and precarity of animals becomes a potential value, a model for an ethics of what Anne-Lise François has called "recessive" (173) action or noninstrumental agency. Peter Singer observes that "the interest a being has in continued life . . . will depend in part on whether the being is aware of itself as existing over time, and is capable of forming future-directed desires that give it a particular kind of interest in continuing to live" ("Animal Liberation at Thirty" 25). Animal precarity is defined by an unreliable hold on "continued life"—related to what I've called textual persistence—and any animal-welfare or animal-rights politics aims to offer greater security to animal life. Yet François's deconstructive ethics also suggests the potential of an approach to textual existence that may be less future-directed, less concerned about narrative extension over time. As creatures lacking the particular human commitment to futurity, animals possess a different relationship to temporality. Perhaps for this reason, a fascination with animal life seems, for Hardy and Schreiner, to have contributed to a restlessly experimental approach to the form of the novel. The very precariousness of animals, their weak hold on linear extension in time, points to a less human-centered, linear, or end-directed approach to narrative and opens up possibilities that emerge more fully in modernism.

Indeed, realism itself as a genre always exists in tension with the representation of animal life, I suggest, in the sense that any tendency toward full characterization of a nonhuman—any claim to a status beyond minor marginality—offers a subtle challenge to realist procedures. Very simply, any textual animal who lays claim to personhood, textual persistence, protagonicity, and so on, threatens to transform a realist text into one of a different genre: in the early and mid-Victorian periods, most likely that of children's literature, fantasy, or allegory. For a famous and emblematic example, consider the opening of *Alice in Wonderland*.

> Alice was beginning to get very tired of sitting by her sister on the bank, and of having nothing to do: once or twice she had peeped into the book her sister was reading, but it had no pictures or conversations in it, "and what is the use of a book," thought Alice "without pictures or conversations?"
>
> So she was considering in her own mind (as well as she could, for the hot day made her feel very sleepy and stupid), whether the pleasure of making a daisy-chain would be worth the trouble of getting up and picking the daisies, when suddenly a White Rabbit with pink eyes ran close by her.
>
> There was nothing so *very* remarkable in that; nor did Alice think it so very much out of the way to hear the Rabbit say to itself, "Oh dear! Oh dear! I shall be late!" (when she thought it over afterwards, it occurred to her that she ought to have wondered at this, but at the time it all seemed quite natural); but when the Rabbit actually *took a watch out of its waistcoat-pocket*, and looked at it, and then hurried on, Alice started to her feet, for it flashed across her mind that she had never before seen a rabbit with either a waistcoat-pocket, or a watch to take out of it, and burning with curiosity, she ran across the field after it, and fortunately was just in time to see it pop down a large rabbit-hole under the hedge.
>
> In another moment down went Alice after it, never once considering how in the world she was to get out again. (7–8)

The Alice of the first two sentences is, at least potentially, a character within a realist novel, "very tired of" its mundane laws of plausibility. But the rabbit's "sudden" appearance, running "close by her," signals a disruption of the realist laws of persons and nonpersons, and implants in Alice a "burning . . . curiosity" that drives her completely out of the—our—world of plausible realism. To fall or go down the rabbit hole has, in the years since Carroll first published his novella in 1865, come to mean something like "to stumble into a bizarre and disorienting alternate reality" (Schulz). This alternate reality is one in which animals talk, have watches, emerge as fully fledged characters, as persons. At one level, this is an obvious insight—animals talk and behave like human beings only in nonrealist genres—but it bears fuller consideration as a marker of realism's commitment to a law of anthropocentrism. These genre rules seem to operate in Carroll's narrative as a constraining limit, such that the bored and sleepy Alice is overcome by a desire to flout or refuse them, to dive into an alternative reality of personified nonhuman beings and to remain "close" to the rabbit who ran swiftly by her. This book, however, does *not* follow Alice—or scholars like Tess Cosslett and Jessica Straley—into that rabbit hole leading from realism to its alternative genres; my own focus is the ways that Victorian realism begins, even at the risk of fracturing, to allow more and more scope for animal life in its representations (while still falling short of the fully counterrealist move to fantasy).

Rae Greiner has made a persuasive case for the centrality to Victorian fictional realism of an Adam Smithian form of "sympathy" produced and defined by the quality that she sums up as "fellow feeling," "a social fantasy in which (as Smith puts it) we 'go along with' others" in a kind of "contentless companionship": "Long designated a genre littered with things and stuff that, simply by being there, produce a reality effect, the nineteenth-century realist novel differs from most novels of the previous century in granting to fellow-feeling—not objects—the task of maintaining reality. By depicting social reality as a product of fellow-feeling, the realist novel portrays the real as both fictive and sympathetic. Fellow-feeling, sympathy's most sustained and important fiction, underwrites reality, deciding what gains significance, and what does not" (10). But with whom precisely can novel readers and characters "go along," feel sympathy for and with? The distinction Greiner draws between the "things and stuff" and "objects" of the novel on the one hand and the genre's sympathy-generating persons on the other is absolutely reasonable; but this book's goal is to complicate such a distinction in order to make a case for a new category of beings that emerge forcefully in nineteenth-century fiction: nonhuman animals who begin to shift further away from "thing" status toward personhood and the possibility of becoming a subject of novelistic, sympathetic "fellow feeling." If not to the point of following the rabbit down its hole, the authors of the texts I examine, and their characters, at least begin to "go along" with nonhumans, to allow them into the space of companionship.

Carroll's White Rabbit notwithstanding, dogs are probably the preeminent domestic animal in the Victorian period, the species so often welcomed and granted pride of place in the Victorian home and the one that seemed closest, in many respects, to the human. The author of an 1881 article in *Temple Bar* magazine titled "Dogs of Literature" declared that "the majority of our masters of literature, and our poets almost to a man, have made dogs their personal friends in real life, in fiction, or in both" (478). But this privileged status also granted to dogs and other pets a potentially troubling ambivalence. If they are almost human, living in the home of the human, are they fully animal? Can they rise to the stature of a protagonist in a novel or even a character? Here the answer is some version of yes and no. In early and mid-Victorian novels like *Wuthering Heights*, *Jane Eyre*, *David Copperfield*, and even *Middlemarch*, pets (canine and other) tend to appear and disappear, sometimes granted names, sometimes not, but generally defining a minorness even exceeding that of human minor characters. They are diminished beings, subsidiary, not quite worthy of plots or more developed narratives. To count as a sympathetic human character in a Victorian novel one must love animals or be capable of loving them—but to love animals *too much* or to love the wrong kind of animals opens one to accusations of eccentricity or pathology, going down the rabbit hole (and this remains true in many respects for us). If one follows the animal too closely, one risks turning into Alice or a "crazy cat lady."[14] But in the work of authors like Hardy and Schreiner in the 1870s and 1880s, animals begin to press at the boundaries of their minorness. In what can be understood as a seeping of some of the procedures of fantastic or children's literature into the realist tradition, these authors hint that certain animals might have stories and narratives of their own (even if they cannot or will not be fully narrated).

Minorness is one aspect of a larger question of individuation: to what degree can an animal count or be recognized as an individual as opposed to an element in a mass of some kind (a herd, a pack, a swarm, etc.)? Derrida asserts that "power over the animal is the essence of the 'I' or the 'person,' the essence of the human" (*Animal* 93); according to this formula, the being who occupies the place of the animal is categorically denied the privilege of any full selfhood. One of the clearest markers of pet status is the bestowal of a name on an animal, an especially distinct marker of individuality (even beyond the shift from *a* to *the*). Yet part of the precariousness of animals is their susceptibility to falling back into group or mass identity—as suggested, for example, by the common practice of a given household granting a succession of pets the same name. Chapter 5, "Using and Pitying Animals in Thomas Hardy," draws on Michel Foucault's arguments about pastoral care as "an individualizing power." The shepherd, in Foucault's formulation, holds the power to discern and name the individual sheep within the larger herd; "He does everything for the totality of the flock, but he does everything also for each sheep of the flock. . . . [T]he shepherd must keep his eye on all and on each, *omnes et singulatim*" (128). Throughout the book, I am especially interested in the animal's tendency to slip between states of individuation—*singulatim*—and undifferentiated group, mass, or totality, *omnes*. This topic raises questions regarding the state's oversight and regulation of "life" and the living; organic life is conceptually shaped and categorized—into different categories of being and different hierarchies of value—according to biopolitical structures and procedures. Indeed, the novel itself, as a literary form, can be usefully considered as one element in Victorian culture's biopolitics, its organization of these categories and hierarchies.[15]

The novels of the Brontës, for instance, were particularly influential, I suggest, in linking novelistic characterization itself with the processes by which an animal who might otherwise have been viewed as simply part of what Derrida calls "the living in general" (*Animal* 12) becomes transformed into a treasured, named pet and an individuated character. For the Brontës, and subsequently for other Victorian novelists, authorship itself becomes emotionally associated with relationships with domestic animals. The bestowal of subjectivity in the naming and care for a pet becomes an analog for the comparable processes involved in the creation of a novelistic character, and the domestic pet becomes an analog for the domestic novel, both proving the sympathetic, humanizing, enculturating potential of the household that possesses them. In chapter 4, for instance, I argue that George Eliot situates such figures as a Maltese puppy and a pair of pet goats within a broader array of life-forms whose position on the life/nonlife, or wild/domestic, continua is ambiguous or precarious. One of the forms of power that Eliot assigns herself as author is to position and situate these various forms of creaturely or domesticated life, to distinguish them from "the living in general."

George Eliot's observation from *Middlemarch*, "It seemed that she had no more identified herself with him than if they had been creatures of different species" (369), captures the process by which what is animal or nonhuman is disavowed (yet always retained, albeit in a marginal position). What Derrida calls the "deranged theatrics of the *wholly other they call animal*" (*Animal* 11) gains its "deranged" intensity from a felt necessity to shore up human identity by disavowing a troubling animality within the human. Giorgio Agamben's conceptualization of "the modern anthropological machine" (*Open* 35) is also useful for understanding a process by which the human repeatedly shores up its own definitional borders through a "dehumanizing": that is, by a rejection of an animal being, essence, or a broader animality that leaves behind a human whose boundaries are rendered temporarily clearer. Agamben suggests that "man" must "recognize himself in a non-man in order to be human" (*Open* 27).[16] I bring the logic of the "anthropological machine" to a consideration of the Victorian novel, which cannot seem to stop representing animals, if only to mark them out as secondary, minor, precarious, and marginal. Yet part of the logic of this process is its failure to complete the task it begins: the animal within the human can never be finally or permanently excluded, for according to the logic of the form, to fully expel the animal would be to become cruel and inhuman. The humane person or the humane literary form must preserve an (always subordinated and marginal) animality.

In a more historical (as opposed to theoretical) register, such issues can be considered in relation not only to Darwinian thought, and the well-known dismay that followed Darwin's suggestion that human beings were in effect just another species of animal, but also to the rise of the animal-welfare movement and the struggle over the status and permissibility of violence against or cruelty to animals.[17] In a society famous for meat eating (albeit of beef and not the flesh of dogs or cats), these questions were tricky, as they remain today: given that animals are continually slaughtered in huge numbers for meat production, why and on what basis is violence against animals limited and regulated? From the 1822 passing of Martin's Act—the "Act to prevent the cruel and improper treatment of Cattle"—and the subsequent founding in 1824 of the Society for the Prevention of Cruelty to Animals (after 1840 the Royal Society for the Prevention of Cruelty to Animals), to the 1876 passing of the Cruelty to Animals Act, and into the 1870s and 1880s vivisection debates, Victorian culture struggled over these ethical, political, and legislative questions, and this history of reform has been less well-considered—especially in relation to literary history—than most other comparable movements of the period.[18] Kelly Oliver argues that Anglo-American "rights discourse has assumed the Cartesian subject and . . . the Cartesian subject has been constructed through the sacrifice of the animal" (37). One of my aims is to consider how the Victorian novel participated in (and sometimes critiqued) this project of asserting the rights of the human against the animal.

England became especially known in the nineteenth century for its love of animals. Some of the various, often ambivalent and conflicted, manifestations of that love are another recurring concern of this book and can be understood as the reverse or counterpart of the various forms of domination, abuse, and what Derrida calls "disanimalization" so evident throughout the century. Among other things, this book aims to consider the meanings and effects of the noteworthy, sometimes passionate relationships with pet animals in the novels and the lives of the authors I examine. Following Donna Haraway's lead, I ask what are the consequences of taking seriously the proposition that dogs and other domesticated animals functioned as "companion species" within Victorian Britain, their lives deeply imbricated in and influencing human culture and narrative. In the pages to follow, I consider, among others, Emily Brontë's Keeper and the many dogs of *Wuthering Heights*; the favorite "stout well-fed pony" of *Agnes Grey*; Jip in *David Copperfield*, Dickens's own dog Sultan, and the "immense" dogs who "fought for veal cutlets out of a silver basket" in Pip's fantasy version of his first visit to Miss Havisham's; the "tiny Maltese puppy," Sir James's rejected gift to Dorothea, and the "pair of beautiful goats" that Mr. Farebrother "set up . . . to be pets of the village in general, and to walk at large as sacred animals" in *Middlemarch*; the many dogs and cats of Thomas Hardy and his wives and the many domestic animals he depicts, including the doomed sheep of *Far from the Madding Crowd*; Conan Doyle's hound of the Baskervilles; and Doss, the dog in *The Story of an African Farm*. I consider how these animals were loved, valued, marked out as special; what meanings they convey in the texts in which they appear; how they were remembered and written about; how they died and were or were not memorialized; and how they appear in what Woloch calls the "character space" of the Victorian novel.

One characteristic move of the Victorian novel is to mark a division between those characters—often marked out as heartless, selfish, or cruel—who abuse animals and those more ethical or sympathetic individuals who can appreciate, sympathize with, protect, "go along with," and even love animals, or at least certain animals. George Eliot famously writes in *Middlemarch* that "if we had a keen vision and feeling of all ordinary human life, it would be like hearing the grass grow and the squirrel's heart beat, and we should die of that roar which lies on the other side of silence. As it is, the quickest of us walk about well wadded with stupidity" (124). Robyn Warhol summarizes Eliot's point here: "If we could clearly see and feel the details of the ordinary, it would kill us; if we could hear the tiny sounds made by every living thing, we would die of the roar. . . . [Eliot] implies that the very imperceptibility of the ordinary makes these seemingly insignificant details impossible to speak about" (58). It is probably no surprise that I am more interested in the squirrel in this passage than Warhol or most other commentators are. The squirrel can certainly be reasonably read as a figure for a being who necessarily lies beyond sympathy, understanding, or interest: the point of the passage seems to be that to hear this insignificant (nonsignifying, noninterpretable) being's heartbeat would be akin to madness.[19]

And yet, Eliot's famous image is one of those literary figures that, even as it negates or rejects a possibility, in so representing it opens it up for consideration. Eliot wrote *Middlemarch* at a cultural moment—several years before the passing of the revised 1876 Cruelty to Animals Act—when sympathy for animals was becoming increasingly less marginal, more thinkable, and I read this passage as at least posing the questions: what if we *did* listen to the squirrel's heartbeat? How do we determine which beings deserve (and do not deserve) to be heard, to be listened to, valued, sympathized with, cared for? Eliot poses a question very similar to the one Derrida addresses when he admits that some readers "might object . . . that what I am doing is simply an almost limitless broadening of the notion of 'fellow' and that in talking about the dissimilar, the non-fellow, I am surreptitiously extending the similar, the fellow, to all forms of life, all species" (*Beast* 1: 109). True, Eliot seems to be saying that one cannot possibly sympathize with every animal and that to consider doing so, to perform a Derridean act of "hyperbolical hospitality" beyond the human, would be akin to madness; yet this passage also suggests that to "walk about well wadded with stupidity"—closing our ears to the many beings who do not appear to matter very much—is also a moral and a sensory failing.

To cite one small but telling example, consider the puppy that Dorothea is offered but rejects as a gift from a suitor early on in *Middlemarch*: "The objectionable puppy, whose nose and eyes were equally black and expressive, was . . . got rid of, since Miss Brooke decided that it had better not been born." As I demonstrate in chapter 4, *Middlemarch* is in fact filled with marginal or passing references to animals and household pets ranging from puppies to goats that, I argue, are in fact crucially bound up with the novel's very representation of humanness within a broader concept of organic life. It is a mistake to read Eliot's masterpiece with a sense that the definition of *the human* is fixed in place at the onset; instead, we should trace the ways the novel sets into play its own version of Agamben's "anthropological machine" that separates and distinguishes different forms of life, identity, and character. For Dorothea to count as the

novel's protagonist, she must prove at once not only that she is not herself
an animal but *also* that she is the sort of person who may be capable of
love for animals; her straightforward rejection of the pet dog threatens to
align her with the haters and abusers of animals who, since the novels of
the Brontës, had been identified as incapable of the proper sympathy that
defines the human. The human subject, the protagonist, must at least attempt to listen for the animal heartbeat.

Throughout this book, I consider and explore many of the different
ways that Victorian authors and characters grappled with such questions
and considered the species limits to their own sympathy and love. The
story I tell culminates in the work of Thomas Hardy and Olive Schreiner,
who explore in different ways a new possibility: that of what Schreiner
calls "infinite compassion"—that is, of a love and compassion or sympathy that would go beyond the usual species limits, even beyond the sanctioned and limited love of the family pet.[20] In this work from the last few
decades of the nineteenth century, we see new approaches to the question of how one might deploy literature as, in Derrida's words, a "radical
means of thinking the finitude that we share with animals" (*Animal* 28).
Animals finally threaten to move to the center of the hitherto profoundly
anthropocentric form of the Victorian novel, even possibly into the space
of protagonicity; to assert a claim as a fellow to the human. Derrida asks:
"How does one recognize a fellow? Is the 'fellow' only what has human
form, or is it anything that is alive?" (*Beast* 1: 106). This book adds to this
the question: how does one recognize a novelistic character? Can it be
anything that is alive?

This book argues that the Victorian novel and the Victorian home
are two strongly related and codefining cultural forms that position the
domestic animal or pet in comparable ways—at once marginalizing and
alternately, in a sense, sacralizing the animal: that is, rendering that animal symbolically central and foundational. The Victorian literary animal is quite different from the—arguably more prestigious—romantic
or modernist animal. Discussing the "extensive literary phenomenology
of animals," Barbara Herrnstein Smith writes, "One thinks here of the
vivid animal evocations of Hopkins and Rilke, Lawrence and Hemingway,
Faulkner and Moore. A recurrent topos among these and other (largely
modernist) writers is what could be called the ontological thrill of the animal: that is, the sense of a sudden intensification—quickening or thicken-
ing—of Being, as experienced, for example, at the sighting of a large bird
or animal (hawk, deer, bear, or snake) in the wild" (5). As Smith suggests,
when we think of literary animals, our mind probably turns first to such

ontologically thrilling, romantic or modernist depictions of wildness. But my focus here is a cozier, homier variety of animal, one with strong links to the home and to domestication, which I argue was much more significant to the Victorian novel.

The household pet always poses boundary problems. Those exceptional animals we allow through the conceptual cat door of pet status are obviously biologically animal, but the symbolic and cultural positioning of these creatures who share our homes—and sometimes our beds and dinner plates—is less simple. Are pets animal, human? Thing or person? Some combination of these categories? Claude Lévi-Strauss in *The Savage Mind* influentially defined pet dogs as "metonymical human beings" (207), possessing a partial or incomplete personhood. "Having no social life of their own," he writes, dogs "form part of ours" (207). The pet's location in the family circle, "part of" and subsumed in our "life," can seem to offer proof of its falsity to its wild nature, its shift from a natural state to a human culture where it does not belong. Pets are often associated with sentimentality precisely because they can appear preeminent figures of excessive or otherwise improper sentiment, as recipients of affect that should properly belong only to human beings. In *A Thousand Plateaus*, for instance, Gilles Deleuze and Félix Guattari vilify pets as sentimentalized possessions, describing "the family animal or pet" as "the Oedipalized animal as psychoanalysis sees it, as the image of the father, etc." (244). The theorists present themselves as instead interested in animals as embodiments of wildness, vitality, and "becoming," all qualities antithetical to those associated with pets: "Ahab's Moby-Dick is not like the little cat or dog owned by an elderly woman who honors and cherishes it. Lawrence's becoming-tortoise has nothing to do with a sentimental or domestic relation" (244). "There is always a possibility that a given animal, a louse, a cheetah or an elephant, will be treated as a pet" (241); after all, the authors imply witheringly, there are a lot of sentimental old ladies out there. Deleuze and Guattari's scorn is directed at those who would treat animals as pets: domestic, feminized, Oedipalized, "cherishe[d]," and confined to the home. If the proper destiny of the animal lies in a dynamic "becoming" within a state of wildness, in this view it finds a lifeless stasis and enclosure in front of the family hearth.

In its celebration of the laws of packs and swarms, *A Thousand Plateaus* elevates a modernist or postmodernist, masculine wild animal, satisfyingly other to human culture, at the expense of what clearly seems a sentimental premodernist or nineteenth-century feminized domestic pet. (Donna Haraway singles out Deleuze and Guattari's attack on the household pet for its "misogyny, fear of aging, incuriosity about animals, and horror at the ordinariness of the flesh" [*When Species* 30].)[21] And, indeed, Victorian British culture *did* in fact raise pet loving to new heights and can lay claim to a fundamental role in the construction of the modern family pet—along with Christmas, the Angel in the House, and the realist novel, among other inventions and influential adaptations—as a cherished object of sentiment. As Ritvo points out, "[b]y the middle of the nineteenth century what has been called the Victorian cult of pets was firmly established. *Punch* frequently satirized the foolishness of dog lovers who fed their pets from the table, dressed them in elaborate outfits, and allowed them to inconvenience human members of the household" (*Animal* 86). For Deleuze and Guattari and to others who follow their lead in theorizing animals and animality as offering possibilities of otherness beyond the human, the Victorian cult of pets is problematic precisely because it so foundationally emblematizes the link between pets and a sentimentalized home. What we might call the posthumanist critique of the sentimentality of pet keeping is not, however, I would suggest, so much completely wrong as too limited in the conclusions it draws. The antisentimentalist position on pets is correct in recognizing the link between pets and a highly affective vision of the home but fails to recognize a deeper point: that this very way of understanding domesticity, one invented or at least mass produced in the Victorian period—and whether or not one dislikes or approves of it—*always relied in the first place* on the existence of pets in the home and on the page. That is, the Victorian cult of domesticity and of family life does not retroactively sentimentalize the animal as pet; that very vision of domestic space and of domestic writing is crucially constituted by the pet, which operates as a defining and conceptually necessary supplement of affect to the home. As Susan Pearson writes, in the nineteenth-century American context, "both domestic pets and children were positioned as family-constituting beings that attracted emotional investment and care" (37). That a home permits the luxury of love for an animal in fact proves and ratifies its domesticity. In some sense, then, the conceptual categories of the sentimental home or domestic space cannot exist without the presence of the pet, that being that, as an object of extravagant, excessive, potentially "sentimental" love, demonstrates the power and potency of affect within the home.

This pet-dependent home is at once material and discursive, existing in space but just as much in language and in print. Hilda Kean observes that "from the 1850s the number of books published specifically on pets and their care escalated" (47) and that, while there are no books listed in the British Library catalog with "pets" in their title before 1800, there "are 11 between 1821 and 1860" and "49 between 1861 and 1880" (224). Victorian Britain became famous for its affinity for both long domestic novels and domestic pets, and there is a deeper logic than one might assume to the association Kean notes between pets on the one hand and books about or depicting pets on the other. As pets and pet keeping became increasingly popular and culturally visible, their literary representation naturally flourished, but a more substantial cultural binding linked these two forms, pet and book, as repositories of potentially excessive (elaborate, inconvenient, escalating) sentiments that are excessive precisely because directed at something other than a human person. Novels and pets become in the Victorian period not just instances or proofs of domesticity but constitutive of the concept. The sentimental Victorian home is created and maintained through the excessive affect lavished on and in print narratives and on pet animals.

Consider, for instance, the preface to Jane Webb Loudon's *Domestic Pets: Their Habits and Management* (1851), in which the author depicts herself as writing not just about pet animals but in a space defined by their presence: "Now . . . that I chance to have a short interval of leisure, I have taken up the subject in earnest, and with my favourite dog lying at my feet, a cat purring on a sofa at my side, and two gold fish swimming merrily about in a vase before me, I sit down to write about the animals I am so fond of; and fortunately for the interest of my book, thousands of other people are equally fond as myself" (iii). Loudon explains how books are like pets and vice versa, both objects of affection and interest produced and defined by the light of the domestic hearth within an interior space of edifying leisure. Loudon writes with no other human companion, yet in a state of sociability, enclosed in a private space yet connected by bonds of sentiment to a mass print readership of "thousands of other people . . . equally fond as myself." Her pet loving becomes an element of and a spur to literary production, and her writing a testament to and multiplication of her fondness. For Loudon and for many of her peers, the writing or reading of a book about pets was simply an explicit instance of a broader tendency to view print culture as embedded in a context of domestic family sentiment—and one that crucially included animals as, among other things, proofs of the expansive, incorporative powers of such sentiment. In Loudon's comments, we can see a distinctly mid-Victorian representation of writing and of literature as not simply domestic but as including a necessary sentimental nonhuman supplement within domestic space: "with my favourite dog lying at my feet."

Victorian literature, especially the genre of the realist novel, was preoccupied with a project of measuring and testing the boundaries and limits of the family, asking: who belongs as an enfranchised occupant of domestic space, who may be represented as domesticated, a friend to man,
native to the home and within the genres of the home? One key proof
of the power of domestic feeling or fondness was its capacity to draw
in figures from outside to inside, to seize on those lacking satisfying or
proper domesticity—orphans, criminals, the poor, animals, the geographi-
cally and ethnically peripheral—and grant domesticity to them through
a humanizing process that displays its power precisely in going beyond
the already sanctioned. This book argues that many of the greatest and
most cherished works of Victorian fiction—*Jane Eyre, Wuthering Heights,
Agnes Grey,* Gaskell's *The Life of Charlotte Brontë* (if we can include that),
*David Copperfield, Great Expectations, Bleak House, Middlemarch, The
Descent of Man,* and *The Variation of Animals and Plants under Domestication* (if we can include those), *Far from the Madding Crowd, Tess of the
D'Urbervilles, The Hound of the Baskervilles,* and *The Story of an African Farm*—turn out to be, to a surprising degree, interested in the various
ways animals are brought into the home as pets or denied access to that
domestic space in gestures of inclusion or exclusion that can express larger
structures of belonging or nonbelonging. Some of these novels (*Wuthering
Heights, David Copperfield, Tess, The Story of an African Farm*) contain
extensive representations of actual pets and other animals, while others
(*Great Expectations, Bleak House*) play out related concerns less in terms
of literal representations than in their patterns of imagery, allusion, and
reference. But just as animals were surprisingly central—economically,
emotionally, and culturally—to Victorian Britain, so are pets and other domestic animals surprisingly prominent within Victorian literature as potent symbols and proof of the inclusivity of family feeling and its power to
draw selected potential outsiders into a charmed interior circle where sentiment becomes supercharged. Not any animal can become a sanctified
pet, of course; as Loudon explains, "the four-footed domestic pets I have
written about at length in this work, are dogs, cats, and squirrels . . . I have
slightly mentioned monkeys, though I think the latter so mischievous and
disagreeable that they scarcely deserve to be called Domestic Pets" (iv).
The pet is a conceptual category strongly defined by what lies outside of
it; any pet implicitly stands in relation to a far greater number and mass of
animals who are not and cannot be pets—and who therefore cannot matter and can only be matter (or meat).

Dickens's Jip, Dora's spaniel dog in *David Copperfield*, can serve here as just one representative example of the tendency of pets to leave traces across the pages of Victorian texts. Dora attempts ineffectually to maintain the family financial account book, a synecdoche for the household itself:

> When she had entered two or three laborious items in the account-book, Jip would walk over the page, wagging his tail, and smear them all out. Her own little right-hand middle finger got steeped to the very bone in ink; and I think that was the only decided result obtained. . . . [S]he would bring out the immense account-book, and lay it down upon the table, with a deep sigh. Then she would open it at the place where Jip had made it illegible last night, and call Jip up, to look at his misdeeds. This would occasion a diversion in Jip's favour, and some inking of his nose, perhaps, as a penalty. Then she would tell Jip to lie down on the table instantly, "like a lion"—which was one of his tricks, though I cannot say the likeness was striking—and, if he were in an obedient humour, he would obey. Then she would take up a pen, and begin to write, and find a hair in it. . . . And then she would give it up as a bad job, and put the account-book away, after pretending to crush the lion with it. (595–96)

Dora claims that he is "like a lion," but of course the joke is that he is so thoroughly domesticated as to be as little like a wild animal as one could imagine. Here we see a process comparable to that by which Darwin distinguished between the heroic little monkey and the fierce baboon, the domestic or domesticable animal—a potential friend to man—and the one who cannot become such a friend. Like Jane Loudon's favorite dogs, cats, and goldfish, Jip occupies the same household space as does the text, walking over the pages and serving as a writing instrument: a kind of animated, four-legged ink pen.[22] As Jip ruins David and Dora's housekeeping and steps all over their pages, he becomes a figure for affection and sentiment—as emotions that are textually constructed or induced. "Jip *would* bark at me, . . . gnash[ing] his teeth with jealousy," David complains when he is first courting Dora. "If he had the least idea how I adored his mistress, well he might" (445). To reach Dora, David must find a way to displace or at least join Jip in his adoration of her. *David Copperfield*, like Loudon's *Domestic Pets*, is characteristically Victorian in the way it defines and oversees a realm of domestic sentiment that offers certain persons and creatures, privileged characters and pets, a wealth of affection and value denied to those outside the boundaries of the home so defined. "I couldn't care for any other dog but Jip" (644), Dora declares, prompting her aunt to declare of her (not Jip!), "Why, what a sensitive pet it is!" To be a Victorian "pet," a "petted thing," is, among other things, to be an object of *literary* attention and affection, to be allowed into the space of the home and of the literary genres defining and buttressing that space of "subjectivity-saturated" (Lynch 10) powerful feeling or love. Dora may claim that Jip is one of a kind, but part of the power of both novels and pets is their capacity for serial extension and the subsequent addition of a replacement or supplement. There is always potentially room for one more within this economy, at once expansive and limited, of household sentiment.

Following this introductory chapter, *Minor Creatures* turns to chapters on the Brontë sisters, Charles Dickens, George Eliot, the fiction of Thomas Hardy and of Arthur Conan Doyle, and a final chapter on South African novelist Olive Schreiner. The book's chapters trace a narrative arc from a cluster of "high Victorian" novels—revealing a new sympathy to animals in chapter 2 and worry about the limits of that sympathy in chapters 3 and 4—to a collection of later nineteenth-century novels that embody or move toward naturalism and early modernism: deepening the question of sympathy in Hardy, animal agency and the dissolution of human-animal boundaries in Schreiner. I tell a story in which the realist novel wants to incorporate nonhuman otherness—but only to a point; the more that boundary truly begins to break down, the harder it is to write a realist novel at all (at least in the familiar sense). Jane Bennett defines posthumanist thought as aiming "to find new techniques, in speech and art and mood, to disclose the participation of nonhumans in 'our' world" ("Systems" 225). In this book I consider the question of whether the Victorian realist novel was a purely human world and what room it found for the participation of nonhumans, especially those minor creatures whom it alternately embraced as friends and companions or rejected and expelled as brutes or mere animals.

Animal
of a
Pendulum
agency

(in

novel

Figure 2 Emily Brontë's diary paper, entry of Thursday, July 30, 1845. From Clement K. Shorter, *Charlotte Brontë and Her Circle* (London: Hodder and Stoughton, 1896), 152.

CHAPTER TWO

Petted Things: Cruelty and
Sympathy in the Brontës

She knows how to hang puppies,
that Emily.
—Anne Carson, "The Glass Essay"

In the opening pages of *Jane Eyre*, when John Reed bursts into the family breakfast room looking for Jane and cannot find her, he calls out to his sisters, and labels Jane in a surprising manner: "tell mama she is run out into the rain—bad [X]!" (9). If asked to guess what that noun X is in John Reed's phrase, what comes to mind? Jane is viewed by the Reeds as an orphan, a quasi-servant, akin to a rebellious slave, as a deceitful liar, as a "caviller" (8), as an ungrateful "dependent" (11), an "interloper not of [their] race" (17), an "uncongenial alien" (17), among other designations. But it is none of those specific concepts that John Reed references here; rather, he labels her a "bad *animal*."

This chapter argues that this identification of Jane Eyre as an "animal" (she is later compared to, among other images, a bird in a cage and a slaughtered lamb) offers a clue to a much broader discourse and logic that informs all of the novels published by the Brontë sisters in 1847. We know from friends and biographers like Ellen Nussey that "[t]he Brontës' love of dumb animals made them very sensitive of the treatment bestowed upon them" (429); their novels were written in conversation with an emergent set of social, political, and philosophical questions regarding the human treatment of animals. Even when the question of cruelty to animals is not an explicitly represented topic, questions and issues surrounding human responsibility to animals structure the Brontës' work more fundamentally than has been recognized. The Brontës, I will suggest, understood the creative process by which an author invests a fictional character with life as one fundamentally related to the imaginative act by which a human being grants ethical stature to the animal. It was therefore through the Brontës' drawing on the discourse of animal suffering and of cruelty to animals, I argue, that Victorian narrative and characterization developed some of their signature techniques and tropes. In *Agnes Grey*, *Jane Eyre*, and *Wuthering Heights*, the domestic animal emerges as symbolically central yet still marginal, a supplement to the home and to the human that proves the sympathetic potential of those categories. After the novels of the Brontës, to be capable of love for animals becomes a prerequisite of protagonicity; yet to love animals too much remains a threat to that status. One must learn to "go along with" animals but not to follow them down the rabbit hole.

In her analysis of the implications of the figure of the governess in Victorian culture, Mary Poovey argued that "the governess was asked to stabilize the contradiction inherent in the middle-class domestic ideal" (128) by, among other things, specifying and defining the boundary "between 'well-bred, well-educated and perfect gentlewomen,' on the one hand, and, on the other, the 'low-born, ignorant, and vulgar' women of the working class." I argue, however, that Anne Brontë's *Agnes Grey* also suggests a different boundary fixed by the governess: that between the human and the domesticated on the one hand and the animal, nonhuman, and/or nondomestic(ated) on the other. Indeed, Brontë's novel positions Agnes's authority as governess such that it must repeatedly define and assert itself via what we could think of as species sovereignty or sovereignty always expressed in relation to a spectrum of dominated forms of life. As Poovey and others have argued, the discourse around the Victorian governess reveals much about the meanings of middle-class ideals of gender, but I suggest that it also tells us something about how gender was constructed in relations to figures of species and animality. I invoke Poovey's work here in part to demonstrate how often the scholarship of the past few decades, in its elucidation of the power dynamics of gender, race, or class, has tended to neglect or to leave to one side the no less salient category of species.

My use of the concept of sovereignty draws from Jacques Derrida's discussion in *The Beast and the Sovereign* of the historical and philosophical links between the concept of sovereignty and of species. Derrida concludes a reading of the dynamics of species and sovereignty in Hobbes with a discussion of the ways he elevates both the "sovereign" (that is, the "master, king, husband, father")—and "ipseity" itself, meaning a sense of indivisible selfhood—while "below, subjected to his service," are "the slave, the beast, the woman, the child" (*Beast* 1: 30). In a state of nature, "it is the mother . . . who controls the child" (29) by virtue of her indisputable maternity; in civil society, however, with its system of sovereignty, the "absolute right of the father" (29) displaces the mother and situates her on the side of the ruled, along with children and beasts. "[T]he beast was often the living thing to be subjected, dominated, domesticated, mastered, like, by a not insignificant analogy, the woman, the slave, or the child" (66). Kelly Oliver echoes Derrida's claims in her argument that "the discourse of rights" itself, in Anglo-American culture, "developed in relation to owning animals. . . . Much of what we take to be constitutional rights began, in one sense or another, with the domestication, use, and owning of animals" (37). And Monica Flegel argues that the "presence of pets in the home fully supported the conception of the paterfamilias as individual representative of male power writ large; including animals within the family meant the ruler of the home embodied masculine authority over both lesser humans and beasts" (97–98).

Considering Derrida's, Oliver's, and Flegel's comments in relation to Poovey's arguments about the governess in Victorian culture allows us to see that the power or authority of the Victorian governess existed in an ambiguous and difficult relation to hierarchies of household, gender, and of species authority. The governess was forced to wield a fundamentally "divisible" authority (in Derrida's terms), a problematic household authority that altogether lacked the "ipseity" or "indivisible," unquestionable right of power associated with sovereignty.[1] Poovey cites Lady Eastlake writing in her famous 1848 *Quarterly Review* piece on *Vanity Fair* and *Jane Eyre* that the governesses' situation, more than any other social ill, "'painfully expresses the peculiar *tyranny* of our present state of civilization'" (qtd. 132). Recognizing that the surplus of well-educated governesses willing to work at servant wages was at once a result of (Poovey's words) the "volatile fluctuations of the modern, industrializing economy" (132) and a necessary solution for it (in allowing middle-class families to educate their children cheaply), Lady Eastlake declared that "'[w]e need the imprudencies, extravagancies, mistakes, or crimes of a certain number of fathers, to sow that seed from which we reap the harvest of governesses'" (132). Eastlake's imagery at once positions the governess in relation to sovereignty (via "tyranny") and to a metaphorics of what we could call life and the living. Citing—along with Lady Eastlake's image of a "harvest" of governesses—an 1844 article in *Fraser's* that characterizes governesses as "plants in a hot-house" who either "snap yearly from the stalk" or "prolong a withered, sickly life," Poovey argues that "the image of the short-

lived or barren plant elaborates the causal connection between the governess and the lunatic by metaphorically tying both to a vitality stunted,
silenced, driven mad by denial and restraint" (130).

Poovey discusses this "vitality" only briefly, but I suggest that the paradox of the governess can be found precisely in her ambiguous status as
both dominated being and supposed master of the creatures of the household, situated unstably on the boundary of a series of power relationships
of gender, class, and also of species. Her plantlike "vitality," in the *Fraser's* piece, suggests her proximity to "life" itself as the basic currency of
power, the object of social domination. Political power itself, in the state
or household, derives from a biopolitical exercise of control over the animal life or vitality of subjects. Derrida's argument suggests that in a state
of nature, the mother possessed mastery over the children but that this
mastery was displaced in civil society by the artificial or invented new
form of power of the father/king, that of "sovereignty," which newly positions women with the children and animals in subjugation. *Agnes Grey*
positions its protagonist as placed in a somewhat impossible position as a
governess who is, as a servant, one of those "living thing[s] to be subjected,
dominated, domesticated, mastered"—yet is also expected, by job description, to master and control all the living things within the home. Agnes's
story becomes, importantly, a matter of asserting her mastery over the
animal life of the household, although she achieves this less by assertions
of power than via acts of sympathy with the nonhuman. Indeed, as this
book will argue throughout, to have power as a human being in Victorian
culture, or to possess characterological status as a character in Victorian
literature, *virtually requires the potential exercise of authority over an
animal*, whether this authority be dominating or sympathetic. One proves
one's status as a primary person in relation to a secondary animal, an animal rendered secondary (this is one implication and element of Derrida's
recurring stress on the figure of the animal as "following" man). The writing and reading of novels at once and variously participates fully in and, at
times (especially in the second half of the nineteenth century), begins to
resist this logic by pointing to less domineering possibilities for human-
animal relations.

Following the idyll of the novel's opening pages, when Agnes lived
happily in modest prosperity with her parents and sister, the household of
Agnes Grey is disrupted by a bad investment and the subsequent mental
and physical weakening of the head of the household, Agnes's father: "The
useful pony phaeton was sold, together with the stout well-fed pony—the
old favorite that we had fully determined should end its days in peace,

and never pass from our hands; the little coach house and stable were let, the servant boy, and the more efficient (being the more expensive) of the two maid servants was dismissed" (9). We see an emphasis—which recurs throughout the novel—on the household animals or pets as not extraneous but basic and essential to the totality of the domestic whole. The "peace" of the household and even its very definition *as* a household seems to have relied importantly on the "old favorite" pony's well-being. The domestic exception to the rule, the pony's happy life becomes proof of the household's humanity and restraint. Unlike most animals, the pony was "well-fed" rather than food itself. The pony is positioned somewhere between the "things" and objects of the household on the one hand and the human family members on the other: and, indeed, the pony seems more a member of the family than the "maid servant" whose absence is mostly lamented due to her "efficiency."

Efficiency as a principle may in fact be positioned *against* the kind of love of animals the novel promotes, in that love and care for animals is, at least beyond the degree to which it is profitable or linked to household supplies like eggs, meat, or wool, always in some sense extravagant, excessive, operating in an affective gift economy, going beyond what is useful or practical. One could even invert the terms here to hypothesize that in this novel, the gift of extravagant feeling, or of sympathies going beyond what is efficacious, becomes specifically linked to love or caring for animals. Loving animals is an affective stance valued for its *inefficiency* and thus linked at once to the aesthetic and to one idealized version of the domestic; its value is a countervalue, a value incommensurable with household and public economies, in which animals can only count as material or labor. To be able to *love* an animal, to claim it as a pet rather than to eat it (or to otherwise *use* it), is a show of resources, both emotional and otherwise.

To hold onto the pony, to "never" let it "pass from our hands," is now, in *Agnes Grey*, revealed as a practice of the lost way of life of a household whose nonhuman creatures lived in "peace" and continuity with the humans. For the sake of economy, "we sat with our feet on the fender, scraping the perishing embers together from time to time, and occasionally adding a slight scattering of the dust and fragments of coal, just to keep them alive" (9): expressed here metaphorically is a larger principle that the vitality of the household is measured by its skill and effectiveness (if not "efficiency") in *keeping alive*, in maintaining vitality. And with the decline of the father, that which was kept alive, not permitted out of the family's hands, is no longer safe but is instead marked by breaks, absence, and departures.

This state of rupture and can also be considered as a crisis of household sovereignty: who has authority over the household? Brontë stresses that the mother's power and efficacy are linked—if only from a "perverted" perspective—with the father's decline: "The very willingness with which she performed these duties, the cheerfulness with which she bore her reverses, and the kindness which withheld her from imputing the slightest blame to him, were all perverted by this ingenious self-tormenter into further aggravations of his sufferings" (9). "Being so clever and diligent herself," Agnes's mother "was never tempted to trust her affairs to a deputy, but on the contrary, was willing to act and think for others as well as for number one" (9). So, after the weakening of the father, the mother is now the real sovereign—or at least a usurper or replacement for the sovereign: it's not clear if she can in fact possess this role non-"perversely." To return to Derrida's formulations, we see a difficulty regarding the indivisibility of sovereignty, which in his account is crucially linked to "ipseity": "the concept of sovereignty will always imply the possibility of this positionality, . . . this autoposition of him who posits or posits himself as *ipsei, the (self-) same, oneself*" (*Beast* 1: 67). For Agnes's father, it does seem to be the case that once his authority begins to break down, it collapses in a recursive and self-perpetuating, "perverted" perception of weakness that shatters not just his authority but his very subjectivity or sense of self-possession.

For Agnes, there is a problem here regarding her own position in the family in relation to power and sovereignty. She is eighteen years old, "a woman in my own estimation" but "still a child in theirs." And to the mother, the holder of the power, Agnes is allied less with mature agency than with a realm of play and leisure associated with the most immature domestic pets:

> "Then let me help you."
> "You cannot indeed, dear child. Go and practice your music, or play with the kitten." . . .
> [T]hey liked better to see me prosecuting my studies, or amusing myself—it was time enough for me to sit bending over my work like a grave matron, when my favorite little pussy was become a steady old cat. Under such circumstances, although I was not many degrees more useful than the kitten, my idleness was not entirely without excuse. (10)

We see again a household pet operating as a point of reference for the family, which defines and assesses itself in reference to the animals it takes

in, contains, and manages. They had "fully determined" that "the stout
well-fed pony . . . should end its days in peace, and never pass from our
hands" (9): that was one vision of domestic happiness, and a figure of luxury or wealth, an expectation that the family would be able to oversee
the pony's entire lifespan. Agnes's own maturity is, somewhat similarly,
keyed to that of the kitten, her own abilities and responsibilities measured
against its feeble powers. (And the image of the "favorite little pussy"
turned "steady old cat" assimilates her own biological timescale to that of
the cat.) To exist in a form "not many degrees more useful than a kitten"
is to occupy a position of luxurious dependence and almost absolute weakness. One may and should care for a helpless kitten—but to become akin
to a kitten goes too far.[2]

Following the financial collapse of her father's and thus the family's fi-
nances, Agnes's domestic idyll truly ends, and she enters into a new career
as a domestic governess. She soon discovers, to her dismay, that the household in which she finds employment is a veritable hell for nonhuman living creatures: the poor discipline and chaos of the household leads to or
even promotes, again and again, acts of violence against birds, mice, and
other small creatures. Agnes discovers that the favorite "amusement" of
her young charge, Tom, is to mutilate and torture baby birds:

> "And what do you do with them, when you catch them?"
>
> "Different things. Sometimes I give them to the cat; sometimes I
> cut them in pieces with my penknife; but the next, I mean to roast
> alive."
>
> "And why do you mean to do such a horrible thing?"
>
> "For two reasons: first, to see how long it will live—and then, to
> see what it will taste like." (20)

Agnes tries to convince Tom of the evil of such behavior: "But don't you
know it is extremely wicked to do such things? Remember, the birds can
feel as well as you, and think, how would you like it yourself?" Tom, however, rebuts her moral argument by denying that sympathy can occur beyond the boundary of species: "Oh, that's nothing! I'm not a bird, and I
can't feel what I do to them" (20).

We remember Agnes's "well-fed" pony and the sense of luxury and of
going beyond efficiency or economy that accompanied love of animals in
her childhood home. Now, she expresses a willingness to pay what little
she has, or far beyond it, for the possibility of seeing the animal secure
its revenge: "he treated them so brutally that, poor as I was, I would have

given a sovereign any day to see one of them bite him, provided the animal could have done it with impunity" (42). In her comfortable childhood, to love an animal and treat it as a pet or companion was a kind of gift, an excessive going beyond the usual laws that would treat animal flesh as material for use or consumption. Now Agnes is in effect willing to spend her last sovereign—to pay any price, even beyond an economic measure of value—to turn the tables on Tom. Driven by his continued sadism toward animals, and his parents' toleration of his cruelty, Agnes finally performs her own act of violence against the set of baby birds she knows will be tortured by this "little tyrant" if they live: "I got a large flat stone, that had been reared up for a mouse-trap by the gardener, then, having once more vainly endeavored to persuade the little tyrant to let the birds be carried back, I asked what he intended to do with them. With fiendish glee he commenced a list of torments, and while he was busied in the relation, I dropped the stone upon his intended victims, and crushed them flat beneath it" (43). Anne Brontë here raises a set of ethical and representational questions concerning the limits and requirements of sympathy with animals, cruelty or violence to animals, and the depiction of such violence. We learn of Agnes's character, her compassion, through her objection to, at once, the sadism of Tom Bloomfield—whose "face twisted into all manner of contortions in the ecstasy of his delight" (42) as he plans his tortures— and to the cruel indifference and lack of compassion on his mother's part: she views Agnes's intervention with disapproval, concluding that "a child's amusement is scarcely to be weighed against the welfare of a soulless brute" (45). That the very rock Agnes uses for her mission of mercy was to be used by the gardener as a mousetrap suggests how thoroughly this society is suffused by violence to animals: this is not simply the quirk of a single family but, it is implied, a characteristic of the society more generally. Agnes modernizes the household by denying the pleasures of a "little tyrant" who embodies a premodern ethics and power that takes the wrong kind of pleasure in the killing of animals. Tom's sadism toward animals is echoed in Charlotte's depiction of John Reed's "tyrannies" in *Jane Eyre*: "John, no one thwarted, much less punished; though he twisted the necks of the pigeons, killed the little pea-chicks, set the dogs at the sheep, stripped the hot-house vines of their fruit" (15). In the Yorkshire world of the Brontës, tyranny manifests itself through gratuitous cruelty to animals.

The scene of animal cruelty becomes an ethical theater in which at least four roles stand out: the cruel sadist, who enjoys inflicting pain; the coolly indifferent actor—the gardener—who weeds out pests without a

care; the cruelly indifferent observer, who can witness the sadistic act and
the animal's pain without feeling; and the feeling observer who acts in
response to the abuse or responds to it with strong compassion and sympathy. Yet the sheer power of the image of the stone crushing the baby
birds produces an additional unresolved tension in this passage. If we respond with horror, at least we respond; it is difficult to cordon off a reader's proper dismay at such a scene from an undercurrent of voyeuristic
fascination. The exercise of power over the animal is fundamental to this
novel's—and the Victorian novel's, more broadly—project of organizing
and hierarchizing life and of sorting out the categories of person and non-
person, character and noncharacter. Such scenes of violence performed to
and on the animal have become necessary to the novel, which must repeatedly stage the self-definition of the human character via such acts of
aggression. This is to say that the Victorian novel needs such acts of cruelty in order to condemn them, in order to prove its own investment in a
sympathetic and humane ethics.[3]

Agnes Grey, along with its companion novels *Wuthering Heights* (with
which it was issued in a single volume) and *Jane Eyre* (published a few
weeks earlier), was published, in 1847, at a moment when an animal-
welfare or anticruelty movement was taking its place as a powerful social
force in England, twenty-five years after the founding of the Society for
the Prevention of Cruelty to Animals.[4] In this year, the Vegetarian Society
of Great Britain was founded (Thomas 297), and Marshall Hall published
a controversial series of articles on animal experimentation and medical
ethics in the medical journal *The Lancet*.[5] In response to criticism accus-
ing him of "unjustifiable cruelty," Hall defended his approach to animal
experimentation:

> Is it right to "kill and eat," to preserve strength and health; and is it
> not right to perform experiments, with all the precautions which I
> have laid down, to promote that very science, on which not only the
> preservation, but the restoration, of strength and health depend! Or,
> if the animal is to be destroyed, is any more lenient mode of killing it
> known than that inflicted by asphyxia . . . ? May I ask the writer in the
> last number of the Medical and Chirurgical Review, how it will please
> him henceforth to dispose of superfluous puppies and kittens? (58)

Hall's comments suggest how easily the language of medical ethics, on
the topic of animal experimentation, overlaps with or crosses into a discourse of "sensibility" we associate with literature and fiction. Both kinds

of writing and thinking at this historical moment struggled to define the meaning of cruelty to animals, the limits of "leniency" toward other species, and the difficulty of ethical action in a world containing, perhaps, too many objects of potential sympathy. If we must kill animals, how may we do so without harming or hardening ourselves?[6]

When we think of animal characters in literature today, we probably think first not of realist fiction but of modern cartoons, comics, and children's books. As soon as we consider the likes of such cartoon animals as Garfield, Marmaduke, and Heathcliff, however, we will notice a surprising connection to the realm of classic Victorian fiction. That one of the most famous characters in Victorian fiction somehow migrated into a popular 1970s American cartoon is not a meaningless echo, I suggest, but a link that can point us toward important insights regarding the animality of Victorian fiction. The September 2001 London *Guardian* obituary for the cartoonist George Gately explains how, in 1973, Gately invented his most successful creation: "According to his brother, George was 'toying around with something based on a household pet' when he came up with a stylish cat and, rather incongruously, named him after Emily Brontë's romantic hero" (Hiley). We would probably all second the judgment that the cartoon cat Heathcliff's name seems somewhat "incongruous," but we can also notice the parallels that must have brought the name to mind for Gately. "The pugnacious Heathcliff," a "fat cat with attitude," the obituary reminds us, was "nominally owned by the Nutmeg family . . . but was very much his own character. . . . [S]elf-assertive . . . and underhand, he demanded the best food and the best seat in the house, then went out to terrorise the other pets in the neighbourhood. . . . But Heathcliff also had a gentle side, which he showed most willingly to a Persian cat named Sonja." Mutatis mutandis—the Earnshaws become the Nutmegs, Catherine becomes the Persian cat Sonja—perhaps this was the Heathcliff 1970s America required.

So, Heathcliff becomes a household pet, a cat with attitude (and is there, in fact, really any other kind?). If we can accept Heathcliff's pethood, then perhaps it will not take much of a leap to realize that Jane Eyre is, or began her existence as, a dog: not Heathcliff's Great Dane companion Marmaduke, but rather an ugly, ungainly, but passionately loyal dog named Clumsy. In her 1842 school notebook kept in Belgium, Charlotte Brontë sketched what seem to have been early notes toward *Jane Eyre*, the novel she would publish five years later, in an extract titled "The Two Dogs." The outline for a story begins with a husband bringing his wife a puppy as a gift. As the puppy matures, he loses favor. "Tell how he grows ugly in growing up; how his limbs enlarge. . . . Madam's disgust for him; the rebuffs he suffers. . . . Clumsy, for that is what she calls him now, banished to the yard; his degradation; detail his privations, the change in food and company" (*Belgian Essays* 60). We can read this as an early prototype of young Jane in Mrs. Reed's home, enduring her disgust and rebuffs, then banished to the "privations" and "change in food and company" of Lowood. Next, a rival appears, a pretty poodle named Zephyrette, "a well-bred dog, placed above all animals of her kind." This is, of course, the predecessor of Blanche Ingram, the embodiment of conventional—and shallow—female beauty and virtue. In the end, Clumsy, having suffered "privations" and "rebuffs," demonstrates the superiority of loyalty and strength of character to superficial graces and appearance. When two robbers enter the house, the faithless Zephyrette flirts with them whereas Clumsy fights them to the death with all the fierce loyalty Jane would later show to Rochester. Charlotte ends her notes with a reminder of the central lesson to be learned regarding character: "At that sight the master's regret over his conduct toward Clumsy and the preference given to the thankless Zephyrette." When this story would become *Jane Eyre*, of course, Clumsy would achieve a more satisfying triumph over the Zephyrette character.

The late work of Jacques Derrida, in which he turned his attention to issues of species, animality, and human-animal distinction, offers a compelling framework for considering the issues at stake in Charlotte and Emily Brontë's—as well as, more broadly, Victorian fiction's—representation of animals and animality. Derrida defines Western metaphysics as characterized by what he calls *carno-phallogocentrism* ("Eating Well" 280), an ideology in which "carnivorous virility" defines powerful subjectivity. Such an ideology demands a category of the nonhuman living: that which is alive but can be objectified as consumable meat.

"Can the voice of the friend be that of an animal?" Derrida asks. "Is friendship possible for the animal or between animals? Like Aristotle, Heidegger would say: no. Do we have a responsibility toward the living in general? The answer is still "no," and this may be because the question is formed, asked in such a way that the answer must necessarily be "no" according to the whole canonized or hegemonic discourse of Western metaphysics or religions" (280). Derrida goes on to argue that Western thought has always allowed "a place left open, in the very structure of these discourses . . . for a non-criminal putting to death." The "carnivorous sacrifice" is fundamental to these discourses and cultures. This is to say that Western culture is fundamentally structured by the necessity of the sacrifice and execution of the animal, that which is both living and nonliving, sentient yet a thing. Animals are like things or objects in that they may be owned, but unlike objects in that they *can* be killed; like human beings in that they are sentient, but unlike human beings in that they *may* be killed. Derrida argues that we demand such (non)things, beings permitted to be killed, in order to demarcate the human.

Such historians as Keith Thomas, Harriet Ritvo, Brian Harrison, James Turner, and Hilda Kean have vividly narrated the history of eighteenth- and nineteenth-century English attitudes toward animals—a history that permits us to test the more specific historical relevance of Derrida's broad claims. A major transformation occurred around the turn of the nineteenth century as a country that had been strongly associated with sports involving cruelty to animals such as bullbaiting and cockfighting, came increasingly to define itself—led by Evangelicals and middle-class reformers—by opposition to such cruelty.[7] It would seem, however, that it was not simply that cruelty to animals became newly defined as particularly un-English but that it became defined as particularly English—or rather, particularly bourgeois English—to *witness*, with condemnation and sympathy, the spectacle of cruelty to animals. We might draw an analogy with Foucault's famous argument about the history of sexuality and its supposed repression: here, too, that which is apparently being repressed—cruelty to animals—becomes increasingly discussed, represented, imagined. The mistreatment of animals becomes charged with new energies as the object of a national discourse. A class relationship is routed through a species relationship and vice versa, and the human and humane becomes defined not only *against* the animal, as in earlier centuries, but also in sympathy with the animal. As we've seen in *Agnes Grey*, the narrative of animal suffering—somewhat resembling in this the model Freud later defined in his 1919 "A Child Is Being Beaten"—opens up at least three distinct subject positions: the sadistic perpetrator of cruelty, the feeling witness, and the cruelly indifferent bystander.

The dynamic I discuss resembles the Victorian "scene of sympathy" as defined by Audrey Jaffe as marked by "a confrontation between a spectator 'at ease' and a sufferer" in which "the sufferer is effectively replaced by the spectator's image of him or herself" (2). Jaffe defines Victorian sympathy as fundamentally visual and middle class. The normative sympathetic subject is a middle-class observer, the object of sympathy a "deserving 'victim'" who "displaces attention from the destructive consequences of industrialization and the rise to power of the middle class" (21). In Jaffe's account, the scene of sympathy "involves a spectator's (dread) fantasy of occupying another's social place" (8); when the object of the gaze is other than human, however this dread may be at once mitigated—the animal *has* no properly "social place"—and, potentially, intensified. To whatever degree the animal *is* permitted a "social place," is enculturated or allowed to approach the human, this opens the possibility of a more disturbing reversal: that is, of the human spectator taking the place of the animal.

Ritvo bases her analysis of the history of the RSPCA in part on her interpretation of the society's lavish annual reports, filled with narratives of cruelty to animals. "Lurid reports" of the torments of animals, Ritvo writes, "often provided emotional guidance by recording the reactions of upstanding witnesses" (*Animal* 141). Readers could, for example, "imagine themselves among the crowds that had gathered to cry 'shame' on a carman beating his horse with a shovel" (142). As Ritvo's analysis suggests, these RSPCA reports, published annually from 1824 but especially influential from the 1840s on, typify an important genre of Victorian writing and one that bears consideration as an intertext of the novel in this period. To be a literate middle-class Englishperson by midcentury was to develop one's sensibility and sympathy through the vicarious experience of reading narratives of animal suffering, which allow the reader to stake a claim to his or her own humanity. The description and redescription of accounts of animal suffering became a familiar discursive mode accompanied by characteristic tropes, metaphors, and characters.[8] A response to Marshall Hall's 1847 letter to *The Lancet* cited earlier, for example, offers a characteristic example of the antivivisectionist version of this rhetorical mode, which often takes advantage of the technique of reciting an experimenter's description, framing it in a condemnatory commentary:

One would suppose, from the tone of that letter [Marshall Hall's], . . . that the experiment which 'called forth our censures had been instituted upon an animal that was deprived of sensation. That such was not the case on the occasion referred to is abundantly obvious from the very terms in which Dr. Hall's coadjutor has described the experiment in question: "In a spaniel dog, a portion of the skull was removed by the trephine; . . . The immediate effect was paralysis of the opposite side of the body; the animal, when placed on the ground, falling on that side, and being unable to rise. It managed, however, to struggle to the wall and corner, when, on being raised, it supported itself by leaning the paralyzed side against it. . . ." Can it be conceived that the infliction of such horrible suffering (for the animal, it would seem, was

quite sensible at the commencement of the experiment) is necessary
for the elucidation of any important truth . . . ? ("Reply to Dr. Marshall Hall")

The shock and moral outrage raised by such narratives—describing both
cruelty to animals on the streets and the horrors of vivisection and scientific experiment on animal subjects—became, I would suggest, linked to
the moral purposes of reading itself. Consider, for example, an 1836 letter
by the young Quaker W. E. Forster describing his mother: "[S]he has been
reading these dreadful things about galvanized frogs and impaled dogs,
etc., till she is the same herself as if she had a continual shock of galvanism about her" (qtd. in French 24). These are effective (and affective) narratives indeed, triggering forms of powerfully mimetic sympathy.

England, over the course of the nineteenth century, contained a growing and influential minority of citizens who cared about animals' welfare,
advocated against their cruel treatment, and even chose not to consume
animal flesh. The record of legislation from the 1822 Martin's Act to the
1876 Cruelty Against Animals Act can be read as one of progress and effective reform, as at least some of the more blatant forms of animal abuse became increasingly discouraged and condemned. Derrida's argument, however, asks us to supplement this narrative of reform and decreasing general
abuse of animals with recognition of the ways the nation may have repudiated its own continued investment in "carnivorous virility" through the
definition of a special *limited* category of beloved animals—domesticated
pets that were to be treated as friends or fellows and in need of protection.
Victorian culture, at the point that it has apparently achieved domination
through industry and technology over the forces of nature, redefines itself
through its creation of a special category of protected animals, animals
associated with pastoral qualities who become the victims of unenlight-
ened English people.[9] This is still carno-phallogocentrism, then, but one
that hopes to make up for killing and eating the living by protecting a
symbolic subcategory of animals not to be eaten or mistreated: that is,
the dogs, cats, and horses that received the lion's share of the RSPCA's
attention and that became increasingly vested with subjectivity in Victorian writing. Of these abused animals' fate at the hands of cruel English people, the founder of the SPCA, Lewis Gompertz, wrote in 1824:
"Their wants are disregarded, their desires curbed or destroyed, and their
bodies cut or disfigured, when it suits those persons' purpose so to do"
(7).[10] The animal becomes newly defined as a being possessing "wants,"

"desires," and possibly even rights, and the suffering or torture of animals became privileged occasions for the display of powerful affect—particularly sympathy—within narrative. These domesticated animals define a new subcategory of animals that are mournable, nameable, memorable (or in Judith Butler's terms, "grievable"; *Frames*)—animals that are afforded a limited exemption from the otherwise capacious category of "animal"— meaning creatures that can be used virtually at will for human purposes, as meat, entertainment, wool or hide, and so on.[11] My point here is not so much to cast a skeptical eye on the Victorian animal-welfare movement for its compromises; short of aiming to ban meat eating, it would always have needed to choose its battles and to focus on some areas for potential reform at the expense of others. Instead I note the necessity, in any animal-welfare politics, of drawing distinctions between different categories of animal and forms of harm or abuse.

The narratives of animal suffering and animal rescue defined by the annual RSPCA reports set the agenda for new genres of Victorian writing investing certain privileged animals with subjectivity and the characteristics of human beings. These genres emerged from earlier eighteenth-century depictions of animals, especially in children's literature, but they also mark a new, distinctly Victorian routing of feeling through animal and pet characters. A subgenre of melodrama called the "dog drama" was a staple on the London stage from the early part of the century through the 1850s (Turner 164). Joseph Taylor's 1804 *The General Character of the Dog* was, Keith Thomas claims (108), England's first sentimental book about dogs, but the category soon took off: Books filled with "heartwarming and enlightening anecdotes about dogs" (Ritvo, *Animal* 85–86) became increasingly popular during the first half of the nineteenth century. The "dog anecdote" becomes a recurring feature in a magazine like *Chambers's Edinburgh Journal*—which all three Brontë sisters read enthusiastically— through the 1840s. As I have already hinted, I want to argue that the work of Charlotte, Anne, and especially Emily Brontë might be influenced by— and even perhaps instances of—such a new Victorian genre of dog or pet narrative. For the Brontë sisters, narrative and fiction itself raised the same questions of sympathy, antipathy, cruelty, and scapegoating—and of the bounds of the human as defined by and against the animal—that RSPCA narratives of animal cruelty posed. *Wuthering Heights* in particular I see as underpinned by a framework of such issues, which were for Brontë fundamentally linked to animals, pets, and the ethical problem and narrative resource of the suffering animal.

A CARNIVOROUS RACE

Charlotte was more than commonly tender in her treatment of all
dumb creatures, and they, with that fine instinct so often noticed, were
invariably attracted towards her. . . . [S]he quickly noticed the least
want of care or tenderness on the part of others towards any poor brute
creature. . . . The feeling, which in Charlotte partook of something of
the nature of an affection, was, with Emily, more of a passion. Some
one speaking of her to me, in a careless kind of strength of expression,
said "she never showed regard to any human creature; all her love was
reserved for animals." The helplessness of an animal was its passport
to Charlotte's heart; the fierce, wild, intractability of its nature was
what often recommended it to Emily.
—Elizabeth Gaskell, *The Life of Charlotte Brontë*

Elizabeth Gaskell begins her biography of Charlotte Brontë in ethno-
graphic mode by defining the habits, practices, and qualities of the "interesting . . . race" (60) of people out of which the Brontës emerged, a Yorkshire "race," which Gaskell defines in part by its investment in cruelty
to animals. Gaskell's invocation of the category of "race" seems linked
to her vision of an eighteenth-century society in which divisions of class
are trumped by the allegiances of species. She depicts a society organized
around the "savage delight" of such spectacles as bullbaiting and cock-
fighting. She describes, for instance, a local squire who went to amazing lengths to end his life as a spectator to animal suffering. His "great
amusement and occupation had been cock-fighting. When he was confined
to his chamber with what he knew would be his last illness, he had his
cocks brought up there, and watched the bloody battle from his bed. As his
mortal disease increased, and it became impossible for him to turn so as
to follow the combat, he had looking-glasses arranged in such a manner,
around and above him, as he lay, that he could still see the cocks fighting.
And in this manner he died" (68). Here we see one of the primary subject
positions defined by the theater of animal cruelty: that of the cruel spectator who watches but does not intervene or sympathize. Yet the squire is
far from indifferent: he is a fascinated voyeur, unable to tear his eyes away
from the sight of animal violence to the point that he constructs a sadistic
theater of cruelty in order to enjoy it to his final moments.

The Brontë sisters appear strikingly eccentric and at odds with their
surroundings amid this culture of animal cruelty, possessed of special
virtues and talents that seem importantly linked to their repudiation of

carnivorousness. A family acquaintance commented: "[T]here never were such good children. I used to think them spiritless, they were so different to any children I had ever seen. In part, I set it down to a fancy Mr. Brontë had of not letting them have flesh-meat to eat" (87). (Interestingly, Patrick Brontë protested this detail in Gaskell's biography, apparently afraid of being blamed for his children's physical weakness, and it was omitted in the text's third edition.) A classmate of Charlotte at Miss Wooler's school observed, "She always showed physical feebleness in every thing. She ate no animal food at school. It was about this time I told her she was very ugly" (130).

The sisters, living amid a "race" of carnivorous virility, repudiate meat, violating the law that decrees that the "virile subject" is the one who "does not want just to master and possess nature actively" but who "accepts sacrifice and eats flesh" (Derrida, "Eating Well" 280). We might even consider a link between the sisters' social marginalization—due, in part, to their eccentric relationship to English carnivorousness and animality—and their creation of such fictional characters as Clumsy the dog and, later, their better known human characters. In such a figure as Clumsy or Jane Eyre, Charlotte Brontë invests life and sympathy into what had been viewed as dumb and unfeeling. The imaginative process of granting subjectivity to an animal serves a compensatory function. Fictional characterization itself becomes associated with a larger project of giving life to the nonliving, voice to "suffering dumb creation," that might be understood as a negotiation with carno-phallogocentrism. This is part of the process Richard French describes, within Victorian antivivisectionist politics and discourse, as an "attempt to infuse some kind of spirit into a materialistic . . . world" (383). While antivivisectionism came fully into its own as a reform movement only in the 1870s, English opposition to what was usually depicted as Continental physiology and animal experimentation was well established by the 1840s.[12] If Yorkshiremen and rough cart drivers take animal life, the Brontës (and their readers) give life, grant subjectivity to the animal or the nonliving through fictional characterization. The Victorian creation of affective fictional narratives and sympathetic characters becomes deeply bound up with sympathetic thinking about animals. The fictional investment of characters with sympathy becomes part of a general attempt to redeem a carnivorous and cruel society through feeling. The investment of special feeling into privileged domesticated animals becomes an occasion for the proof of special sympathies on the part of those more sympathetic individuals who refrain from treating their pets cruelly and who can sanctify the home with love for a pet. (And yet, outside of children's literature or fantasy, no animal can in fact achieve protagonicity in a realist novel; the limits remain in place.)

As Charlotte did, Emily Brontë also wrote an essay in Belgium on household pets. In it, she argues about feline character with a fine lady who insists that human beings are less cruel than cats:

> "But," says some delicate lady, who has murdered a half-dozen lapdogs through pure affection, "the cat is such a cruel beast, he is not content to kill his prey, he torments it before its death; you cannot make this accusation against us." More or less, Madame. . . . You yourself avoid a bloody spectacle because it wounds your weak nerves. But I have seen you embrace your child in transports, when he came to show you a beautiful butterfly crushed between his cruel little fingers; and at that moment, I really wanted to have a cat, with the tail of a half-devoured rat hanging from its mouth, to present as the image, the true copy, of your angel. (*Belgian Essays* 56–58)

In this almost Baudelairean prose fragment, Emily Brontë powerfully questions the distinctions Victorian society posits between different forms of the taking of animal life and between the human and the non- or inhuman. She suggests that a shrinking from "the blood sacrifice" distinguishes modern Victorian society from its more openly brutal past but questions whether more civilized forms of bourgeois violence against the animal can be in fact exempt themselves from the same category of cruelty. This delicate lady's "affection" to her pets is itself murderous, and, like Anne Brontë's Mrs. Bloomfield, she encourages cruelty to animals in her child and thereby turns such cruelty into a national and familial inheritance. What is startling and slightly disconcerting in Emily's passage is the final statement of desire for an "image" of cruelty to "present" to the woman. The cat with the rat in its mouth who is a "true copy" of the young boy is civilization's guilty conscience, a reminder of the fundamental carnivorousness of Englishness. Emily's "image" has something in common with Anne's of Agnes's rock falling on the baby birds, crushing them in a blow: both images share a reformist desire to reduce violence to animals, or induce some truer recognition of it, through the depiction of such an act. But whereas Agnes's act of violence is clearly marked as regretful, a last-ditch emergency measure to forestall future torture, Emily seems uncomfortably to relish the picture she sketches of the cat with a tail hanging from its mouth as an image of a child's violence. There is, one must admit, an aesthetic charge in such a scene or image, a representational force inherent in the depiction of violence to the animal. Presented with such an image, we must respond emotionally; not to do so would be to fail a basic test of our fitness as readers.

CREATURE HEATHCLIFF

Emily's essay invites a consideration of the ways her later novel *Wuthering Heights* is structured by similar questions of animality, cruelty, and pethood. Heathcliff in particular becomes, in the novel, the test case for the human treatment of animals. The question Isabella Linton asks, "Is Mr. Heathcliff a man?" (136), seems one Brontë intends for us to consider with a certain literalness. Critical attention to Heathcliff since the 1980s has tended to focus on the ways Brontë depicts him as racially or ethnically "other," pointing to such evidence as Nelly Dean's attempt to reassure Heathcliff that "A good heart will help you to a bonny face, my lad . . . if you were a regular black. . . . You're fit for a prince in disguise. Who knows, but your father was Emperor of China, and your mother an Indian queen, each of them able to buy up, with one week's income, Wuthering Heights and Thrushcross Grange together? And you were kidnapped by wicked sailors, and brought to England" (56). Brontë's insistent *animalization* of Heathcliff has received much less recent attention, probably because such a figurative strategy is often seen simply as a component of the dehumanization we associate with racism.[13] Susan Meyer, for example, characterizes Heathcliff as "pronounced upon as if he were a specimen of some strange animal species" but then immediately subsumes his animalization into the topics of race and ethnicity: "Heathcliff is subjected to the potent gaze of a racial arrogance deriving from British imperialism. . . . As the Lintons inspect the adolescent Heathcliff . . . they return him, with the power of the gaze of empire, to the status of racial property . . . and fix him into the role of inferior racial outsider" (97–99). The arguments of Meyer and other critics who have attended to the dynamics of race and imperialism in *Wuthering Heights* were and are convincing and necessary, but I want to think more literally about what it means that Heathcliff, whose hair is like "a colt's mane" (57), is so forcefully associated with animals; *species* is as salient as race as a category by which to consider Brontë's depiction of the character and should not be reduced to or considered *only* as a subcategory of race. In recent decades, we have tended to view Victorian rhetoric that dehumanizes and animalizes certain characters or human beings primarily as one aspect of racialization, presuming that to view someone as animalistic is more importantly a way to define him as nonwhite. But the human-animal distinction bears consideration as operating according to a logic of its own that is not *only* a matter of defining normative whiteness.

Gaskell, in her biography of Charlotte, cites an 1840 letter in which Charlotte describes her own pleasure in imaginative creation: "It is very edifying and profitable to create a world out of your own brains, and people it with inhabitants, who are so many Melchisedecs, and have no father nor mother but your own imagination" (201). What I would underline here is Charlotte's emphasis on the status of the fictional character as a kind of orphan, lacking father or mother, born ex nihilo: Melchisedec was a Biblical priest "[w]ithout father, without mother, without descent, having neither beginning of days, nor end of life" (King James Bible 7:3). Heathcliff is such a Melchisedec. No matter what Nelly might speculate about his origins and human parents, they cannot be known; within the world of the novel, he is a foundling, an orphan, an "unreclaimed creature" (102). As Nelly admits to Lockwood in a less whimsical mood on being asked what she knows of Heathcliff's history: "It's a cuckoo's, sir—I know all about it; except where he was born, and who were his parents, and how he got his money" (33). To assign Heathcliff a particular racial status is to attach him to human history, lineage, and parentage, but his *failure* to attach to such traditions or grounds for social identity is what is most basic to his existence. He has something in common with Shakespeare's Caliban, as Julia Lupton describes that character: "As a monstrous exception to the human norm, Caliban's creatureliness propels him into the conceptual space occupied by ideas of national and racial difference. . . . Yet Caliban's exceptionality . . . also prevents him from becoming the articulate representative of a single race or culture" (3). Heathcliff is a "cuckoo" or animal in his outsider status to human categories of being and belonging (and, of course, he is cuckoo-like, in Nelly's view, in his opportunistic/parasitic invasion of Wuthering Heights). As a Melchisedec, in Charlotte's sense, his life stands as a testimony to the inevitable exclusions of such categories.

Heathcliff's entrance to the Earnshaw household offers a preeminent instance of what Derrida calls the "deranged theatrics of the *wholly other they call animal*" (*Animal* 11). Derrida argues that the very term *animal* is at once a logical and an ethical affront, a gross conceptual error: "They have given themselves the word in order to corral a large number of living beings within a single concept: 'the Animal,' they say" (*Animal* 32).[14] Thus the "deranged theatrics" to which Derrida refers: to be an animal is to be an other in the most fundamental sense, to embody in one's abjected body the "absolute alterity of the neighbor or of the next(-door)" (11) and an utter lack of ethical or political recognition. Heathcliff, even as he becomes a human character, remains throughout the novel essentially such an animal, a being of "absolute alterity" and unsolvable lack of paternity or origins. Brontë defines Heathcliff as a feral pet, a resistant animal brought into the family circle who rebels against the hypocrisy of the boundary lines drawn to separate different forms of what Derrida calls "the living in general" (*Animal* 12; "Eating Well" 280). His body becomes an experimental object for investigation into pain and suffering, and the suffering he and Catherine cause one another becomes a "spectacle" by which observers and readers may test their powers of sympathy. Finally, Heathcliff becomes, himself, a kind of vivisector, turned monstrously cruel in a demonstration of the corrupting effects of the abuse of the helpless animal body.

DOGS LOST AND FOUND

Kathleen Kete points to the particular importance, in midcentury thinking about pets, of the trope of the lost dog as a signifier of the dangerousness and cruelty of urban life and of modernity itself. Animal lovers in Paris advocated the creation of private refuges or homes for dogs as an alternative to the Parisian pound, established in 1811 and described as "the morgue for things" by the *Revue Britannique* (Kete, *Beast* 19). Dogs not claimed from the pound were hung or sold to the vivisectors who always needed animal bodies for scientific experimentation. In England, too, the figure of the lost or abandoned pet became a prominent indictment of modern urban life. "Professional dog stealers would abscond with a cherished animal, then offer to restore it for a price. In 1844 individual Londoners paid from £2 to £50 to ransom favorite pets" (Ritvo, *Animal* 86). (This was the fate of Elizabeth Barrett Browning's spaniel Flush, as later immortalized by Virginia Woolf.) In this context, the young Heathcliff, found by Mr. Earnshaw "starving, and houseless, and as good as dumb, in the streets of Liverpool" (35) becomes an analog for the lost pet, needing hospitality and offering human characters the opportunity to demonstrate their sympathy and kindness or lack of those qualities. Mr. Earnshaw in effect gives (social) life to the nonliving by adopting Heathcliff from the streets as a pet. Nelly Dean immediately dehumanizes Heathcliff by referring to him as a thing, "it," and tries to get rid of him by "put[ting] it on the landing of the stairs, hoping it might be gone on the morrow." Heathcliff's adoptive brother beats him so badly his arm turns "black to the shoulder" and, underlining the implied metaphor, addresses him

Figure 3 *Keeper—from Life*, 1838. Pencil and watercolor on paper. Drawing by Emily Brontë. Brontë Parsonage Museum, Haworth, Yorkshire, UK/Bridgeman Images.

as "dog" (37) as he hits him with a heavy iron weight. As Terry Eagleton writes, "Heathcliff's presence is radically gratuitous. . . . He is available to be accepted or rejected simply for himself, laying claim to no status other than a human one" (102). We might add that Brontë particularly stresses this ethical dilemma by problematizing the very category of human status in her depiction of the character.

Heathcliff had a real-world pet predecessor in the Brontë family—a dog owned by Emily named Keeper. Gaskell tells us that the dog was received as "a gift to Emily." As Heathcliff does, Keeper enters the household as a gift, with the "radical gratuitousness" of the household pet whose body and existence is wholly at the mercy of his owners. "With the gift came the warning. Keeper was faithful to the depths of his nature as long as he was with friends; but he who struck him with a stick or whip, roused the relentless nature of the brute, who flew at his throat forthwith, and held him there until one or the other was at the point of death" (268). Like Heathcliff, Keeper is both and alternately friend and brute, human and

animal, subject of affection and bitter enemy, embodying the "absolute alterity of the neighbor" and the dilemmas of care, friendship, and kinship.
The connection between the dog and fictional character suggests how for
the Brontës characterization itself was fundamentally linked to the conceptual processes by which "the living in general" becomes a pet or by
which different living creatures are sorted out into various categories: to
be killed, to be allowed to live, to be loved. For the Brontës both pets and
literary characters are gratuitous, creative inventions, bestowals of subjectivity generating new responsibilities, debts, and emotions. Authorship
thereby becomes emotionally associated with relationships with domestic
animals.

Gaskell relates the remarkable story of how Emily was forced to discipline Keeper for his habit of lying on the beds upstairs at Haworth parsonage: "He loved to steal upstairs, and stretch his square, tawny limbs,
on the comfortable beds, covered over with delicate white counterpanes."
The dog violates domestic boundaries and threatens to allow dirt and natural disorder to soil the pure whiteness of an interior space defined by its
exclusion of all that is "outside" a privileged human community. Emily
finally announced that, if Keeper once again violated the household arrangements, she would punish him in such a way that he would never do it
again. When the servant Tabby reported that Keeper was once more in his
favorite spot, Emily's face turned pale and she headed upstairs:

> Down-stairs came Emily, dragging after her the unwilling Keeper,
> . . . growling low and savagely all the time. The watchers [Tabby and
> Charlotte] would fain have spoken, but durst not, for fear of taking off
> Emily's attention, and causing her to avert her head for a moment from
> the enraged brute. She let him go, planted in a dark corner at the bot-
> tom of the stairs; no time was there to fetch stick or rod, for fear of the
> strangling clutch at her throat—her bare clenched fist struck against
> his red fierce eyes, before he had time to make his spring, and, in the
> language of the turf, she "punished him" till his eyes were swelled up,
> and the half-blind, stupefied beast was led to his accustomed lair, to
> have his swelled head fomented and cared for by the very Emily her-
> self. (269)

"The generous dog owed her no grudge," Gaskell explains, and "loved her
dearly ever after." This passage may be read as one scene of origin for the
zero-degree emotions of *Wuthering Heights*, in which brutal or even sadistic punishment precedes loving treatment and care, not in the spirit

of antithesis but of necessary origin. Emily imaginatively transforms the "half-blind, stupefied beast" Keeper into Heathcliff, defining this character as an animalized human being, a creature invested with all the contradictory and sometimes cruel emotions that go into the definition of the *pet*. Also important in this passage are the presence of "the watchers," those who observe the scene of animal violence: they are necessary players in any such scene, those witnesses who respond emotionally—or fail to do so—and so allow the violence to be transformed into reported narrative.

Gaskell's scene of Emily's abusively loving relationship to Keeper also has certain parallels with Brontë's depiction of Catherine's bond with Edgar Linton. Consider, for instance, the scene when Nelly describes Edgar's behavior after Catherine slaps him in a fit of frustrated rage. "You've made me afraid and ashamed of you," the shocked Edgar tells Catherine, as he begins to leave, vowing never to return. But as Catherine sobs, Edgar cannot bring himself to depart:

> The soft thing looked askance through the window—he possessed the power to depart as much as a cat possesses the power to leave a mouse half killed, or a bird half eaten—
>
> Ah, I thought, there will be no saving him—He's doomed, and flies to his fate!
>
> And so it was: he turned abruptly, hastened into the house again, shut the door behind him. (72)

Brontë effects a counterintuitive reversal, as the seeming victim—Edgar, who has just been struck, and whom she describes as powerless and "doomed"—is figured as a cat unable to abandon a half-devoured creature. The image of Edgar does not exactly make sense here—shouldn't *he* be the "mouse half killed, or a bird half eaten"? The implication seems to be that love, or erotic fascination, are disconcertingly similar to a predator's devouring of a prey animal. (As we will see in a subsequent chapter, George Eliot is fascinated by the scene of one creature's devouring or absorption of a weaker one, a dynamic that has something in common with Brontë's image here.)

Brontë foregrounds the category of the pet in the important earlier scene where Heathcliff and Catherine spy on the Lintons at Thrushcross Grange. This scene at once posits and deconstructs the opposition between the natural and the cultural, inside and outside, uncivilized and civilized—distinctions on the border of which stands the figure of the pet.

Heathcliff and Catherine are wild things, like animals, in their androgynous idyll in the moors. Peering into the Lintons' home, they see a "civilization" that is most vividly defined by its abusive relationship to those pampered animals that define the "inside" of culture by their difference from "the living in general" or ordinary wild animals:

> And now, guess what your good children were doing? Isabella . . . lay screaming at the farther end of the room, shrieking as if witches were running red hot needles into her. Edgar stood on the hearth weeping silently, and in the middle of the table sat a little dog, shaking its paw and yelping, which, from their mutual accusations, we understood they had nearly pulled in two between them. The idiots! That was their pleasure! to quarrel who should hold a heap of warm hair, and each begin to cry because both, after struggling to get it, refused to take it. We laughed outright at the petted things, we did despise them! (46)

Brontë suggests both that the Lintons are themselves "petted" or spoiled "things"—and that their brutal form of "affection," like that of the lady in Emily's essay, requires a nonhuman animal object or pet.[15] If this is not quite a scene of carnivorous sacrifice of the sort Derrida defines, it resembles one in the way it defines the human in relationship to a suffering animal. Brontë clearly draws here on the discourse of cruelty to animals and of vivisection. In Heathcliff's description of the Lintons at home, we have a "little dog" sitting in pain "in the middle of a table," "nearly pulled in two." The innocent dog was a stock figure in antivivisection literature, as when activist Frances Power Cobbe quotes from a physiology handbook recommending the sedation of dogs in order to plunge them "into a state of immobility which permits us to place them on an experimenting table without tying or muzzling them" (qtd. in *Modern Rack* 40). And although the "red hot needles" running into flesh are displaced here into the metaphorical ones piercing the shrieking Isabella, their presence as figurative instruments of torture is powerful.

This scene leads to Catherine being attacked and seized by the Linton's bulldog Skulker, who is the opposing counterpart to the petted poodle in the Lintons' version of civilized domesticity. Little Isabella responds to the sight of Heathcliff by saying: "Frightful thing! Put him in the cellar, papa. He's exactly like the son of the fortune-teller, that stole my tame pheasant" (48). Brontë defines the Lintons' domestic space as a sorting house for animals: some are thrown in the basement, some are "petted" and domesticated as useless pets, others are positioned as sentinels and

guards against any uninvited creatures around the premises. We might recall, from Ellen Nussey's reminiscences of the Brontës, the family tabby,
"Tom," who was "everybody's favorite" and "received such gentle treatment it seemed to have lost cat's nature, and subsided into luxurious ami-
ability and contentment" (Nussey 429). Heathcliff himself suffers, early
on, in part from having become Mr. Earnshaw's pet, "his favorite" (39), in
a manner that prompts jealousy in Hindley. The sorting of animals into
pet and nonpet, favorite and unfavored, is a fundamental gesture of the
world of *Wuthering Heights*, beginning with one of Heathcliff's first utter-
ances, advising Lockwood to take care: "You'd better let the dog alone. . . .
She's not accustomed to be spoiled—not kept for a pet" (5).[16] Brontë makes
a mordant joke about the logic of choosing petted "favorites" among animals when Lockwood, attempting to charm Cathy Linton, points to "an
obscure cushion full of something like cats" and asks if "your favorites
are among these?" (8)—only to discover that what he was pointing to was
in fact "a heap of dead rabbits" (9). This detail hints at a grim underlying
logic contained within the procedures of pet keeping: that is, that those
animals we deny "favored" status—either unwanted particular animals
or entire species—are at immediate risk of being turned into meat or mere
flesh.

In the introduction, I discussed what I called a logic of sentimental domestication in Darwin's *Descent of Man*, by which the "heroic little monkey" is marked out from the "fierce baboon" and indeed from the human
Fuegian "savages" whom Darwin glimpses with a shudder on the shore.
As I suggested, animality and domestication become, in that text, shifting and often unstable markers of nearness or closeness to personhood.
Wuthering Heights is witheringly critical of sentimental domestication—
frequently drawing attention to the hypocrisies, blind spots, and incon-
sistencies by which certain animals (or human beings) are judged to be
domesticable and others are banished to a state of wildness (or turned into
mere flesh). Yet it too employs its own system and discourse of domestication, of bringing the nonhuman or noncultural into the space of culture.

THE MOURNING DOG

Brontë associates Heathcliff with a certain type of pet, a familiar Victorian icon of loyalty. In his extravagant mourning for Catherine, Heathcliff
closely resembles a stock figure of Victorian magazine writing, the faithful
dog whose loyalty exemplifies passionate attachment and presses against
the boundary dividing everyday life and death. *Chambers's Edinburgh*

Journal—one of the Brontë sisters' favorites magazines—of the mid- to late 1840s contains numerous anecdotes and accounts of dogs who mourned their masters so intensely that they refused to leave the gravesite. In an 1846 article, for example, we hear of a "dog which I knew, . . . which attended every funeral that took place in that village and neighborhood. . . . he would look anxiously on while the body was being interred; and that melancholy duty over, he would immediately trot away home, or set off for another funeral" ("Funeral-Fancying Dog"). And in an 1844 issue we are told of a woman whose dog disappears soon after the death of her child. One day she "with a mother's feelings went to take a mournful look at her child's grave. On going to it, she found to her great astonishment her lost dog. It was lying in a deep hole which it had scratched for itself over the child's grave, probably hoping to get a little nearer to the object of its affection. It was in an emaciated state from hunger, but neither hunger, cold, nor privation had expelled its love, or diminished the force of its attachment" ("Jesse's Scenes" 300). The figure of the dog in such magazine writing stands for a persistent loyalty and a fierce "force of . . . attachment" that refuses to respect the niceties of human ceremony or the dividing line between the everyday world and the grave. Brontë depicts Heathcliff as, among other things, such a creature. Isabella suggests to him, "Heathcliff, if I were you, I'd go stretch myself over her grave and die like a faithful dog" (176). He does in fact keep vigil over Catherine's body: "Mrs. Linton's funeral was appointed to take place on the Friday following her decease; and till then her coffin remained uncovered, and strewn with flowers and scented leaves, in the great drawing-room. . . . Heathcliff spent his nights, at least, outside, . . . a stranger to repose" (167). Finally, like the dog who dug into the child's grave "hoping to get a little nearer to the object of its affection," he digs into Catherine's coffin: "I got a spade from the toolhouse, and began to delve with all my might—it scraped the coffin; I fell to work with my hands; the wood commenced cracking about the screws, I was on the verge of attaining my object" (289). Gaskell's biography contains a very similar account of the reaction of Keeper to Emily's death: "As the old, bereaved father and his two surviving children followed the coffin to the grave, they were joined by Keeper, Emily's fierce, faithful bull-dog. He walked alongside of the mourners, and into the church, and stayed quietly there all the time that the burial service was being read. When he came home, he lay down at Emily's chamber door, and howled pitifully for many days" (358). In representing Heathcliff's inconsolable mourning for his dead beloved, Emily mobilized a set of both personal and cultural associations linking pet dogs with a force of attachment transcending usual human limits. Keeper, we might finally say, *is* Heathcliff and vice versa (which means that Cathy is also in some sense Keeper).

ANIMAL PAIN AND VIVISECTION

Brontë associates Heathcliff with animality in his introduction to the family as a rescued creature, a lost animal reclaimed from the urban streets, and in his resemblance to the iconic figure of a loyal dog in his mourning for Catherine. She further does so by defining Heathcliff as a sufferer and inflictor of pain. Heathcliff's body, in Brontë's narrative, becomes the testing ground for the effects of physical pain, and his response to pain offers a rebuke to the failures of a social system that mistreats the unwanted or marginal animal. "He seemed a sullen, patient child," Nelly observes unsympathetically, "hardened, perhaps, to ill-treatment: he would stand Hindley's blows without winking or shedding a tear, and my pinches moved him only to draw in a breath and open his eyes, as if he had hurt himself by accident and nobody was to blame" (36). James Turner has argued that for the Victorians "the suffering animal was the avatar of pure, simple, unmitigated pain" (82).[17] The first effective application of nitrous oxide as an anesthetic in the late 1840s (166) was thus greeted with particular enthusiasm by early antivivisection activists.[18] Turner's analysis suggests how closely such issues became bound up with the very questions of sympathy and imaginative projection that are fundamental to Victorian fictional narrative: "Animal experimentation became the principal focus for the anxiety and dread stirred in Victorian minds by the thought of pain. The common use of dogs as experimental animals only made matters worse. One could all too readily imagine oneself in the place of a pet who shared hearth and home. Even easier was to picture oneself in the shoes of the fellow human being doing the vivisecting, knife in hand poised over the trembling pet" (88). Turner's language recalls the scene from *Agnes Grey* where the young torturer Tom Bloomfield rejects Agnes's demand that he imagine and sympathize with the sufferings of a bird: "I'm not a bird, and I can't feel what I do to them" (20). If we see Tom's response as blithely stupid and unimaginative at best, monstrously cruel at worst, we can also admit that imagination and sympathy beyond the species barrier may not be quite as simple or natural as either Agnes Grey or James Turner imply.[19] But what seems incontrovertible is Turner's point that the Victorians were increasingly inclined to attempt such sympathy and to relish narratives that promoted or enabled such imaginative acts.

Heathcliff's relationship with Catherine becomes marked by experiences of pain and suffering, which we can read in the context of the 1840s' particular way of thinking about the *witnessing* of the suffering of living creatures. "I shouldn't care what you suffered," Catherine tells Heathcliff. "I care nothing for your sufferings. Why shouldn't you suffer? I do!" (158) Nelly adds, "The two, to a cool spectator, made a strange and fearful picture," saying of Heathcliff, "I did not feel as if I were in the company of a creature of my own species" (159–60). Brontë has defined Nelly, in effect, as an excessively "cool spectator," far too quick, in her dismay at Heathcliff's behavior, to other him as inhuman and, in effect, to brand him as a "brute." If she is not quite like the Yorkshire squire Gaskell described, who spent his last moments on earth peering at a cockfight through his looking glass, neither is she a sufficiently sympathetic onlooker. In our own emotional response to this scene, we distinguish ourselves as being in that category of affective readers who shrink from brutality and suffering. As narrator, Nelly comes to play the role of unfeeling witness, cruel "brute" who sees suffering but fails to understand it, and who is quick to draw distinctions of "species" to distance herself from pain.[20] Heathcliff's pain invites our pity and curiosity, as well as our judgment of Nelly's failure to experience such feelings as strongly as we do.

Nelly *is* eventually moved to tears by Heathcliff's reversion to thinghood. As he stands, soaked through, leaning against an oak tree, mourning Catherine, a pair of birds regard "his proximity no more than a piece of timber." Now at last Nelly weeps: "we do sometimes pity creatures that have none of the feeling either for themselves or others." Nelly continues to set the standard by which we will measure our own response as superior. She can only blame Heathcliff for his own capacity for pain, can only misunderstand him as anesthetized or feelingless, rather than as extravagantly feeling. Finally, in a culminating moment in the novel, Brontë defines Heathcliff explicitly as an animal suffering abuse at the hands of man: "He . . . howled, not like a man, but like a savage beast getting goaded to death with knives and spears" (167).[21] Heathcliff may seem here more a bull in a pre-Victorian bullbaiting than a dog in a modern vivisection—yet the force of antivivisectionist discourse was precisely to deny the ethical difference between two such forms of cruelty to animals.

At least since William Hogarth's 1751 *Four Stages of Cruelty* prints—showing the progress of a boy who begins by torturing cats and dogs and ends at the gallows for murder—it had been a truism of English culture that cruelty to animals led to cruelty and violence against human beings (see, e.g., Thomas 151). Heathcliff becomes a perfect test case of this belief in his figurative transformation into that dreaded figure in Victorian

culture, the vivisector.[22] Nelly has commented that Hindley's early treatment of Heathcliff "was enough to make a fiend of a saint" (65). Heathcliff
hangs Isabella's pet dog; more than this, however, he very explicitly describes himself as a kind of physiologist, an *experimenter* on the living.
Seeing Isabella as herself a stand-in for her pet, Heathcliff complains that
"I've sometimes relented, from pure lack of invention, in my experiments
on what she could endure, and still creep shamefully cringing back!" (151)

Brontë characterizes Heathcliff as at once subject and object of vivisection, as suffering animal and sadistic animal abuser. Described by
Catherine as a "pitiless, wolfish man" who would "crush" Isabella "like a
sparrow's egg" (102) (perhaps by contrast to Catherine's own dreamy examination of various bird feathers "according to their different species" [122]),
Heathcliff becomes inhuman both in his own animality and in his cruelty
to animals. Observing Cathy Linton and his own son Linton Heathcliff,
Heathcliff reflects on his own penchant for cruelty: "It's odd what a savage feeling I have to anything that seems afraid of me! Had I been born
where laws are less strict, and tastes less dainty, I should treat myself to a
slow vivisection of those two, as an evening's amusement" (270). Isabella
describes Heathcliff's favored mode of violence to be less "knocking on
the head" than "[p]ulling out the nerves with red hot pincers," a procedure calling for "coolness" (172) (and one that recalls the younger Isabella
"shrieking as if witches were running red hot needles into her" [46]). "I
have no pity! I have no pity!" Heathcliff pronounces. "The worms writhe,
the more I yearn to crush out their entrails! It is a moral teething, and
I grind with greater energy, in proportion to the increase of pain" (152).
When he "stare[s] hard at the object of discourse, as one might do at a
strange repulsive animal" (105), he has taken a position resembling that
of the Yorkshire squire who watches the animals kill one another through
looking glasses on his own deathbed. Having once occupied the position of
object of torture, Heathcliff has eventually taken up the instruments himself. (And he passes on his tendencies as an inheritance to his son, about
whom he declares, "He'll undertake to torture any number of cats if their
teeth be drawn, and their claws pared" [275].)

"AS WE READ OF THESE HORRORS . . ."

Victorian antivivisectionism was, like so many other nineteenth-century
reform movements, to a significant degree a print-culture phenomenon.
As Cobbe reminisced in her autobiography of the early days of the movement, "our society from the first issued an almost incredible multitude

of pamphlets and leaflets" (613). The horrors of vivisection would be met with texts and images that decried these horrors in part by reproducing them, exposing them through publication: "Sometimes it would appear as we read of these horrors—the baking alive of dogs, the slow dissecting out of quivering nerves, and so on—that it would be a relief to picture the doer of such deeds as some unhappy, half-witted wretch, hideous and filthy of mien or stupefied by drink, so that the full responsibility of a rational and educated human being should not belong to him, and that we might say of him, 'He scarcely understands what he does'" (606). We are reminded of the 1836 letter describing a woman's reaction to reading antivivisectionist literature as making her feel "as if she had a continual shock of galvanism about her" (qtd. in French 24). Taken to a limit, the end point of such a discourse is to place the reader herself on the operating table. Animal cruelty discourse defines the sensitive, feeling reader as one who feels in her own body the shocks and pains of the helpless animal subject. In these animal narratives—which can at times become melodramas of beset animality—readerly subjectivity, sentimental domestication, and middle-class humanity are defined according to a logic of cruelty and sympathetic witness that *requires* a suffering creature.

The Victorian novel becomes more fully *embodied* in the Brontës' work in part because of the ways their novels position the suffering animal and the human witness; to read these texts is necessarily to fall into a process of somatic suffering—and witnessing—that is at once sympathetic and sensational. Offering the reader at once the opportunity for vicarious sympathy at Heathcliff's sufferings and appalled dismay at his cruelties, Brontë's depiction produces a "continual shock" in the sympathetic reader, for whom the very experience of reading the novel becomes something like that "slow vivisection" Heathcliff yearned to perform on his enemies. Brontë seems to scorn a too-easy sentimental domestication, the creation of helpless "petted things," but she does—no less than her sister Anne Brontë—require a scene of the spectacle of a suffering animal. *Wuthering Heights* redefines the humane reading subject as the one who can most strongly feel the pain of the animal on the operating table, most powerfully respond to the force of that "bloody spectacle."

of excitement, up t
the little creatu
floor, to be ex
ens, and sh
and little
ly over
could
bu

Charles Dickens with his Dogs.

Figure 4 *Charles Dickens with his Dogs*. Illustration from *Some Noted Princes, Authors, and Statesmen of Our Time*, edited by James Parton (New York: James Y. Crowell, 1885), 42.

CHAPTER THREE

Dying like a Dog in Dickens

The dogs that are brought in suffer from distempers, from broken limbs, from infected bites, from mange, from neglect, benign or malign, from old age, from malnutrition, from intestinal parasites, but most of all from their own fertility. There are simply too many of them. When people bring a dog in they do not say straight out, "I have brought you this dog to kill," but that is what is expected: that they will dispose of it, make it disappear, dispatch it to oblivion. What is being asked for is, in fact, *Lösung* (German always to hand with an appropriately blank abstraction): sublimation, as alcohol is sublimed from water, leaving no residue, no aftertaste.

—J. M. Coetzee, *Disgrace*

ROASTED AT A SLOW FIRE: BECOMING MEAT IN *BLEAK HOUSE*

In a piece titled "A Monument of French Folly" in the March 8, 1851, issue of *Household Words*, Charles Dickens offers an extended, bitingly satirical comparison of the slaughterhouses of London's Smithfield Market with the cleaner, better run, and more humane such markets to be found in Paris. This piece is one of a number of texts, including both *Oliver Twist* and *Great Expectations*, in which Dickens returns to a depiction of Smithfield Market as an appalling scene of unhygienic animal death. Smithfield embodies for Dickens a recurring cluster of images and concerns regarding death and the body. The market becomes for him the place where the body is disrespected and abused, loses all integrity or individual wholeness, and transforms into sheer meat. As meat, bodies are subdivided and treated as fungible, processed matter; they are broken or ground down into small parts and sold, often in a diseased or unwholesome state. Of course, what saves the market from seeming utterly nightmarish and Gothic in Dickens's descriptions is that *human* bodies are exempted from its processes. The import of the satire of "A Monument of French Folly," after all, is that the French way of slaughtering animals is far superior to the English approach. Yet Dickens's descriptions seem animated by a sense that Smithfield's spectacle of animal bodies and animal death is so powerful as to put into question any belief that human beings could remain confidently exempt. Smithfield appears to inspire in Dickens, indeed, a fearful understanding that to possess *any* body is to run the risk of having that body destroyed, broken down, shamed, and turned into meat—a sense that human-animal distinctions may not be powerful and stable enough to protect the human observer from the terrible fate of animal bodies transformed into meat. In viewing the processes by which cows are turned into beef or sheep into mutton, the human observer feels a mixture of sympathy, relief that he or she is (or should be) safe—and an underlying fear that this safety may be unreliable.

Slaughterhouses in England, Dickens writes in *Household Words*, are "for the most part, unventilated and dirty; and, to the reeking walls, putrid fat and other offensive animal matter clings with a tenacious hold." Identity and agency break down here; rather than any individual creature, we find disgusting by-products, "offensive animal matter" that clings to the wall with a troublingly animated tenacity. The "tenacious hold" can be read, perhaps, as what is left when a concept like agency or will is dehumanized; there is no person, identity, or individual being here, simply fat, "matter" that "clings" to the wall in a blind, pointless (and indeed harmful) purpose. We see a logic of deindividuating "swarming" here that at once describes the animals brought to be killed and the human beings in the neighborhood of the market: "All these places are surrounded by houses of a poor description, swarming with inhabitants. Some of them are close to the worst burial grounds in London."

Bodies do not remain whole here but combine in masses, corrupting and decomposing in Gothic scenes of horror:

> In half a quarter of a mile's length of Whitechapel, at one time, there shall be six hundred newly slaughtered oxen hanging up, and seven hundred sheep—but, the more the merrier—proof of prosperity. Hard by Snow Hill and Warwick Lane, you shall see the little children, inured to sights of brutality from their birth, trotting along the alleys,

mingled with troops of horribly busy pigs, up to their ankles in blood—but it makes the young rascals hardy. Into the imperfect sewers of this overgrown city, you shall have the immense mass of corruption, engendered by these practices, lazily thrown out of sight, to rise, in poisonous gases, into your house at night, when your sleeping children will most readily absorb them, and to find its languid way, at last, into the river that you drink.

Dickens's suggestion is that the poor hygiene of the markets, situated as they are in crowded and dirty human neighborhoods, threatens to produce infections that may cascade outward in the form of cholera and other diseases. But underlying the concern about literal infection seems a broader intuition that the scene of animal slaughter produces a contagion of deindividuation and corporeal decomposition.[1] Dickens dwells in gruesome detail on the physical processes required to transform animal bodies into meat and other by-products: "cattle-slaughtering, bone-crushing, blood-boiling, trotter-scraping, tripe-dressing, paunch-cleaning, gut-spinning, hide-preparing, tallow-melting, and other salubrious proceedings." Through such processes, bodies become "bone," "trotter," "hide," and so on, rendered into vast arrays of flesh hung to drip into the sewers. Nobody and no body seems entirely safe. In Smithfield, bodies become creaturely and drop out of the protected zone of culture.

In another depiction of Smithfield, in *Oliver Twist*, Dickens describes the "stunning and bewildering" sensorium of "market-day," which "confound[s] the senses" in its overwhelming cacophony of sound and overflow of "filth and mire":

The ground was covered, nearly ankle-deep, with filth and mire; a thick steam, perpetually rising from the reeking bodies of the cattle, and mingling with the fog, which seemed to rest upon the chimney-tops, hung heavily above. All the pens in the centre of the large area, and as many temporary pens as could be crowded into the vacant space, were filled with sheep; tied up to posts by the gutter side were long lines of beasts and oxen, three or four deep. Countrymen, butchers, drovers, hawkers, boys, thieves, idlers, and vagabonds of every low grade, were mingled together in a mass; the whistling of drovers, the barking dogs, the bellowing and plunging of the oxen, the bleating of sheep, the grunting and squeaking of pigs, the cries of hawkers, the shouts, oaths, and quarrelling on all sides; the ringing of bells and roar of voices, that issued from every public-house; the crowding,

pushing, driving, beating, whooping and yelling; the hideous and dis-
cordant dim that resounded from every corner of the market; and the
unwashed, unshaven, squalid, and dirty figures constantly running to
and fro, and bursting in and out of the throng; rendered it a stunning
and bewildering scene, which quite confounded the senses. (203)

As in "A Monument of French Folly," Dickens stresses the impression of
promiscuous crowding and improper mixture in Smithfield. It is difficult
to distinguish body from environment, as bodily steam "mingle[s]" with
the fog such that, Dickens implies, one cannot be sure that what appears
to be fog is not some distillation of blood or other substance emitted by
the "reeking bodies" of the animals. The cries, "grunting and squeaking,"
"bleating" of sheep, dogs, and pigs mingle with the "cries" and "roars"
of the market's human workers to create, too, an aural effect of mingled
combination in which human and animal conjoin in one dismaying cacophony. In *Great Expectations*, when the guilt-ridden Pip enters Smithfield, he says that "the shameful place, being all asmear with filth and
fat and blood and foam, seemed to stick to me" (163), as the "offensive
animal matter" seemed to "cling to the walls" in the *Household Words*
piece. Smithfield produces a miasma of sound, "filth and fat" that weak-
ens human-animal distinctions, overwhelms the senses, and reminds a
visitor of the dependence of nineteenth-century modern life in England on
a continual process of converting and processing living animal bodies into
useful products.

Bleak House (1851) shares with the *Household Words* essay on Smithfield market of that year a strain of imagery relating to bodily decomposition and a concern with the possibility that whole, self-possessed bodies
will be processed and transformed into meat and other by-products, that
characters will be reduced into bodies. This theme is probably most famously represented in Dickens's infamous depiction of the "spontaneous
combustion" of Krook, who leaves "smears, like black fat!" (512) spread
disgustingly throughout his room and even, via the chimney, the entire
building he occupied. As in the slaughterhouses from *Household Words*,
here "to the reeking walls, putrid fat and other offensive animal matter
clings with a tenacious hold" following Krook's strange explosion. The
London cattle market also specifically registers its presence in the novel
at various moments. When Peepy goes missing, Esther inquires after him:
"[T]he cook supposed that he had 'gone after the sheep.' When we repeated,
with some surprise, 'The sheep?' she said, O yes, on market days he sometimes followed them quite out of town, and came back in such a state

as never was!" (216). This "state as never was" refers to Peepy's typically filthy and less than presentable physical appearance but can be read more broadly as a state of proximity to animality. In this novel, as elsewhere in Dickens, to be symbolically intimate with or proximate to animals—and especially to "follow" or "go after" them, a bit like Alice following the rabbit down the hole—is to fall into a state of questionable or precarious humanness (a state that Dickens implies is, however, inescapable). We see this most clearly in Jo, a character who resembles Peepy in his migratory habits, his dirtiness, and his eccentricity to any centered location, social status, or human identity. "It must be a strange state," the narrator observes of Jo,

> not merely to be told that I am scarcely human . . . , but to feel it of my own knowledge all my life! To see the horses, dogs, and cattle, go by me, and to know that in ignorance I belong to them, and not to the superior beings in any shape, whose delicacy I offend! . . . Jo and the other lower animals, get on in the unintelligible mess as they can. It is market-day. The blinded oxen, over-goaded, over-driven, never guided, run into wrong places and are beaten out; and plunge, red-eyed and foaming, at stone walls; and often sorely hurt the innocent, and often sorely hurt themselves. Very like Jo and his order; very, very like! (258)

Jo and the cattle are "over-driven" and "never guided," which is to say that they are *impelled* along a path, forced to walk, yet are paradoxically not "guided" in this path. Dickens wrote in the *Household Words* piece that "the beasts have to be worried, and goaded, and pronged, and tail-twisted, for a long time before they can be got in" to a slaughterhouse; the march of cattle to Smithfield seems to have become iconic for him as a representation of animal life as a literal and figurative "plung[ing] . . . at stone walls," an activity of blind, self-destructive movement without progress. Jo, who in his illness later in the novel "is like some wounded animal that had been found in a ditch" (493), most fully embodies this state in *Bleak House*.

Jo's famous phrase, "they dies more than they lives, according to what *I* see" (492), referring to "people" generally, suggests a vision of organic or biological life itself as backward-directed, tending toward death. *Bleak House* often suggests a social world and a physical environment in which death cannot easily be distinguished from life, as in this description of Lady Dedlock: "her exclamation and her dead condition seem to have passed away like the features of those long-preserved dead bodies some-

times opened up in tombs, which, struck by the air like lightning, vanish
in a breath" (466). In this world, profit and wealth often seem to accrue to
those who can take control of the processing of the living into dead things:
whether meat, parchment, tallow, or the like. The hypocritical reverend
Mr. Chadband, for example, is himself a kind of processing plant for the
"conversion of nutriment . . . into oil"; "in beginning to eat and drink, he
may be described as always becoming a kind of considerable Oil Mills or
other large factory for the production of that article on a wholesale scale."
The lawyer Tulkinghorn is like "a dingy London bird among the birds at
roost in these pleasant fields, where the sheep are all made into parchment,
the goats into wigs, and the pasture into chaff" (661). Derrida suggests that
political man's sovereignty consists in part in "raising himself above the
animal and appropriating it, having its life at his disposal" (*Beast* 1: 51),
and he notes that in *Robinson Crusoe*, "the skin of beasts" is "the origin
of . . . [Crusoe's] technology and supremacy as a man" (*Beast* 2: 55); *Bleak
House* depicts an eerily industrialized scene of the mass appropriation and
processing of animal life.

Dickens's reference to parchment foregrounds the ways his own tools
of authorship rely on animal life; the novel conveys an uneasy sense that
a novelist, whose work is imprinted on large amounts of printed paper,
participates in and relies upon an industrialized factory system for the
conversion of living animals into material of various kinds. In a reference
to London's transition from a coach-based to a railroad system of transportation, Dickens portrays technological and social progress as an ongoing
process of devouring and violent consumption, with each new invention
or system processing and destroying the previous one: "Mr. George se-
dately marches to a street of little shops lying somewhere on that ganglion
of roads from Kent to Surrey, and of streets from the bridges of London,
centering in the far-famed Elephant who had lost his Castle formed of a
thousand four-horse coaches, to a stronger iron monster than he, ready to
chop him into mince-meat any day he dares" (438). To be an elephant or
any creature of flesh is, for Dickens, to be susceptible to being chopped
into mincemeat, a substance that implies both extreme subdivision and
the possibility of promiscuous mixture (mincemeat was often a combination of chopped meat and other ingredients such as fruit and spices).

One culmination of this line of imagery comes in Dickens's descriptions of the creepy Mr. Vholes and his legal chambers, which I would argue
serve as a symbolic center of the novel's interest in the transformation of
living creatures into meat. "A smell as of unwholesome sheep" in his of-

fices, "blending with the smell of must and dust, referable to the nightly (and often daily) consumption of mutton fat in candles, and to the fretting of parchment forms and skins in greasy drawers" (621).[2] When Vholes and Richard Carstone return to Vholes's office or "den," Dickens offers a remarkable image of the lawyer as in effect a self-scalping cannibal, that is, a human being who eats himself and turns not only the bodies of others but also his own into meat: "Mr. Vholes, and his young client, and several blue bags hastily stuffed, out of all regularity of form, as the larger sort of serpents are in their first gorged state, have returned to the official den. Mr. Vholes, quiet and unmoved, as a man of so much respectability ought to be, takes off his close black gloves as if he were skinning his hands, lifts off his tight hat as if he were scalping himself, and sits down at his desk" (623). This image may be an improvised follow-up to a previous image of cannibalism, the point of which was to satirize a tendency to argue against reform and the elimination of pernicious occupations (such as Vholes's) on the grounds that to do so will necessarily create unemployment: "As though, Mr. Vholes and his relations being minor cannibal chiefs, and it being proposed to abolish cannibalism, indignant champions were to put the case thus: Make man-eating unlawful, and you starve the Vholeses!" (632). This is, of course, among other things, a prime example of Dickens's sheer obsessive imaginative fecundity: having introduced the image of a cannibal into his text, he cannot let it rest but must develop its symbolic implications in a subsequent image. More than this, however, Dickens's riffing on cannibalism symbolically explores one of *Bleak House*'s central preoccupations, that of the tendency of life toward voracious consumption, most obviously visible in everyday life in the preparation and consumption of animal meat. "Might sovereignty be devouring?" Derrida asks; "Might its . . . absolute potency be . . . a power of devourment (mouth, teeth, tongue, violent rush to bite, engulf, swallow the other, to take the other into one-self too . . .)" (*Beast* 1: 23). In "these pleasant fields, where the sheep are all made into parchment, the goats into wigs, and the pasture into chaff," every living being is a potential morsel for another; every being may be once "nutriment" and the useful "oil" produced out of it. Animal life in *Bleak House* is precarious because it is so available for exploitation, processing, transformation, and consumption. Tom Jarndyce used to describe the experience of his Chancery case as "being ground to bits in a slow mill; it's being roasted at a slow fire" (71); part of the horror of the experience of the case is the sense that, by participating in it, one is slowly consumed, like a juicy steak or other piece of meat, by some devouring being.

DYING LIKE A DOG IN *GREAT EXPECTATIONS*

These thematics in *Bleak House* recur throughout Dickens's later work, as he frequently returns to images and ideas relating to anxieties of dehumanization and fears of animalization. It is as if some of the possibilities opened in Victorian culture for sympathy toward animals now operate as a source of anxiety or a potential threat that Dickens must manage. Definitions that had once seemed more settled—of human versus nonhuman, subject versus object, and so on—now began to seem less secure, more prone to slippage.[3] More and different kinds of nonhumans seemed to become conceptually "nearer" to the human, offering the threat that even as the animal might become humanized or domesticated, so the human might become animalized. *Great Expectations* is, of course, a novel about memory, structured around Pip's attempt to remember the past and to give it narrative shape. But at the novel's core, I'll now suggest, lies a fear of being forgotten or misremembered, of "perishing out of all human knowledge," a fate that Dickens specifically links to the state of being an animal, or of being animalized. The entire work plays out the tension of its opening scene, where Dickens contrasts two possible fates: that of being remembered and memorialized, as Pip's parents are in the letters inscribed on their tombstones, or alternately of being obliterated and forgotten—not remembered but dismembered and cast aside, as Pip fears he will be when Magwitch threatens to cut his throat in the graveyard. Dickens, I will argue here, associates this threat of creaturely obliteration, of being destroyed so as to leave no remnant or residue, with the fate of the dog. To be a dog is in this novel to lack a narrative, to fail to take hold within others' language and memories, to lose all solid form, somewhat like those "Dogs, indistinguishable in mire" (13) in the opening paragraph of *Bleak House*. Dogs are preeminent examples of the category Lévi-Strauss defined as "metonymical human beings" (207), pet animals who are inconsistently treated as part-humans, partially incorporated in human society. Pet dogs, in British culture, typically possess a tantalizingly incomplete identity: they are granted a name and a place by the hearth in the family circle but only temporarily, only as long as their human master permits it.[4] Their identity and ethical status are fundamentally unstable and dependent, in a manner that Dickens's novel powerfully evokes. The novel begins with the protagonist "call[ing] himself" Pip, but among the first names he is called by another is "young dog" (4). To be a dog is, in *Great Expectations*, to possess and to typify—in a novel deeply concerned with the precariousness of identity—a precarious or threatened identity, an identity falling short of the standard of full-fledged novelistic protagonist or even minor character. We saw in the Brontës that love for an animal or pet could function emotionally as a "gift," as excessive, and as fundamentally linked with the aesthetic processes of novels: pet keeping and novel writing became codefined as procedures of extravagant affect directed to the animal. In Dickens we see a more anxious dynamic in which every human character seems at risk, vulnerable to the precariousness that defines animal life.

In Dickens's novel, the possibility or threat of being seen or treated as a dog bears a strong correlation to an anxiety about being forgotten.[5] Peter Singer, in a discussion of the philosophical basis for animal rights, observes that "the interest a being has in continued life . . . will depend in part on whether the being is aware of itself as existing over time, and is capable of forming future-directed desires that give it a particular kind of interest in continuing to live" (25). If we consider this idea in relation to the form of the Victorian novel, we might contemplate the problem Dickens and other novelists faced when they turned away from the early nineteenth-century form of the sketch to the more extended novel. The vivid personalities and urban types that Dickens, in his guise as Boz, could sketch in passing and leave behind, had now to be sustained and developed as novelistic characters, possessing new reservoirs of interior experience and expectations of futurity. A represented animal gains special significance in this context as, among other things, a reminder of the lot of those pre- or nonnovelistic characters formerly left behind undeveloped and not able to "continue to live," a preeminent instance of an undeveloped character failing to exist over time. Animals generally lie on the wrong side of a division separating those ephemeral beings who will be forgotten and whose stories are brief from those entitled to continued life, development, and full-fledged narrative treatment.

Pip begins both the novel and his identity as a memory-bearing subject, filled with fear in a graveyard, misreading the language on a gravestone. His task is to write himself into a permanent, stable relationship with death and memory so that future readers will properly understand him and do justice to him when he can no longer speak for himself. His task must be to avoid the fate of those personalities or semicharacters in a sketch by Boz who enter the reader's consciousness with vivid force but soon depart, leaving no residue. In this context, Dickens's representation of animals and his use of figurative language comparing humans to animals reflects a concern that individual identity, personality, and memory might *not* be retained: that all one's individuating characteristics might slip away into formlessness and an abyss of forgetfulness or misremem-

bering that would threaten the possibility both of novelistic form and of
continuing identity over time.

Philosophers and theorists have long debated the problem of how to
consider animal communication in relation to human language, considering whether animal signs or gestures deserve to be understood as
a kind of language or signifying.[6] Recent work in animal studies, especially work engaged in conversation with the writings of Emmanuel Levinas, has also dedicated considerable attention to another category, that of
the "gaze" as the marker of subjectivity or of a significant otherness, an
otherness that might make ethical claims on a human subject.[7] In *The
Animal That Therefore I Am*, Derrida returns insistently to a "moment
when, caught naked, in silence, by the gaze of an animal, for example the
eyes of a cat. . . . I have trouble . . . overcoming my embarrassment" (*Animal* 4); "Nothing," he adds, "will have ever given me more food for thinking through this absolute alterity of the neighbor or of the next(-door) than
these moments when I see myself seen naked under the gaze of a cat" (11).
For Derrida, the gaze between a languageless animal and a human being
encapsulates the ethical and political problem of recognition and reciprocity. The stare of his pet cat becomes, for Derrida, an embodiment of the
problem of responding to mute or nonsignifying otherness; in this book,
indeed, he announces his turn to the question of the place of the animal in
Western thought as the major topic of what has turned out to be his final
body of work.

The link between Derrida's argument and a work of Victorian literature is closer than it might at first appear. Derrida, who had rarely if
ever in his previous work analyzed texts by Victorian British authors, announces, early in the essay, that "[a]lthough I don't have time to do so, I
would of course have liked to inscribe my whole talk within a reading of
Lewis Carroll" (*Animal* 7). Derrida's analysis of his cat's gaze resonates, in
particular, with Dickens's effort in *Great Expectations* to think through
questions about the boundaries and definition of self-definition, naming,
and autobiography.[8] These questions as routed through representations of
the animal are manifested most obviously, perhaps, in the literary trope
of personification, the figurative granting of personhood to things or creatures normally not given that status.[9] At least since Dorothy Van Ghent's
classic 1950 essay "The Dickens World: A View from Todger's," critics
have devoted considerable attention to the importance within Dickens's
work of human/thing reversals. But although Van Ghent herself actually
begins her essay with a reference to pets, the allusion is fleeting and par-
enthetical: "Things, like animal pets, have adopted the disposition and ex-

pression of their masters" (419). And while it makes sense to think about the broader topics of reification, thingification, and the pathetic fallacy in Dickens in relation to a range of nonhuman things including animals, animal personification also operates according to its own logic. One of the first animals personified in *Great Expectations* is a black ox who fixes Pip with a stare very much as the cat does Derrida:

> The cattle came upon me with like suddenness, staring out of their eyes, and steaming out of their nostrils, "Holloa, young thief!" One black ox, with a white cravat on—who even had to my awakened conscience something of a clerical air—fixed me so obstinately with his eyes, and moved his blunt head around in such an accusatory manner as I moved round, that I blubbered out to him, "I couldn't help it, sir! It wasn't for myself I took it!" Upon which he put down his head, blew a cloud of smoke out of his nose, and vanished with a kick-up of his hindlegs and a flourish of his tail. (16–17)

Pip finds himself confronted and "fixed" by an accusatory, fleeting gaze, a gaze that follows him: the ox "moved his blunt head around . . . as I moved round." Part of the accusation here is a mimicry and a paralleling. The head is "blunt," suggesting the physiognomic difference between cattle and person, yet that head also tracks Pip with an insistence that seems full of meaning to Pip, prompting his blubbering, apologetic response. There is something communicative, even perhaps human, in the way the ox's head follows Pip. This passage is exemplary of the novel's engagement with animals and animality in several respects. One is the suddenness with which the cattle come in and out of the field of vision and Pip's consciousness. In this novel of abrupt entrances and exits, these creatures' hold on our attention is especially fleeting. If these are characters, they are characters without a past or a future, "coming upon" our protagonist and coming into personification with startling abruptness and then "vanishing" in a "cloud of smoke."[10]

A second factor here is the animals' ambiguous relationship to speech. Lévi-Strauss observes that "even when one talks to cattle, their character as objects never allow them to be anything but *what is spoken about*" (207). But in Dickens's passage, the cloud is at once that which blocks vision—the ox seems almost to escape in a smokescreen—and also the animal's speech: Pip sees the cattle as *speaking* collectively "out of their nostrils." The steam that their breath becomes in the cold air presents itself as a form of accusatory language—albeit language emitted through the nose rather than the mouth—before transforming back into a cloud. The animal's abrupt "vanishing" can be seen as following on the devolution of what was, briefly, seen as speech, back into mere breath. To vanish would seem to be characteristic of the animal: to vanish is to fade back into the misty realm without personification, language, or characterization, the formless life of cattle. Such a vanishing poses an implicit threat to Pip, given his own worries about naming and individuation: he fears that he himself, like any animal, may slip away into such an abyss.

Another scene of animal-human confrontation or similitude follows soon after, as Pip watches the convict eating the food Pip has stolen for him.

> I had often watched a large dog of ours eating his food; and I now noticed a decided similarity between the dog's way of eating, and the man's. The man took strong sharp sudden bites, just like the dog. He swallowed, or rather snapped up, every mouthful, too soon and too fast; and he looked sideways here and there while he ate, as if he thought there was danger in every direction, of somebody's coming to take the pie away. He was altogether too unsettled in his mind over it, to appreciate it comfortably, I thought, or to have anybody to dine with him, without making a chop with his jaws at the visitor. In all of which particulars he was very like the dog. (19)

Here too Dickens describes a "decided similarity" between human and animal, a similarity underlined when the description ends by returning to the claim that the man is "very like" the dog.[11] The question of human likeness to or difference from the animal is, of course, a fundamental one in both ethical and biological thinking on animal-human relations. Erica Fudge argues that "[w]e are horrified that there is a kinship between us and them (a kinship that we have, of course, in part produced through our own desires), and we wish to wipe it out; annihilate it" (8). Cary Wolfe asks, "Who is 'like' and who is 'same,' who the original and who the copy, who the human and who the animal?" (*Animal Rites* 180). Alice A. Kuzniar discusses a melancholia that she views as inherent to the human-dog relationship, precisely because of its merging of closeness with difference: the dog lover is "saddened by the inevitable disjointedness and nonsimultaneity between herself and the extimate species," *extimate* meaning "that which is exterior to one yet intimately proximate" (8). Wolfe suggests that a truly ethical stance toward the animal can depend neither on a claim for the animal's similarity to us nor on a self-interested hope for reciprocity: "why should not the supremely moral act be that directed toward one, such as the animal other, from whom *there is no hope, ever, of reciproc-ity?"* (199).[12] The ethical act toward the animal must be a freely given one, according to this logic, a gesture of pure generosity or hospitality, not de-manding a prerequisite of speech or a communicative or comprehending gaze in return.

We see something like such an act in Joe's response to Magwitch. Dickens's depiction of Magwitch's capture develops an ongoing logic in the novel linking the state of being like a dog or animal to a denial of comfort and hospitality. After Magwitch has been taken, Joe extends a gesture of hospitality to the convict: "We don't know what you have done, but we wouldn't have you starved to death for it, poor miserable fellow-creatur" (39). More than simply offering kindness—Joe has also told Magwitch he was "welcome to" the pie he had eaten—Joe is making an importantly open gesture of forgiveness and inclusion here. Derrida asks, "Does one give hospitality to a subject? to an identifiable subject? . . . to a legal subject? . . . Or is hospitality *rendered*, is it *given* to the other before they are identi-fied" (*Of Hospitality* 29), "whether or not the new arrival is the citizen of another country, a human, animal, or divine creature" (77)? Joe's hospital-ity to Magwitch, decidedly not a "legal subject," takes the form of what Derrida defines as such an "unconditional, hyperbolical hospitality" (75).

Joe's hospitality is made not on the grounds of a privileged "human" status but on that of sharing the broad category of "miserable fellow-creatur." That is, he does not aim to pluck Magwitch from the ranks of the inhuman, undeserving of hospitality or kindness, to restore him to the ranks of human but instead makes a claim for general kinship or com-monality.[13] We recall Rae Greiner's definition of Smithian realist sympa-thy as a matter of "going along with" another; Joe is placing Magwitch within the category of those with whom one can go along. If Joe and Mag-witch are "miserable fellow-creatur[e]s," Joe himself has no particular status above that of creature; and, in fact, he has just a sentence earlier repudiated his own status as a propertied owner of the pie Magwitch de-voured: "God knows you're welcome to it—so far as it was ever mine." Joe can be seen to be undermining the division between the propertied (Lockean) human subjects who are entitled to food, comfort, and hospital-ity, and those dehumanized others who are treated as animals: "No one seemed surprised to see him, or interested in seeing him, or glad to see him, or sorry to see him, or spoke a word, except that somebody in the boat growled as if to dogs, 'give way, you!'" (40) The very next sentence in the novel underlines Dickens's implication that Magwitch, as a despised prisoner, has been animalized: "By the light of the torches, we saw the black Hulk lying out a little way from the mud of the shore, like a wicked Noah's ark." Noah's ark was a boat of the saved, those to be remembered, while all other living creatures were destroyed, erased from memory. The prisoners on the Hulks are treated as animals and as without dignity: the hunt for Magwitch on Christmas day, offering the spectacle of a human being run down like an animal, is a profanation of the joyful day in its mockery of any claim to an inclusive human community.[14]

Dogs are generally linked, in *Great Expectations*, both with degradation and humiliation and, in a different register, with imagination, lies, and figurative language. When Jaggers asks Joe if he keeps a dog and adds "Bear in mind, then, that Brag is a good dog, but Holdfast is a better" (135), he at once tropes on dog names and invokes a supposed canine quality that might exist in tension with the verbal act of troping: that of steadfastness, fidelity, and honesty. If dogs are conventionally seen as being "true," faithful pets, notably lacking in deceit or duplicity, this might seem to render them inappropriate vehicles for metaphor or other figurative language. Yet one of Pip's most memorable lies involves the invention of imaginary dogs, as Dickens seems to imply a sharp contrast between associations of dogs with fidelity or truthfulness and Pip's own imaginative, mendacious relation to language. Dickens links dogs with both social humiliation and metaphoricity when Pip, following his distressing first visit to Miss Havisham's, can find no language to explain what he feels about the visit, and so tells an outrageous string of lies that culminates in a description of four "immense" dogs who "fought for veal cutlets out of a silver basket" (66). These powerful dogs recall Pip's earlier comparison of Magwitch to "a large dog of ours"; dogs are clearly, for Dickens, strongly linked with eating and food and, perhaps, more generally with the state of hunger or material need. These dogs can also be seen as Pip's wishful transformation of the scene that took place earlier at Satis House, where Estella emphasized Pip's low status in a manner familiar to him—through the socially encoded rituals of a meal: "She came back, with some bread and meat and a little mug of beer. She put the mug down on the stones of the yard, and gave me the bread and meat without looking at me, as insolently as if I were a dog in disgrace. I was so humiliated, hurt, spurned, offended, angry, sorry—I cannot hit upon the right name for the smart—God knows what it was—that tears started to my eyes" (61). Estella and Miss Havisham reward Pip's lower-class status, his "coarse hands" and "thick boots" (59), with "insolent" treatment fit only for that most degraded creature, "a dog in disgrace." Pip's fantasy dogs are, then, an effort at compensation, a reversal of the shameful treatment: the "dog in disgrace" expands to become four "immense" dogs dining sumptuously on a cut of meat Pip has doubtless never tasted, a veal cutlet.[15] These imagined dogs are grandiose and extravagant, the most impressive creatures Pip can come up with. If, as Derrida suggests, the power of the human is defined by its mastery of the animal, the master of such dogs would be impressive indeed. Yet their actions also hint at some of the pathos and limitations of animal identity. Fighting for pieces of meat, they seem proxies for Pip, embodying his feelings of figurative and literal hunger and prefiguring his subsequent fisticuffs with the pale young gentleman (later Herbert Pocket). At Satis House, Pip must earn his keep through a performance of degraded status; whether by "playing" or fighting in response to Miss Havisham's explicit or implicit commands, he resembles the dogs in his pet-like subordination. Even in Pip's fantasy version of his visit to Satis House, in which he dines sumptuously on "cake and wine on gold plates" (66), he consumes only on command: "I got up behind the coach to eat mine, because she told me to."

The link between dogs and lies or metaphorical language leads to the novel's implication that to be a dog is to occupy a shadowy realm of incomplete identity, identity that may not possess permanence or leave permanent traces. The power of those immense dogs corresponds to their fundamental weakness: that is, they exist only in Pip's language and imagination. In this sense they are no different from any literary character, yet they lack the support of the conventions of realism that grants "real" characters continuity and persistence. As we've also seen in his depiction of the disappearing cattle, Dickens is broadly interested in what it means to be a "character" that lacks robust substance, agency, or continuity. When Pip arrives at Matthew Pocket's lodgings at Barnard's Inn, he is disappointed: "I had supposed that establishment to be an hotel kept by Mr. Barnard, to which the Blue Boar in our town was a mere public-house. Whereas I now found Barnard to be a disembodied spirit, or a fiction" (171). The emptying out of "Mr. Barnard" to "disembodied spirit" exemplifies a central anxiety in the novel, that of finding oneself or another to be in fact nothing but a spirit, a fiction, a made-up name in someone else's narrative (a concern hinted at in the novel's inaugural sentences, when Pip explains that his name is less Christian or proper than a nickname, a single syllable by which he "came to be called" [3]). Pip's fabulous dogs are paradigmatic of such a status and, indeed, perhaps more broadly of the animal or pet in much of Victorian fiction. Denied proper place within the novel's diegesis, they exist only in a realm of shame and fantasy, skulking in the disavowed corners of the plot.

DYING LIKE A DOG

The culmination of the novel's logic regarding the likeness between humans and animals and the fear of being treated as or forgotten like a dog occurs in the scene of Orlick's attack on Pip. This is characterized by Eve Kosofsky Sedgwick as "one of several very powerful [scenes] in this paranoid novel to bring men together under a wildly exacerbated homosocial bond of rivalry" (131). But the most salient category here, a category posing special boundary problems, may be species more than gender. Like Bentley Drummle, another of the novel's villains, who "would always creep in-shore like some uncomfortable amphibious creature" (*Great Expectations* 201), Orlick seems to emerge from moist places, his form indistinct: "When we came near the churchyard, we had to cross an embankment, and get over a stile near a sluice-gate. There started up from the gate, or from the rushes, or from the ooze (which was quite in his stagnant way), old Orlick" (129). Orlick is a figure of ambiguous and amphibious animality who poses a threat in his metonymic relation to the oozy marshes of Pip's upbringing, that site of primordial origins where—in this just post–*Origin of Species* novel—human identity may become indistinct, its boundaries blurred or undefined, disconcertingly creaturely.

Orlick's attack on Pip foregrounds the problem of human-animal resemblance and constitutes a terrifying fulfillment of Pip's deepest fear: that he will disappear and be forgotten or misremembered like a dog or a minor character. Pip seems to have fallen back into a premodern state of pure nature and animality, a state of "constant antagonism" and fundamental enmity, as Orlick, "with his mouth snarling like a tiger's" (420), continually reminds Pip: "Oh you enemy, you enemy!" Derrida suggests that Crusoe "is afraid of the pre-social and pre-institutional savagery that would have him die without a funeral. . . . He is afraid of dying like a beast, if a beast is indeed . . . a living being that dies without a funeral and without mourning" (*Beast* 2: 145). Orlick's revenge on Pip may be seen as a revenge of the animality that has always been defined as the abjected other of the human.

Orlick calls Pip not just "enemy" but also a much more specific embodiment of a traditional enemy to mankind: "wolf" (419). Orlick is at once placing Pip back in the ancient wild past and rendering him the predator, the savage and irreducibly wild beast whose death at the hand of man may be just or necessary; in Derrida's terms, as the "rogue" animal "who does not even respect the law of the animal community, of the pack, the horde, of its kind" (*Beast* 1: 41). Orlick's rhetorical animalization of Pip suggests Colin Dayan's characterization of dogs, in the light of their place in Anglo-American legal history, as "[p]owerful metaphors for the extremities of abuse, adoration, and prejudice" (230). "Whether we consider public rituals of physical death or secret practices of psychic elimination," Dayan writes, "dogs figure ubiquitously" (16). Orlick's greatest threat resides in his claim that he will not only kill Pip but dispose of his body so thoroughly that he will be "misremembered" after death. Dickens defines Pip's possible fate here precisely as a form of dehumanization or even inhumanization, an annihilation so complete that it would prevent any true memory of Pip to outlive him. Orlick boasts,

> "I won't have a rag of you, I won't have a bone of you, left on earth. I'll put your body in the kiln—I'd carry two such to it, on my shoulders— and, let people suppose what they may of you, they shall never know nothing." . . . The death close before me was terrible, but far more terrible than death was the dread of being misremembered after death. And so quick were my thoughts, that I saw myself despised by unborn generations—Estella's children, and their children—while the wretch's words were yet on his lips. (420)

Orlick's next words emphasize that what he proposes to do to Pip is, specifically, to treat him like a common animal, "standing outside the concerns of civil life" (Dayan 214), who is entitled to no gravestone, elegy, or full-fledged narrative memory: "Now, wolf," said he, "afore I kill you like any other beast—which is wot I mean to do and wot I have tied you up for."[16] We recall Audrey Jaffe's definition of the scene of sympathy as one that "involves a spectator's (dread) fantasy of occupying another's social place" (8); the dread of taking the just barely social place of a dog is, of course, yet more threatening than any fear of decline in human social class.

Orlick's definition of Pip as "like any other beast" emphasizes Pip's grouping in the expansive category of animal, of which there are always *too many*. As my chapter epigraph from J. M. Coetzee suggests, essential to the category of the animal is an excessive multiplicity: a multiplicity that is, in Woloch's argument, also fundamental to fictional minorness: the abundance of minor characters defines the special status of the protagonist. There are always more fish in the sea, more dogs in the pound, yet this superabundance of nonhuman creatures is linguistically subsumed into a single term, the animal, a catchall concept including "*all the living things* that man does not recognize as his fellows, his neighbors, or his

brothers" (Derrida, *Animal* 34). For an animal to be treated as an individual is, then, to receive a kind of gift or dispensation, to be temporarily
selected and individuated from the undistinguished masses of animal life.

We recall Pip's early observations that Magwitch was "very like the
dog." Such "likeness" between animal and human, according to Joe and
perhaps Pip's own logic, offered a route to an ethical recognition of the
animal other as deserving of hospitality and kindness. Yet here Orlick's
rhetorical gesture sweeps Pip into a realm of mute and nonsignifying helpless animality. It seems appropriate to that logic that, once Orlick has defined Pip as "like any other beast," Pip senses his human status abandon-
ing him so completely that he fears not simply his dehumanization but
what might be called his *in*humanization in a transformation into pure
vapor: "I knew that when I was changed into a part of the vapour that had
crept before me but a little while ago, he would do as he had done in my
sister's case." Orlick threatens—to adopt the language Coetzee uses to describe the destruction of dogs in *Disgrace*—to sublimate Pip "as alcohol is
sublimed from water, leaving no residue"; to turn him into sub-substance,
a disembodied spirit, something below the level of form.

Dickens conjoins Orlick's physical threat—to break down and destroy
the body—to a threat to Pip's reputation or presence in memory. "I was
within a few moments of surely perishing out of all human knowledge,"
Pip declares. To be so treated would be to have one's individuality, claim
to a name or to agency, evacuated. To be misremembered would seem to
resemble in some respects the state of being *dis*membered, perhaps like
the "veal cutlets" fought over by Pip's fantasy dogs. To be dismembered
is to be reduced to a state of unindividuated mass without features, mere
matter, something like a piece of meat—that into which any animal, even
a pet, can be instantly transformed. The body of any dead human being is
considered deserving of special treatment and burial, but, as we've seen
in the discussion of Smithfield Market, a dead animal becomes mere fungible flesh or meat and, as such, available for others' use and profiteering
(and cutting into pieces). E. M. Forster famously defined novel characters
according to a distinction between the flat minor character and the round
protagonist or other developed character; Dickens seems to evoke the possibility of a state below even that of flat character—perhaps that of road-
kill or slab of meat.

The form of *Great Expectations* enacts a hope that narrative might
serve as a source of memory, atonement, and forgiveness. As chapter suc-
ceeds chapter, Pip gives accumulating form and continuity to his experience and grants it extension in time and memory. As with any autobi-

ography, the fact of narration attests to, if nothing else, the survival of
the narrator and his "continued life," a continuation we multiply and re-
inforce in the act of reading. In the confrontation with Orlick, the narrative undergoes a crisis of animalization as it approaches a brink of
misremembering, forgetting, and shockingly sudden loss of the status of
a subject or character. I earlier cited a Dorset farmer who wrote in 1698
that "my old dog Quon was killed, and baked for his grease, of which he
yielded 11 lbs" (Thomas 102). "Quon," the name of the farmer's old dog,
is a variant of the word *whone* or *one*. We might take Quon's fate to be in
a general sense emblematic of that of the dog in Victorian culture, who is
granted the right to be "one," to possess a name and character and history
like any other whole subject, but who, as a "creature," may find that subjectivity abrogated with no warning, transformed into grease or vapor of
the sort that clings to the walls in Smithfield Market. This is what Orlick
threatens Pip with as well, the promise of such a final abyss, with neither
rag nor bone left to attest to his former existence on earth. To endure this
fate would be to become an impossibility as a protagonist or narrator and
would mark the collapse of the very form of the novel we read.[17] So, as we
read *Great Expectations*, we are continually made aware of the human-
animal distinction as defining a set of ethical challenges—can one grant
hospitality, or even life, to the animal? Can one welcome the animal into
human space? The distinction signals a terrifying threat: of a loss of identity, language, narration, memory.

As a coda to this analysis of Dickens's fiction, I want briefly to consider Dickens's own enthusiastic experience as a dog owner. In his biography of Dickens, Peter Ackroyd notes that as the author moved from house
to house, he always brought with him certain objects to place on his writing desk, including a bronze figurine of "a dog fancier, with the puppies
and dogs swarming all over him" (a figure that Alex Woloch cites [178] as
emblematic of Dickens's sense of himself as swarmed by his own minor
[human] characters). In Dickens's later prosperous years, he took on something of the identity of a country squire with a whole pack of dogs, most of
which had been given to him as gifts. His favorite was an Irish bloodhound
named Sultan given to him by Percy Fitzgerald; Dickens's passionate relationship with the dog recalls in some respects that of Emily Brontë's with
her dog Keeper.

Fred Kaplan writes of Sultan that

He had become his master's favorite, partly because of his affection-
ateness, partly because he rejected and detested everyone else. "So

accursedly fierce toward other dogs" that he had to be muzzled to be taken out, he attacked everything moving or still. . . . The price of such total love was the problem of having to deal with his creature's unmitigated enmity to the rest of the world. To Dickens, he was the finest dog he had ever seen. "Between him and me there was a perfect understanding," [Dickens wrote.] Breaking his muzzle frequently, though, he came home "covered with blood, again and again." One day he swallowed an entire blue-eyed kitten, afterward suffering "agonies of remorse (or indigestion?)." When he seized the little sister of one of the servants, Dickens flogged him. The next morning he took the dog to the meadow behind the house, accompanied by a half dozen men with guns and a wheelbarrow. Sultan bounded out cheerfully, anticipating "the death of somebody unknown." He paused, meditatively, with his eyes on the wheelbarrow and the guns. "A stone deftly thrown across him . . . caused him to look around for an instant, and then he fell dead, shot through the heart." (502)

I've argued that the Brontës influentially associated novelistic authorship with pet keeping, as two linked practices of giving life and individuality to that which had seemed either lifeless or as possessing a lower-order, non-individuated life. The novel and the home can both bestow a new value on those beings who are given pride of place within them, rendered part of culture rather than nature, domesticated. The scene of Dickens's execution of his beloved Sultan also can be read as suggesting a counterpart to this bestowal of life—that is, the forcible removal of that gift. Dickens as author and dog owner/fancier asserts for himself the sovereign right to remove life, to kill the pet or the character. The author must at once cultivate and care for life, grant individuality and "continued life" to the animals of his household as well as to the characters in his novels, but must also know when best to terminate that life. For Sultan no less than for any of the many characters whom Dickens killed off, the position as "favorite" or "pet" depended on the master's whim.

CHAPTER FOUR

Middlemarch's Brute Life

ABSORBING, SWALLOWING, DEVOURING

In the final pages of George Eliot's novel *Middlemarch*, the narrator has this to say about her protagonist, Dorothea Brooke, and Dorothea's marriage to Will Ladislaw: "Many who knew her, thought it a pity that so substantive and rare a creature should have been absorbed into the life of another" (513). Such imagery echoes earlier passages in the novel where Eliot traces a process by which one being absorbs, incorporates, or "enwraps" another in an act of violence or aggressive appropriation. "Middlemarch, in fact, counted on swallowing Lydgate and assimilating him very comfortably" (99). "We cannot be sure that any natures, however inflexible or peculiar, will resist this effect from a more massive being than their own. They may be taken by storm and for the moment converted, becoming part of the soul which enwraps them in the ardour of its movement" (468). Mrs. Cadwallader defines Mr. Vincy as "one of those who suck the life out of the wretched handloom weavers in Tipton and Freshitt" (204). Or here, in an image drawn from scientific investigation, where Eliot points out that what might appear through a microscope to be "active voracity" on the part of a devouring organism might in fact be a more passive (if not ultimately any less voracious) receptiveness: "under a weak lens you may seem to see a creature exhibiting an active voracity into which other smaller creatures actively play . . . , a stronger lens reveals to you certain tiniest hairlets which make vortices for these victims while the swallower waits passively at his receipt of custom" (38).[1] In such images of absorption, life sucking, and swallowing, Eliot's language recalls the descriptions by her companion George Henry Lewes in his 1859 *Sea-Side Studies* of the habits of the sea sponges, jellyfish, anemones, and other marine creatures he gathered for study: portraits of organisms the boundaries of whose individual form are indefinite, who are prone alternately to active "absorption" or dissolution of others, or of being so assimilated themselves. As we've previously seen in such locations of human-animal brutality, mixture, and domination as Smithfield Market, the Bloomfield family where Agnes Grey serves as governess, and Thrushcross Grange, here life lives on life, life sucks life from or feeds on other beings.

Sally Shuttleworth asserts that "*Middlemarch* is a work of experimental science" in which Eliot turns for inspiration to the "dynamic methodology of experimental biology" (143). Richard Menke has argued convincingly that we should understand Eliot and Lewes as working collaboratively, from the 1850s onward, to develop experimental, innovative forms of fiction, natural history, and physiology.[2] In this chapter I read *Middlemarch* as deeply interested, along similar lines as Lewes's accounts of his natural history research, in the representation of a biological concept of life and of the living being, creature, or organism. Eliot and Lewes are both fascinated by what happens when one life-form is absorbed or subsumed into another, one form incorporated into a larger, more powerful, or more enduring one, a process that raises questions about the boundaries of any individual form—with consequences for the delineating of character. They also both explore, yet more fundamentally, the definition of life or the living itself and the questions—which can be at once biological and ethico-political—of what counts as life, how precisely to mark the moment when life transforms into death or nonlife, and what responsibility one owes to the living. Environmental biologists Lynn Margulis and Dorion Sagan assert that to be an organism is to be the product of "the co-opting of strangers, the involvement and infolding of others . . . into ever more complex and miscegenous genomes" (205).[3] Does the more powerful creature owe anything to the less powerful?

Throughout *Sea-Side Studies*, Lewes dwells with curiosity on the processes by which an organism appropriates the life of another. Sometimes this process is fairly straightforward, as a larger or more powerful creature simply devours a smaller one: "We have just climbed up a ledge, and looked down into a pool. . . . There, now, we have settled into a position in which we can work. Look at that *Gem*, with its lovely tiger-tentacles; it has just swallowed a small fish, and is now, while digesting, opening its arms for more. . . . What queer creatures!" (21) At other moments, Lewes is surprised by incidents of *failure* to devour or absorb, moments when one life-form declines to incorporate another that would seem to offer it the promise of sustenance. Here, for example, Lewes tries to discern whether a sea anemone will, as many naturalists had asserted, eat a crab:

I remember once accidentally dropping a tiny crab on the expanded oral disc of a Crassicornis, whose mouth was wide open; and very amusing it was to see the little creature rush into the open mouth, settle himself comfortably there, and begin twittering his antennae, as crabs do when their alarm subsides. The *Crass* never moved: owing to the insensibility of the stomach, he was quite undisturbed by this refugee. . . . The crab remained twittering for some minutes. I touched him, and he retreated deeper down into the cavity. Looking into the pan some time after, I found he had crawled away. (133)

As Lewes himself gathers up his bucketfuls of seaside creatures to be displayed in bottles in his collections or to be cut into pieces on his dissecting table, he dwells on the ways that these creatures mark out or efface the border between themselves and others by eating one another or declining to do so.

Lewes's seaside researches also raise basic questions about the definition of life or nonlife. Examining the wriggling tentacles of a medusa or marine worm severed from its body, Lewes considers whether "Motion" or motility suffices as a sign of life and concludes that this is not the case.

[L]et us try to be precise in our language. Life is a complex term, indicating complex phenomena. . . . An animal grows, reproduces, and dies; these are the three capital facts of its organism. Out of these issue many derivative and secondary phenomena, one of which is Motion. In some animals, motion can scarcely be said to have any existence. . . . We may therefore conceive Life without Motion, and Motion with Life; and thus, with some plausibility, ask whether the movements exhibited by the tentacles of the Terebella and Medusa ought to be received as indications of life? Here I get myself into a fix. The thought arises that what I observe in these tentacles is owing to a surplus residue of vitality, retained by them, not to any central source of self-renewing vitality, such as the organism possesses; consequently, inasmuch as these tentacles neither grow, nor reproduce themselves, they fail to fulfill the primary conditions of Life; in other words, they are not alive, in spite of movements, apparently spontaneous, during a whole week of independent existence. (58–59)

Lewes's line of thinking clarifies that it is no simple matter to define what is living and what is not; to pose the question leads one quickly to more subtle questions regarding residues of vitality, the possibility of "spontaneous" movement and "independent existence" without true life, and the distinction between a subsidiary organ and the organism on which it depends, both of which possess "vitality" but only the latter of which is truly living.[4] (We can hear an echo of Lewes's investigations into the relation of organic parts to a whole in Lydgate's assertion that living bodies "are not associations of organs which can be understood by studying them first apart, and then as it were federally" [95].)[5] In *Middlemarch*, Eliot investigates similar questions regarding the definition or status of life and nonlife, the process of absorption or incorporation of one organism by another; and, more emphatically than anything we see in *Sea-Side Studies*, she further stages a set of ethical dilemmas raised by these topics.

Questions regarding the domination of or submission to the other in *Middlemarch* have primarily been considered in reference to gender. After all, the full sentence I cited earlier about Dorothea is "Many who knew her, thought it a pity that so substantive and rare a creature should have been absorbed into the life of another, and be only known in a certain circle as a wife and mother." In the marriage plot of *Middlemarch*, Dorothea is an impressive young woman who makes a terrible marriage to an older man who is defined in part by his extreme lack of vitality; he somewhat resembles the individual tentacles of Lewes's anemone in that while possessing apparent signs of life, including motility, he cannot reproduce himself and is, perhaps, not fully human or alive. As Mrs. Cadwallader puts it with her characteristic vividness, defining Casaubon precisely as one of Lewes's specimens, "Somebody put a drop [of his blood] under a magnifying-glass, and it was all semi-colons and parentheses" (45). Dorothea is apparently freed from the marriage trap by her husband's sudden death but finally marries again and, as we've seen, takes up "wifely help" for the cause of her second husband's political career. For many readers of the novel, even if Will Ladislaw may be infinitely preferable to Casaubon, it is still slightly disappointing that Dorothea ends up as a helpmeet. We may prefer Will as an organism or "life" into which Dorothea is to be absorbed but still feel some regret that absorption must occur at all. Why cannot Dorothea exist as a proudly individual being?

Of course, whether this absorption has truly occurred is debatable, as Eliot's sentence contains some self-limiting irony: Dorothea is "only known *in a certain circle* as a wife and mother" (my italics), but we, as Eliot's wiser readers, understand that "the effect of her being on those around her was incalculably diffusive." Perhaps to see Dorothea as truly "absorbed into the life of another" is to underestimate the opportunities her marriage affords for agency, but it seems to me that Eliot does ultimately imply that it would be a sentimental illusion to insist that the strong and admirable individual or "substantive and rare . . . creature" can hope to avoid eventual absorption into other beings. In this thoroughly biologized novel, "there is no creature whose inward being is so strong that it is not greatly determined by what lies outside it" (514). This is a Darwinian point about the absolute codependency of all beings on those other beings with which they live in relation: "what lies outside" the creature is not only environment but also other creatures who threaten to supplant or usurp its own place.

Darwin, of course, introduced the most influential of several major assaults in the nineteenth century on the doctrine of the self-sufficient, autonomous, liberal individual—and Eliot's thinking partakes of this Darwinian critique of the liberal self. In Darwin's—and, I believe, Eliot's—view, being and form cannot or should not be understood apart from an ongoing process and network of affiliation, competition, and struggle for possession of environmental niche. I am, in part, making a familiar point about interrelationship, and Eliot's reliance on a Darwinian model of "the excessively complex and radiating affinities by which all the members of the same family or higher group are connected together" (Darwin, *Origin* 431). But what I want to add to this well-known argument is a sharper sense, in this web of interrelation, not simply of struggle and competition but also of an agonistic drama in which two organisms face or confront one another and threaten to injure, harm, or absorb the life of one into the other, as with the tiny crab and the *crassicornis*. As Darwin puts it, "it should be remembered that the competition will generally be most severe between those forms which are most nearly related to each other in habits, constitution, and structure" (121). Closeness and affinity are often spurs to violence, aggression, and even willful extermination. Beings continually "encroach on places occupied by other beings" (116); the inevitable dependency of every being or form on those closest to it is difficult to wall off conceptually from the ever-present threat of destruction by those same beings.

Derrida posits as the "fundamental phantasm" that haunts Robinson Crusoe that "he is afraid of dying a living death by being swallowed or devoured into the deep belly of the earth or the sea or some living creature, some animal" (*Beast* 2: 77). *Middlemarch*, too, articulates a vision of the individual being as constituted by its dependency on others, a dependency that is inextricable from a threat of possible absorption into or injury or destruction by another. The individual organism is for Eliot, as for Darwin, fundamentally and ontologically precarious, permeable, and subject to aggression at the hands (or teeth, digestive tract, etc.) of another. We all will at some point, it is implied, be confronted by a greater organism who threatens to absorb or to kill us. These ideas have specific consequences for our conceptualization of character for Eliot. The full-fledged human character, particularly the protagonist, is always delineated in relation to other less robust beings who may be incorporated into the stronger one. This dynamic, I believe, leads to two corollaries for Eliot: first, that the formally robust character is always defined in relation to the weaker minor character (this is more or less the Wolochian point about minorness); secondly, that the ethically admirable character is the one who will sometimes *forgo* the absorption, incorporation, or destruction of the lesser creature. Every living being potentially maintains a pastoral relation to other creatures, overseeing their lives and determining which to permit to live.

The institution of marriage is especially important for Eliot in the way it foregrounds the risk of injury, the threat of absorption, and—more positively—the necessity of responsibility and care in relations with other beings. For, if being with others is always to live with the risk of injury, then the care of others in order to avoid or minimize injury emerges as an especially crucial ethical practice.[6] For Eliot, one of the most admirable forms of ethical choice is represented by the spouse who accepts his or her responsibility for the "fragile" life of the partner who may be a lifelong burden, as in Lydgate's final acceptance of Rosamond: "he had chosen this fragile creature, and had taken the burden of her life upon his arms. He must walk as he could, carrying that burden pitifully" (493).

Marriage was Victorian culture's most symbolically powerful institution of transindividual relation; marriage was the quintessential test of what happens to an individual who gives up a putative autonomy in order legally and ritually to merge with another. Needless to say, this institution was asymmetrical when it came to gender; absorption into another and abdication of individual status in marriage was far more thorough for women than for men, to say the least. As a legal definition from 1853 puts it, "husband and wife are treated at Common Law as one person indivisible, the personal and separate existence of the wife being legally considered as *absorbed* and consolidated in that of her husband, from which it is judicially indistinguishable" (qtd. in Graver 216; my italics).

An early aside in the novel nicely evokes the ways Eliot associates marriage with ethical questions of care, responsibility, and the potential to injure. When Dorothea says to her sister Celia, "I am engaged to marry

Mr. Casaubon," these are the next words in the novel: "Perhaps Celia had never turned so pale before. The paper man she was making would have had its leg injured, but for her habitual care of whatever she held in her hands. She laid the fragile figure down at once" (31). Eliot's imagery here subtly implies the risks in this process for Dorothea, as Celia and her paper man come into vision here as a model of the stakes of interrelation and codependency. The paper man, I would suggest, functions as a figure for the individual being in *Middlemarch*, a fragile figure who is at grave risk of injury by another should that other fail to offer the necessary care. Eliot hints here that while Celia handles the objective material world with care and even tenderness, Dorothea lacks these habits of attention and may injure both herself and vulnerable others in her intimate relationships.

Casaubon's own language, describing his vision of the responsibility he took on in marrying, suggests the involvement of the institution of marriage with questions of the care of a living being who is susceptible to injury: "In marrying Dorothea Brooke, I had to care for her wellbeing in case of my death. But wellbeing is not to be secured by ample, independent possession of property; on the contrary, occasions might arise in which such possession might expose her to the more danger" (262). This suggests one way to understand the importance in this novel of plots regarding inheritance and wills. Since marriage enacts a symbolic absorption of one being into another, or a merging of two into one, the death of one spouse introduces a crisis of reindividuation, as the surviving partner becomes vulnerable as she returns to the status of an unencumbered individual—perhaps like the crab crawling out of the maw of the insensible sea anemone. Without sympathizing in the least with Casaubon's grasping attempt to control his wife from beyond the grave, we can acknowledge some truth in his suggestion that the terms of his will contribute to a symbolic redefinition of Dorothea as a single, unabsorbed entity, a transformation always likely to expose the subject to risk.[7]

As I've suggested, it has seemed somewhat ironic or frustrating to many readers that Dorothea ends the novel by being "absorbed" into Will Ladislaw's life, since her drama had previously been to avoid absolute absorption into Casaubon. Paradoxically, though, however oppressed and unfulfilled Dorothea had been in her marriage with Casaubon, one of the primary emotions and concerns Eliot associates with Dorothea in this relationship is a fear that she will injure Casaubon like a helpless animal. Here is one marker of this novel's shared participation in a broader project overlapping with Lewes's work in physiology and animal life and that of novelists such as the Brontës and Dickens who draw, in various ways, on the Victorian discourses circulating around animal welfare and the ethics of human-animal relations. The strong or robust character—capable of protagonicity—is the one who not only *can* absorb and dominate others but also, crucially, possesses the ethical sense of restraint to forgo doing so, at least on occasion. The animal other is in fact critical for the definition of the human character, because this other being represents both the object of domination (animals can always potentially be killed and used) and the object of sympathy and ethical restraint (at least some animals, pets and others, escape this usual fate). This dynamic creates a space for a judgment or moral test of any character: is she or is she not capable of sparing the animal other, of protecting it as friend or fellow? Can she "go along with" the animal, allow the nonhuman creature within the circuits of sympathy and domestication?

SACRIFICIAL ANIMALS

One recurring image of nonsympathy, or incomplete sympathy, in *Middlemarch* is the gaze that examines and categorizes the (human) other as a being of a different species (recalling Heathcliff, who "stared hard at the object of discourse, as one might do at a strange repulsive animal" [105]). "It seemed that she had no more identified herself with him than if they had been creatures of different species" (369); "it was inevitable that . . . he should think of her as if she were an animal of another and a feebler species" (413). We've already considered the novel's famous observation that "if we had a keen vision and feeling of all ordinary human life, it would be like hearing the grass grow and the squirrel's heart beat, and we should die of that roar which lies on the other side of silence. As it is, the quickest of us walk about well wadded with stupidity" (124). Early in the novel, Eliot establishes a pattern of imagery according to which the human relationship to the animal becomes a test case for the care of others and the possibility of autonomy or a companionship that might exist without dependency, as opposed to a parasitic form of relationship in which one being utterly submits to the other.[8]

Eliot marks out Dorothea as a character who is not very interested in animals and who therefore, we can presume, would not listen for that squirrel's heartbeat. When Sir James comes to pay court to the oblivious Dorothea, who believes he is in love with Celia, he brings with him a "white object under his arm, which was a tiny Maltese puppy, one of nature's most naïve toys" (20).

"It is painful to me to see these creatures that are bred merely as pets," said Dorothea, whose opinion was forming itself that very moment (as opinions will) under the heat of irritation.

"Oh, why?" said Sir James, as they walked forward.

"I believe all the petting that is given them does not make them happy. They are too helpless; their lives are too frail. A weasel or a mouse that gets its own living is more interesting. I like to think that the animals about us have souls something like our own, and either carry on their own little affairs or can be companions to us, like Monk here ["the Great St Bernard dog, who always took care of the young ladies in their walks" (18)]. Those creatures are parasitic."

Dorothea having articulated this opinion, "The objectionable puppy, whose nose and eyes were equally black and expressive, was . . . got rid of, since Miss Brooke decided that it had better not been born." Dorothea later seems to feel some misgivings, but "[a]fter all, it was a relief that there was no puppy to tread upon" (21).

This "objectionable" puppy encapsulates a strain of the novel's thinking on mutual dependency, the care of or harm to others in interrelationship, and the risks of injury and violence in intimate relations. The comparison of the Maltese to the Great St. Bernard Monk, who "always took care of the young ladies," highlights that what is at stake here is the problem of "care"; the abject status of the puppy derives from its inability to care for others. Unable to "get its own living," it is therefore also unable to offer care to other beings. The puppy stands unsteadily as a figure of "helpless," "frail," creaturely life defined as "parasitic" and therefore subject to annihilation. Notwithstanding disturbing recollections of Agnes Grey's "large flat stone" that she used to smash the mice, we should not leap to the conclusion that Sir James put this would-be love gift to death in "getting rid of" it—but the creature still seems to represent a category of being that is essentially "fragile" and expendable, quickly banished from the novel.[9] A nameless puppy like this, at least with someone like Dorothea around, exists "to [be] tread upon"; it is a potential victim of sacrifice without ritual, a malleable symbol of the vulnerability to injury of organic form or of animal body. (We might recall Marshall Hall's question, "May I ask the writer . . . , how it will please him henceforth to dispose of superfluous puppies and kittens?" [58].) Even taking account of Dorothea's nearsightedness, the puppy seems to exist in part to reveal to us the potential for violence concealed within her powerful ego; she is one of those heroines of the English novel—in a lineage with the likes of Emma Woodhouse and Jane Eyre—whose capacity for self-sacrifice belies their will to power. Dorothea "gets rid of" the puppy in order that she will not be forced to step on and destroy it; its total vulnerability is too tempting an occasion for aggression.[10]

Eliot defines this puppy as an emblematically creaturely, precarious being and, as such, an occasion for ethical reflection on the care and responsibility one owes to the other. Judith Butler comments in a discussion of Levinas, "Is there something about my apprehension of the Other's precariousness that makes me want to kill the Other? . . . If the Other, the Other's face, which after all carries the meaning of this precariousness, at once tempts me with murder and prohibits me from acting upon it, then the face operates to produce a struggle for me, and establishes this struggle at the heart of ethics" (*Precarious* 135). Or, as Derrida puts it in a reading of Plato, "the question of love and friendship is adapted to the desire to eat the other, to a 'you really have to eat the other'" (*Beast* 1: 60). This struggle over whether or not to kill the other lies at the heart of *Middlemarch*, a novel so fundamentally interested in the responsibility to or care for other beings whose presence might thwart or defy one's own will. For Dorothea to count as the novel's protagonist, she must prove that she is the sort of person who may be capable of love for animals; she must deploy in relation to animals what Deidre Lynch, in reference to the love of literature, describes as the "subjectivity-saturated language of involvement and affection" (10). Dorothea's straightforward rejection of the puppy threatens to align her with the abusers of animals who, since the novels of the Brontës, had been identified as incapable of the proper sympathy that defines the human and the humane.

Dorothea's ungracious comments to Sir James about this "parasitic" creature who cannot "ge[t] its own living" resonate with broader themes in the novel regarding autonomy and the possibility of "getting one's own living" as opposed to existing as simply parasitic. Eliot stresses the distinction between moral autonomy and agency, defined in part through work, and living parasitically through or on another. In this context, it is significant that Rosamond is twice defined as a kind of vegetative life and thereby situated, in a continuum of the biological "living," in near relation to Lewes's tentacled sea creatures or even to the molds and algae he scrapes from the rocks on the shore. In book 4, Lydgate muses on arguments "for not deferring the marriage [to Rosamond] too long, as he implied to Mr. Farebrother, one day that the Vicar came to his room with some pond-products which he wanted to examine under a better microscope than his own" (217). As they discuss, Lydgate thinks, "But that exquisite creature herself suffered in the same sort of way—it was at least one delightful thought that in marrying her, he could give her a much-needed transplantation." In this immediate context, Eliot seems to hint that Rosamond—horticulturally considered—might be less the lovely flower she appears than a vegetative variety of "pond-product" or algae perhaps living in the "brown pond" (3) of social convention mentioned in the novel's preface, or she could even be one of those parasitic, leechlike "hidden suckers" Eliot evokes in a chapter epigraph (chapter 53). We might remember this earlier reference when we encounter the novel's final reference to Rosamond and her marriage to Lydgate: "He once called her his basil plant; and when she asked for an explanation, said that basil was a plant which had flourished wonderfully on a murdered man's brains" (513). This is an image from Boccaccio, adapted by Keats, of Isabella planting the head of her murdered lover in a pot of basil, which flourishes as she waters it with her tears: a devastating image of Rosamond as passively murderous, parasitic, and vegetative, straddling the Aristotelean border between life and nonlife.

Eliot implies that marriage can very easily be a form of soul death, with one partner judged as in effect a murderer. As I've said, it is somewhat surprising that, for all the suffering and self-abnegation Dorothea suffers in her marriage with Casaubon, one of the primary emotions that she experiences with him is fear of injuring him. Casaubon is excruciatingly susceptible to such injury: "his intellectual ambition which seemed to others to have absorbed and dried him, was really no security against wounds, least of all against those which came from Dorothea" (26). In the denouement of their marriage, as Dorothea abandons all traces of the admiration she had once felt for Casaubon, she is increasingly filled with dread that she will injure him like a weak animal. At the close of book 4, as she brims with anger and resentment, she comes close to speaking bitterly to him but restrains herself, and she "felt something like the thankfulness that might well up in us if we had narrowly escaped hurting a lamed creature" (266). Just before Casaubon's death, she is on the verge of consenting to his demand that she promise to dedicate herself forever to the continuation of his scholarly labors: "she was too weak, too full of dread at the thought of inflicting a keen-edged blow on her husband, to do anything but submit completely" (298). "She could not smite the stricken soul that entreated hers." When Eliot alludes to "[t]he sword visibly trembling above him" (297), the sword represents death, but it is also a weapon of interpersonal (marital) aggression that Dorothea herself wields or could choose to wield.

A sacrificial pet animal, a kind of scapegoat, dwells at the symbolic center of *Middlemarch*'s labyrinth of imagery: a fragile creature who may be killed in an enactment of the precariousness of organic life or whose sacrifice might alternately be averted in a gesture of generosity or abeyance. This is necessarily a domesticated animal, an animal brought into the Victorian home and turned into a potential proof of the limits of domestic sympathy. Can (domestic, novelistic) sympathy be extended to an animal? Can the Smithian "going along with" that Rae Greiner argues is fundamental to Victorian realism—which can be extended to "illiterates and children, idiots and madmen" and even "the dead" (17)—also include nonhuman creatures? Eliot's image brings to mind Judith Butler's remark: "That we can be injured, that others can be injured, that we are all subject to death at the whim of another, are all reasons for both fear and grief" (*Precarious* xii). In these passages, Casaubon becomes this animal with Dorothea wielding the axe that could deliver a "keen-edged blow"—even as Dorothea also experiences herself to be "yoke[d]" (296), "toiling under . . . fetters" (306) and in danger of saying "'Yes' to her own doom" (298). This implicit figure of the sacrificial animal emerges in a surprisingly literal form in an aside late in the novel when Dorothea visits the Farebrother parsonage. "That house was never dull," the narrator comments. "Mr. Farebrother, like another White of Selbourne, having continually something new to tell of his inarticulate guests and protégés, whom he was teaching the boys not to torment; and he had just set up a pair of beautiful goats to be pets of the village in general, and to walk at large as sacred animals" (483). This reference to the anthropological concept of the sacred animal offers a crucial hint of Eliot's preoccupation with the ethical challenge posed by frail or fragile organic life and the temptation it offers to torment, kill, or sacrifice it. Catherine Gallagher has demonstrated that Eliot offered in her novels "an overtly fictionalized form of anthropological conjecture" that linked "art to sacrifice" (179) and that she shared with the Victorian anthropologist John McLennan, author of the 1865 *Primitive Marriage*, "a view of culture as an attempt to make sense of suffering, especially female suffering, and both thought that the idea of sacrifice had its origin there" (179). Gallagher suggests that for authors like Eliot and Thomas Hardy, well versed in the anthropological research of their day, the very form of the novel was designed to reproduce the "bioeconomic rituals" of our primitive ancestors "with their underlying logic of forfeiting a life to fertilize the world" (183).[11] Here in *Middlemarch* we can glimpse a slightly different although related logic, one in which the ethical challenge posed by the potentially sacrificial creature is to forgo the obvious temptation of slaughtering it—in effect, to sacrifice the profitable sacrifice. In a sense, every domestic animal or pet offers this challenge: do we forgo taking advantage of the vulnerable creature and using it for food or other purposes? As with Dorothea withholding the blow her ego longs to deliver to the wounded Casaubon, we see these goats "walk at large as sacred animals" in an enactment of a domesticating logic of restraint according to which *some* creatures are spared the general "carnivorous sacrifice." Given the biological imperative and urge to seize, devour, and sacrifice the life of the other, Eliot suggests that to learn to forgo this pleasure—not to kill, not to devour or destroy—is one key capacity of the ethical subject.[12] And the realist novel as a form becomes a staging ground for this lesson, with the human protagonist subjected to a test of her capacity for proper domestication: her ability to draw the line between those nonhuman others that are to be destroyed and incorporated, as opposed to those to be spared.

CREATURELY LIFE

I now want to offer some analysis of a crucial scene in the novel, one that resonates powerfully in relation to our own contemporary debates over a variety of topics relating to the boundary between life and death and the ethical problems that spring up at that boundary. I refer to the passages in book 7 where Nicholas Bulstrode, the banker, presides over the prone body of John Raffles, the man who has come to Middlemarch to blackmail Bulstrode with information about fraud and other wrongdoings the banker has committed and long repressed. Earlier, Raffles had visited Bulstrode on a Christmas Day blackmailing mission and had been sent off with a hundred pounds, the promise of further payments, and a stern threat that all such revenue would be cut off if Raffles ever returned.

Eliot insistently defines the obnoxious Raffles as a test of "care" and oversight of a weak "creature" or "being." Raffles is an embodiment of the creaturely as a wounded animal existence, vulnerable to harm—even as he *also* has the capacity and indeed the will (like Casaubon but more sharply) to harm others; that is, he defines a complex coexistence of frailty and threat. Bulstrode, concealing the real facts of his relationship to Raffles, "had told his wife that he was simply taking care of this wretched creature . . . who might otherwise injure himself. . . . He would himself drive the unfortunate being away the next morning" (424). Unfortunately for Bulstrode, however, Raffles is not so easily disposed of, as Caleb Garth later finds him on the road, in physical distress, and brings him to Bulstrode's property at Stone Court: "I saw he was ill: it seemed to me the right thing to do, to carry him under shelter" (429). By a melodramatic turn of events, then, Bulstrode's nemesis is delivered to him in a state of total physical incapacity, setting the scene for one of the novel's major ethical tests.

When Lydgate is called in to offer medical advice, his judgment is that the patient will likely recover but "should be well watched and attended to" (432). What ensues is a kind of parody or travesty of pastoral care of the body. In her 1858 story "Janet's Repentance" in *Scenes of Clerical Life*, Eliot defines the sickroom or deathbed as a paradigmatic site of vulnerability and responsibility: the place "where a human being lies prostrate, thrown on the tender mercies of his fellow," where "the moral relation of man to man is reduced to its utmost clearness and simplicity" (324).[13] Here, Raffles lies prostrate but finds no tender mercy. Bulstrode tries to reassure himself that Raffles can offer him little serious threat; "the chief point now was to keep watch over him" (434) to ensure Raffles does not, intentionally or otherwise, reveal more of his secrets; Bulstrode presents himself to Lydgate and his servants as taking on this task himself out of a generous sense of personal responsibility, but his "keep[ing] watch" over Raffles is a mission not of caretaking but nervous oversight or "management" of a potential threat (Eliot defines Raffles as "manageable" [435] but posing a risk of becoming "more unmanageable" [432]).

The novel is generally interested in and concerned with the plotline or narrative defined by the state of "Waiting for Death," the title of book 3. Raffles becomes the second character in this novel, along with Mr. Featherstone, to be represented as hovering on the border between life and death (we never really see Casaubon in this state—unless we consider him to have always been in it). More than Featherstone's, however, Raffles's passage from life to death is rendered by Eliot in such a way as to emphasize at once his sheer creaturely existence in a precarious position of indeterminacy between these two realms, and the way his situation places him in a state of total vulnerability and subjection to another.

Agamben and others have argued that the categorical and definitional problems posed by the comatose or vegetative human body capture many of our most urgent ethicopolitical dilemmas regarding state power over the individual and the mobilization of "biopolitics." Agamben discusses the discovery by French neurophysiologists in 1959 of a state they dubbed *coma dépassé* or overcoma, "a coma in which the total abolition of relational life corresponds to an equally total abolition of vegetative life functions" (160). This was a category generated and necessitated by new forms of life-support technology that permitted the extension of "life" beyond its previous limits. The physiologists "immediately realized that the significance of *coma dépassé* far exceeded the technicoscientific problem of resuscitation: at stake was nothing less than a redefinition of death" (161). These and other developments, Agamben argues, ensure that "the concept of 'death,' far from having become more exact, now oscillates from one pole to the other with the greatest indeterminacy" (162). "This means that today . . . life and death are not properly scientific concepts but rather political concepts, which as such acquire a political meaning precisely only through a decision. . . . The hospital room in which the neomort, the overcomatose person, and the *faux vivant* waver between life and death delimits a space of exception in which a purely bare life, entirely controlled by man and his technologies, appears for the first time" (164). "The comatose person has been defined as an intermediary being between man and an animal," and "what is at stake is . . . the definition of a life that may be killed without the commission of a homicide" (165).

One might assume that the definition of the life-death boundary was, prior to the twentieth century's new technologies of life, comparatively clear-cut, but Catherine Gallagher and Stephen Greenblatt have argued that the late eighteenth-century discovery "of 'suspended animation,' or 'apparent death' cast doubt on what had for centuries seemed the certain signs of death. . . . There was, in fact, little consensus about the exact nature of the 'essential difference' [between absolute and apparent death]. . . . Bodies that looked quite lifeless might instead be dormant, and doctors were repeatedly cautioned not to trust too readily to appearances. . . . The place that seemingly moribund bodies occupied on the life-death continuum had become uncertain" (191–92). Gallagher and Greenblatt suggest that even in the mid-nineteenth century, long before the many twentieth- and twenty-first-century debates over the definition of the fully living or alive body, the figure of the comatose body hovering in an indeterminate zone between life and death had become highly charged as a figure embodying major ethicopolitical problems and questions. Who defines life and where it begins and ends? Who has the right to name or to end life? These questions, so pressing in contemporary battles over reproductive rights, the ethics of stem-cell research, and medical care of those near death, have a much longer history. And, in the overlap between conceptualizations of the human subject and the literary character, they bear especially on the form of the novel.

In this strand of the plot of *Middlemarch*, Eliot draws on her own and Lewes's speculations regarding the definition of the category of the living and her reflections on the demands of care and responsibility for organic life in order powerfully to stage a scene of a willful and aggressive, albeit passive, killing of that which may not be fully alive to begin with. The category of what we might call the undead or questionably alive seems to extend beyond Raffles himself in this morbid deathbed scene, where even Bulstrode himself "had the air of an animated corpse returned to movement without warmth" (435). The key lines for my purposes (and those from which I've taken the title of this chapter) are, however, the following, as Bulstrode broods on the consequences of Raffles's likely recovery:

> Raffles, recovering quickly, returning to the free use of his odious powers—how could Bulstrode wish for that? Raffles dead was the image that brought release, and directly he prayed for that way of release, beseeching that, if it were possible, the rest of his days here below might be freed from the threat of an ignominy which would break him utterly as an instrument of God's service. Lydgate's opinion was not on the side of promise that this prayer would be fulfilled; and as the day advanced, Bulstrode found himself getting irritated at the persistent life in this man, whom he would have fain seen sinking into the silence of death: imperious will stirred murderous impulses towards this brute life, over which will, by itself, had no power. (437)

Bulstrode's narcissism takes the form of a "murderous" will to power over life itself. In his view, Raffles, like Dorothea's "objectionable" puppy, "had better not been born"; Bulstrode rescinds Raffles's life.

Eliot depicts Raffles as an embodiment of what Eric Santner has defined as the "creaturely," sheerly biological life at once disavowed from the polis and preserved as the object of political power.[14] I suggest that we read the scene of Bulstrode's passive murder of Raffles—the banker allows his servant unwittingly to administer a fatal dose of alcohol to the patient suffering from the throes of alcohol poisoning—as *Middlemarch*'s central test case of the administration of a form of biopolitical power. Bulstrode's fraudulent care of Raffles exemplifies the narcissistic human will to domination of life itself, the drive to seize control over the boundary between the dead and the living. The narcissism of this desire is most obviously (if relatively sympathetically) embodied in the novel in the medical doctor and scientist, Lydgate, who yearns Frankensteinianly to crack the secret of life's basic structure, but in Bulstrode we see a striking further displacement and appropriation of that institutionalized human agency over what might otherwise be seen as belonging to God. (That is, if we understand the practice of medicine as the sole domain in which human beings are normally authorized to assume a godlike role over human life.) Bulstrode's "imperious will" takes the form, specifically, of a willful disregard for medical advice, as Eliot seems to craft an allegory of the modern will to free biopower from either divine sanction or its traditional limited institutional framework in the medical profession. Bulstrode gives free rein to his "imperious will" and "murderous impulses" in order to subjugate, without restraint, "brute life"; as such, he fails the novelistic test of the good protagonistic subject, the one who knows what to allow to live.

The creaturely Raffles in his coma-like state joins the Maltese puppy and other sacrificial animals of *Middlemarch*, along with Lewes's sea anemones and jellyfish, in an array of creaturely life whose position on the life/nonlife continuum is ambiguous or precarious. How do we treat these weak animals within our homes? Raffles becomes, as well, a test case for the power of narrative itself. I have tried to suggest how interested Eliot is in a set of questions concerning the definition and management of life. Who defines life, who can say and determine where it begins and ends? How does one life oversee, control, absorb, or assimilate another? When do or should we forgo the temptation to kill and eat or otherwise use any creature who seems to exist at our disposal? Finally, these questions are also formal and narrative ones as Eliot seems to dwell on her own powers and responsibilities as the author of the world of *Middlemarch* and all the teeming, "palpitating life" (486) it contains. She has singled out Bulstrode as an embodiment of the overweening human will to manage life and to mete out death—but Bulstrode is simply another helpless creature in the grips of the overwhelming creative agency and power of Eliot herself.

One instance of this power making itself known occurs late in the novel when the foolish Rosamond first begins to understand her own implication in the Bulstrode scandal. "Have you heard nothing about your uncle Bulstrode, Rosamond?" her father asks. "'No, papa,' said the poor thing, feeling as if trouble were not anything she had before experienced but some invisible power with an iron grasp that made her soul faint within her" (466). We might interpret this as the moment when Rosamond submits at once to ethical responsibility but also to Eliot's own power as a narrator, which is arguably figured in that "invisible power with an iron grip." One of the dramas of the book relates to our own relation to that power and to the possibility of our own resistance or submission to Eliot's narrative control and force; Eliot herself seems fascinated by the way fictional narrative functions as a godlike force that wields biopower, defines the limits of the living and the nonliving, and in effect assumes responsibility for the creatures it represents. I have suggested that in *Middlemarch* Eliot stages an ethical test or judgment of those human characters who can—or cannot—demonstrate a proper concern for the helpless beings in their care. One might also ask, however, whether Eliot herself passes her own test.

We might speculate that Eliot viewed her own activity of fiction making as a kind of ethical acceptance of the lives of others. As Lydgate "had chosen this fragile creature, and had taken the burden of her life upon his arms" (493), so Eliot takes on her characters—and perhaps readers—as fragile and dependent creatures. We as passive readers are arguably, at risk of total absorption into Eliot's dominating, life-forming narrative power, of "becoming part of the soul which enwraps . . . [us] in the ardour of its movement" (468).[15] For Eliot, I believe, to be "enwrapped" is a paradigmatic form of aesthetic experience: she associates aesthetic "enrapture" with a biological experience of physical incorporation. As we read *Middlemarch*, then, we may be like frail Maltese puppies in danger of being tread on by the giant that is George Eliot, or sea anemones contained in a glass jar on G. H. Lewes's shelf, or, as we end the novel, perhaps we are ourselves like little crabs scrambling out of the maw of the massive being that had temporarily incorporated our own lives. The realist novel offers a series of characterological tests designed to flush out those human characters who are simply cruel, who cannot forgo the incorporation of the helpless creature in their grasp. Yet there is one figure who stands above this stage, to some degree exempt from its judgment: that of the author herself.

Figure 5 Thomas and Florence Hardy with Wessex. Courtesy of the Dorset County Museum, Dorchester, Dorset, UK.

Using and Pitying Animals in Thomas Hardy

ANIMALS IN THE HARDY HOUSEHOLD

Up to this point we have considered some authors (like Emily Brontë) who seemed to feel passionately for animals, at least for select animals, and others (for example, Dickens) for whom animals seemed to "matter"—to signify in important ways in their novels—and yet necessarily to exist on the margins of an anthropocentric worldview. With Thomas Hardy, we come to the first canonical British novelist to take an active interest in the animal-welfare movement—which had itself moved from the margins closer to the mainstream in the decades after the 1824 founding of the SPCA. Hardy was deeply interested in human-animal relations. It has long been a truism to observe that his work is suffused by Darwinian ideas; somewhat less well known is that he had an abiding concern for animals that expressed itself in numerous tangible ways. He accepted an honorary membership in the Wessex Saddleback Pig Society, a group dedicated to the promotion of humane slaughter (*Personal Notebooks* 270); he offered the pig-killing scene from *Jude the Obscure* to the animal-rights organization The Animals' Friend to be republished as a pamphlet (*Life and Work* 289); he wrote in his self-written biography that the "sight of animals being taken to market or driven to slaughter always aroused in Hardy feelings of intense pity, as he well knew . . . how much needless suffering is inflicted" (*Life and Work* 468), and his will left sums of money to two different animal-protection societies "to be applied as far as practicable to the investigation of the means by which animals are conveyed from their home to the slaughter-houses with a view to the lessening of their sufferings in such transit" (468). His entry in the 1928 edition of *Who's Who* offers very few personal details of any kind but did find room to mention that Hardy was "Member of the Council of Justice to Animals; is against

blood-sport, dog-chaining, and the caging of birds" (qtd. in Mallet 465).[1]
The cause of seeking "Justice to Animals" was fundamental to Hardy, but,
with some recent exceptions, scholarship on his work has tended to isolate
it as a biographical quirk.

Gillian Beer has helped us see how Hardy's work can be understood
as offering an ongoing "comedy of propinquity and complementarity" in
which human presence intrudes on, notices, and accompanies the "natural" or the nonhuman world. "The problem of finding a scale for the
human becomes a besetting preoccupation of Hardy's work" (233), Beer
observes, citing as an influence on the author Darwin's assertion that
"the relation of organism to organism is the most important of all relations" (*Origin* 477). George Levine has recently called for greater attention
to a Darwinian inheritance in Hardy's work that manifests itself less in
scenes of "stress, competition, chance, struggle, and suffering" ("Hardy
and Darwin" 36) than in "ethically intense attention to the whole range of
nature, organic and inorganic, in their discovery of narratives latent in all
things" (37). In this chapter I consider further "the relation of organism to
organism" in Hardy's work, considering Hardy's representation of animal
life and animality both as important and as deeply intertwined with his
depiction of human life.

Hardy was not a vegetarian, although he was ambivalent and conflicted about meat eating. Throughout his adult life he became more explicitly and passionately dedicated to the cause of improving the human
treatment of animals. Hardy's biographer Michael Millgate is at least
slightly pathologizing in his analysis of this aspect of Hardy's life, writing
that "[t]hat extraordinary capacity for imaginative identification which
gave such strength to a novel like *Tess* was liable, at the level of everyday
living, to take the form of an almost morbid sensitivity to the sufferings of
others, and especially to the sufferings of animals" (380). Millgate expands
on this:

> For some readers Hardy's especial concern with cruelty to animals has
> always seemed mildly eccentric, beside the main point. And yet Henry
> Nevinson . . . was surely right to identify Hardy's feeling for animals as
> a logical as well as an emotional extrapolation from the wincing raw-
> ness of his response to all forms of suffering. Recalling Hardy's tales of
> the slaughter of game birds and of the hangings, whippings, burnings,
> and other brutal punishments dealt out to human beings in Dorches-
> ter's not-so-very-distant past, Nevinson commented: "These subjects
> have for him a horrible fascination that comes of extreme sensitive-

ness to other peoples' pain. I suppose that if we all had that intensity of imagination we should never do harm to human being or animal or bird, certainly not in cruelty." (413)

Hardy wrote vividly of the sufferings of horses in battle in the Boer war and of cattle in slaughterhouses. He was also particularly troubled by the sufferings of gamebirds, foxes, and other objects of organized hunting. Early in January 1882, after a conversation with a gamekeeper he had met, Hardy made a note that clearly anticipates a famous scene in *Tess* in which Tess kills the wounded pheasants, left behind after a hunt, with her bare hands:

> [T]ells me that one day this season they shot—(3 guns) 700 pheasants in one day—a battue—driving the birds into one corner of the plantation. When they got there they will not run across the open ground— rise on the wing—then are shot wholesale. They pick up all that have fallen—night comes on—the wounded birds that have hidden or risen into some thick tree fall, & lie on the ground in their agony—next day the keepers come and look for them. (They found 150, on the above occasion, the next day)—Can see the night scene—moon—fluttering and gasping birds as the hours go on—the place being now deserted of humankind. (qtd. in Millgate 218)

That eerie, terrible final image of the "fluttering and gasping birds" supports the suggestion that Hardy's "wincing rawness of his response to all forms of suffering" necessarily extended to nonhuman beings. We might even say that Hardy was the first major English author to be fully willing to try to listen to "the squirrel's heart beat," in Eliot's image, to dare to confront "that roar which lies on the other side of silence" by offering sympathy and respect to animals beyond a few select pets.

Hardy's own sense of domesticity and the home was also particularly strongly marked by the living presence of domestic animals. This could be said of other authors like the Brontës and Dickens and indeed of many if not most English people of the era, but the animals in the Hardy household had an unusual degree of latitude and power within the home. Hardy seemed to view the home as a sanctified space not only for marriage and human companionship but also for pet keeping and for other aspects of human-animal relations. I've been arguing that Victorian concepts of both domesticity and fiction virtually required the presence of animals, even if those animals were often marginalized and displaced to preserve a central

space for the (nonanimal) human, that the forms of the Victorian home
and the novel both had to allow a space for the animal, for life outside the
boundary of the human, albeit usually a marginal life. But in Hardy, the
first author I've discussed who took animal welfare seriously and focused
on it as a crucial political-ethical problem, this dynamic begins to shift,
such that the animal within the home and the novel gains more explicit
attention and value. The marginalization of the animal, while still persistent, become less automatic or unthinking, and it begins to seem more
possible for the animal to attain some degree of personhood or character
status. Protagonicity itself seems, potentially, to open to the animal—even
if this change threatens to disrupt or explode the form of the realist novel.

We can see biographical parallels for such shifts in Hardy's writing in
the history of Hardy's two marriages and their practices of pet keeping.
In a reading of Michael Millgate's biography of Hardy, along with Hardy's
letters, one quickly realizes that one of the only topics on which Hardy
and his first wife Emma Hardy could find happy agreement related to their
shared passion for animal welfare and for their own pets.

> Hardy and Emma certainly remained at one in their devotion to their
> cats. One visitor at about this period reported that there were boards
> laid from one piece of furniture to the next, so that the cats could walk
> around the room without descending—or condescending—to the floor.
> Another, startled at Hardy's coming to the door in his stockinged feet,
> was told by Emma, "I never let him wear his boots in the house until
> the kittens are three weeks old, in case they get hurt." A run of fe-
> line disasters in October 1904 began when Snowdove, like so many of
> the Max Gate cats, was cut in two on the railway line. Emma relayed
> this sad news to friends while Hardy wrote to Hamo Thornycroft, as a
> sculptor, to ask where he could get a piece of chisel sturdy enough to
> keep its edge while he carved Snowdove's name on the piece of Port-
> land stone he proposed to place over her grave in the pets' cemetery in
> the Max Gate garden. (401–2)

A few years later, after Emma's death, we find Hardy now married to his
former literary assistant Florence Dugdale, and the famous dog Wessex
has entered the scene. We've earlier considered Dickens's relationship to
his dog Sultan, who became Dickens's favorite "partly because of his af-
fectionateness, partly because he rejected and detested everyone else,"
a human-dog relationship that also recalls Emily Brontë's with her dog
Keeper. Hardy's dog Wessex could hardly muster the ferociousness or gran-

deur of either Sultan or Keeper, but in his own way, he created a comparable dynamic, seeming to operate, like those other authorial dogs, as a sort of familiar or extension of the self—and perhaps even as a Freudian embodiment of repressed instincts.

As Millgate explains:

> Meanwhile the servant problem had again become acute and the viciousness of Wessex—who not only bit postmen and terrorized servants but had once killed a stoat after a long and bloody battle—was prompting talk (neither for the first nor the last time) of having him put to sleep. Hardy, however, persisted in his indulgence of the dog, giving him an eiderdown to lie on in the study and feeding him goose and plum pudding at Christmas, but making no offer to clean up the mess when he was, predictably, sick. Lady Cynthia Asquith . . . reported with perhaps a touch of extravagance that throughout dinner Wessex—the "most despotic dog" she had ever encountered—was "not under, but on, the table, walking about quite unchecked and contesting with me every forkful of food on its way from fork to mouth." . . . Florence . . . had . . . hoped that the new volume would contain a poem about Wessex, but Hardy declared that he could write one only if the dog were dead—a consummation devoutly desired by a succession of servants and postmen but still some years away. Meanwhile, so Florence assured Cockerell, Wessex was bearing up well and continuing to "snarl & growl & fly at people with all his accustomed spirit & sweetness." (489, 501)

The description of Wessex, "not under, but on, the table," subverting all usual human-animal hierarchies, can be read as a distant humorous echo of Dickens's depictions of the chaos of Smithfield Market. (Hardy himself noted "the pandemonium of Smithfield, with its mud, curses, and cries of ill-treated animals," as one of his strongest memories of his first childhood trip to London [*Life and Work* 22].) Throughout the Victorian period and beyond, many writers—and, of course, ordinary citizens—expressed a sense of dismay at the spectacle of unmitigated cruelty on the part of humans toward the animals they exploited or used for food, material, and even companionship. But when animals escape such treatment and seem to shift out of the category of animal into or toward the protected one of human or person, a risk arises of boundary collapse and sheer confusion. The special category of pet, as Lévi-Strauss suggested, at once attempts to resolve such problems and can also amplify them.

Millgate falls back on a very typical claim, describing Hardy and Emma as "this childless couple who increasingly and *almost pathologically* made children of their pets" (283; my italics). But surely there is more to say, and less reductively, about the ways married couples in Victorian culture—and in our own—created forms of intimacy and shared sympathetic endeavor through pet keeping.[2] Even if it is the case that the emotions in pet keeping may seem most intense on the part of childless couples, this is not necessarily proof that there is anything tragically misdirected about the love of animals. Only if we automatically predefine the love of animals as eccentric, sentimental, or a projection of some more properly human-directed emotion can we draw this conclusion. Susan Fraiman's critique of what she characterizes as a phobic disavowal on the part of some strains of animal-studies theorists of excessive "love" or even "liking" (115) of animals as unduly sentimental or feminized also seems relevant here. To love or care for animals *too much* carries a longstanding stigma.

But by the 1870s, as the antivivisection movement gained increasing visibility, concern for animal welfare and dismay at human cruelty to animals became increasingly mainstream, less marginal. In Hardy's work we can see one effect in fiction of such broader shifts. Particularly interesting, in the biographical details Millgate cites, are the ways the Hardy household was literally—architecturally—shaped by its pets' needs and desires, such that the home became increasingly a shared human-animal space in which human needs and priorities had no automatic privilege. Consider, for example, the anecdote about the redesign of the living space to allow the cats to walk to their greatest convenience or Hardy forced to walk around the house in stocking feet for as long as the kittens were in their most vulnerable stage. I read this in relation to another detail Millgate supplies, that "Snowdove, like so many of the Max Gate cats, was cut in two on the railway line" (401). In the glimpses of the pets of the Hardy household, we see a tension between, from the pet's point of view, the hardness, brutality, and harm-dealing violence of the public sphere and the softness and comfort of the home. The softness of Hardy's feet, the elaborateness of the walkways, the soft eiderdown Hardy would give Wessex to sleep on in his study—all of these seem to be poised against the cruel forces in the modern world outside best symbolized by the railway tracks, ready to slice any animal in half.

We have probably all known families or couples of whom one suspects that most of the important decisions about which home to buy, where to live, and how to design the living space are made for the benefit of the pets.

From one familiar perspective, this can seem silly or sentimental, but if we do not dismiss or condemn this approach we can recognize a dynamic in the Hardy household in which Hardy and both of his wives (at different times) collaborated to define an ideal, even utopian domestic space for animals defined by its safety, consideration, softness, and protection from the damaging forces of modernity. The domestic animal seems to become, in the Hardy house, an exemplary figure of the precarious or vulnerable subject, confronted by a public sphere bristling with dangers against which he cannot adequately protect himself. These seem to have been difficult, not altogether happy marriages—not at all happy in the case of Hardy and Emma—and it may have been via only this project of seeking "Justice for Animals" that a successfully shared marital domesticity could be defined. Florence's comment about Wessex, after his death, that *"thousands* (actually thousands) of afternoons and evenings I would have been alone but for him, & had always him to speak to" (524) is a rather poignant one, reflecting her sense of being cut out of her husband's emotional and working life. One affective function of the pets at Max Gate seems to have been to create an emotional buffer or alternative to the coldness and hurt feelings of the human marriage. Hardy and his wives could not be happy together, at least not always or even often, so the household animals like Wessex or Snowdove allowed forms of intimacy and companionship outside of the troubled human couple.

We can choose to see this turn from the spouse to the animal companion as sad, but one might also view it more positively, as an experimental reconfiguration of marriage and of the domestic space, one in which some of the emotional labor of the marriage is taken on by nonhumans. From such a perspective, the care of domestic animals can be viewed as defining a realm in which practices of stewardship, sympathy, intimacy, freedom, and justice are in play in significant ways. Within the home, even after the rise of the RSPCA, one could treat vulnerable, helpless creatures with almost total legal impunity, so it is here that a truly noncoercive ethical practice can emerge. One traditionally skeptical view would have it that to whatever degree such topics are raised in relation to animals, it is only as a kind of diversion from their properly human focus: pet keeping would thus be a sentimental distraction from the vigorous pursuit of such qualities in the human world as—to adapt a phrase from Millgate—"mildly eccentric, beside the main point." But if we resist closing down the topic in this way, we can see how for the Hardys, living with animals offered an opportunity for an experimental, caring, transspecies domestic practice, one governed by dramatic reversals of usual hierarchies of power: such that grown men

tely in stocking feet out of care for kittens, cats clamber on air-
designed for their use, and dogs leap below and above kitchen
king when and where they please.

Even as Hardy experimented in his marriages to allow more room for
the nonhuman, he worked throughout his writing career to discover a
less anthropocentric literary form that would decenter the human and to
find new ways to represent and acknowledge animal or nonhuman consciousness, agency, and being.[3] For Hardy, the challenge—and ultimately,
perhaps, the frustration—of the novel form lay in its intransigent human-
centeredness; by the time he abandoned the novel for lyric poetry after
Jude the Obscure, he had, I believe, concluded that the form of the novel
contained a species-specific logic that could not ultimately be dislodged.[4]
But up to that point he continually searched for ways to, one might say,
animalize the novel, to render it a less exclusively human form, to transform it into a kind of record or "archive of creaturely life" (a phrase I bor-
row from Eric Santner).[5]

A PROSTHETIC DOG

What does it mean to try to read Hardy's fourth novel, 1874's *Far from the
Madding Crowd*, nonanthropocentrically, to take the measure of its creatureliness? I want to begin to answer that question by considering how
this novel seems to think about the ways human beings use animals, specifically in terms of a powerful scene of animal assistance offered to a
human in dire need of help and keeping in mind Donna Haraway's observation on human-animal relations that "[t]o be in a relation of use to each
other is not the definition of unfreedom and violation" (*When Species* 74).
I focus on this novel not because it is unique in Hardy's oeuvre but rather
because it so well illustrates dynamics that are important throughout
much of his fiction.

Can a clear distinction be drawn between the human and the nonhuman living creature? From Descartes through Heidegger to Levinas,
modern Western thinkers have struggled to isolate some fundamental capacity—whether speech, thought, awareness of mortality, or capacity for
future planning—that distinguishes the human. What seems to be needed
here is some term or category that would define the human as separate
from and possessing some priority over the nonhuman. The modern anthropological view of culture, for example, may be said to rest "upon the
idea of the human symbolic appropriation of nature—whether animate or
inanimate" (Ingold 11). This presumption reinforces a more general mod-

ern understanding of human beings as creatures who create and shape the environment in which they live by means of the "symbolic appropriation" of the natural world. The human is distinguished from the rest of the living world, then, by a particular use of that world—a formulation that presupposes a stable distinction between the human and a nonhuman world.

The manipulation of tools, traditionally if mistakenly understood to belong exclusively to humanity, offers one iconic instance of such appropriation or use. A tool allows an exertion of human powers, powers that in the first order manipulate the nonhuman world and in the second order demonstrate and anchor the human/nonhuman distinction. Tools do not simply define the human and its difference from the nonhuman or the animal but extend the human's reach both literally and conceptually. From the first tools used to, say, throw a stone farther than one could with one's arm alone, human beings have created a world of technologies generating the effect of a prosthesis or extension of the human. "With every tool man is perfecting his own organs," Sigmund Freud observed in an oft-cited passage from *Civilization and Its Discontents*. "By means of spectacles he corrects defects in the lens of his own eye; by means of the telescope he sees into the far distance. . . . Man has, as it were, become a kind of prosthetic god" (43–44).

Scholars of Victorian literature and culture have argued in different ways that nineteenth-century Britain was a prosthetic age.[6] Prostheses are typically understood as mechanical-industrial: tools, devices, machines. But we use animals as tools as surely as we do mechanical objects, whether in the form of tools made from an animal (a leather belt or shoe, a wool coat) or in the use of laboring animals (a cart horse, a guide dog).[7] Any of these can be understood as prostheses that extend the human and mark the human being's difference from the animal by incorporating and appropriating the animal in an ongoing, anxious process of defining that difference. I am influenced here by Giorgio Agamben's argument that the "human" is itself constituted by an "anthropological machine . . . at work in our culture" (37) that continually dispels the "nonhuman" or animal from the human, which is in fact defined by that segregating gesture. Human beings use animals to define the nonanimality of the human.

If we think more broadly about the history of human relations with animals and of human domestication of certain species, we can see how a prosthetic logic operates here as well. What is the sheep, the cow, or the dog in its domestication but a projection or extension of human desires and needs? This is most obvious in the human use of substances like wool or leather but is no less evident in the broader manipulation of animal species to serve human needs; in this light, all breeds of domesticated animals are themselves prostheses fundamentally shaped by human beings. I want to suggest, then, that while Freud decreed that in the modern period humanity had "become a kind of prosthetic god," we might also hold a mirror to Freud's phrase to consider the ways that human beings define and buttress their own identity in relation to *prosthetic* dogs and other creatures.

My first brief example comes from Hardy's final novel, *Jude the Obscure* (1895), which begins with the young Jude at work in a field, assigned to scare away crows with the use of a "clacker." This clacker is a simple prosthetic tool, an "anthropological machine" in Agamben's sense: a replacement or extension of the human voice or handclap used to keep birds off the land and to mark territory as a site of purely human culture. This "upland" has been "sown as a corn-field" in a process that lends "a meanly utilitarian air to the expanse," "depriving it of all history beyond that of the few recent months" (8). Hardy suggests that the human "culturing" of this land wipes it of its history in an ugly and mechanical act of erasure. Jude's assignment is to uphold this erasure by scaring away any intruding animals: "The boy stood under the rick just mentioned, and every few seconds used his rattle or clacker briskly. At each clack the rooks left off pecking, and rose and went away on their leisurely wings" (9). As nondomestic animals, these crows must be driven away from the grounds of the human or cultured.

Jude soon begins to question his task: "He sounded the clacker till his arm ached, and at length his heart grew sympathetic with the birds' thwarted desires. They seemed, like him, to be living in a world which did not want them. Why should he frighten them away? They took upon them more and more the aspect of gentle friends and pensioners—the only friends he could claim as being in the least degree interested in him, for his aunt had often told him that she was not. He ceased his rattling, and they alighted anew" (9). Jude throws away his clacker "as being a mean and sordid instrument"—a small-scale refusal to participate in the system that works to mark and protect the human against the category of the animal. As a reward, Jude is himself beaten with the clacker by the farmer, and so treated *like* an animal, in an early demonstration of Jude's inability to find a place in the human community. By failing to drive away the birds, Jude fails to observe species propriety, perhaps as Hardy himself wished to do.

My second example comes from Hardy's earlier novel, 1874's *Far from the Madding Crowd*. In the chapter titled "On Casterbridge Highway," Hardy offers what can be read as a brief, self-contained fiction that crucially revolves around a scene of the marking of an indistinct human-animal distinction. In this chapter, the starving and heavily pregnant Fanny Robin (whose name, of course, links her symbolically to animals) tries to make her way on the highway to the Casterbridge Union for shelter for the night. Hardy stresses her solitude: she has not even a breeze "to keep her company." Like Jude, she represents the human cut off from community, with an implication that there is no solitude, no loneliness so stark as that of the isolated human being who is also, as all modern humans are, alienated from the nonhuman world. Fanny can barely walk, and "she was oddly exercising the faculty of invention upon the speciality of the clever Jacquet Droz, the designer of automatic substitutes for human limbs" (230). Musing on the Swiss clockmaker Droz's mechanical automata, Fanny turns her thoughts to prosthetics. In her weakness, she needs help walking, and she also must crave, more broadly, extension of her humanness, a restoration or replacement of a fully competent identity and body.

Fanny constructs "a material aid" in the form of wooden crutches, but the "crutches, although so very useful, had their limits of power. Mechanism only transmutes labour, being powerless to abstract it, and the quantum of exertion was not cleared away: it was thrown into the body and arms" (231). These prosthetic devices, being purely material and inorganic, possess no energy of their own and add nothing to Fanny's dwindling strength. She falls and desperately cycles through every possible form of prosthetic invention she can imagine: "She thought of sticks, wheels, crawling—she even thought of rolling" (232).

In her hopeless state, an amazing thing happens: "she became conscious of something touching her hand; it was softness and it was warmth. She opened her eyes, and the substance touched her face. A dog was licking her cheek" (233). This natural force, "assignable to no species," is a kind of *bestia ex machina* that takes on the tasks she had imagined as "sticks, wheels, crawling, . . . rolling."[8] Hardy undermines any strict division between the human, cultural, or artificial on the one hand and the natural, organic, or animal on the other by defining this creature as, in some sense, Fanny's "contrivance" or "invention." Or at least he emphasizes the ways that Fanny's successful use of the dog to help her walk is itself an act of invention. "Her friend moved forward slowly, and she with small mincing steps moved forward beside him, half her weight being thrown upon the animal. Sometimes she sank as she had sunk from walking erect, from the crutches, from the rails. The dog, who now thoroughly understood her desire and her incapacity, was frantic in his distress on these occasions" (233).

If Jude's clacker functioned as a mechanism to extend human capacities and to define the human as distinct from the animal, here we see a less dominating, collaborative conjoining of animal and human under the sign of friendship. Fanny's interaction with the mysterious dog reveals a malfunctioning or temporary failure of the anthropological machine—one that hints at changes overtaking the Victorian novel more broadly in this period. Describing the way ivy had grown to offer a picturesque covering for what had been the "grim" architecture of the Casterbridge Union, Hardy remarks that "[n]ature, as if offended, lent a hand" (234). This same phrase could also apply to the appearance of the dog, who in effect "lends a paw" to Fanny and allows her to move toward shelter when she could not of her own power. We could even say that Fanny has become a kind of prosthetic dog. This idyll lasts only for a brief interlude of a few pages, however, ending abruptly when Fanny faints at the door of the Union and is taken in: "'There is a dog outside,' murmured the overcome traveller. 'Where is he gone? He helped me.' 'I stoned him away,' said the man" (234).

We never see the dog again. He is, then, very much like any other animal in Victorian fiction, any of those who remain *a* rather than *the*; wild or only partially domesticated or befriended, brought into proximity to the human but then expelled like Sir James's puppy. The difference here is Hardy's self-awareness of these dynamics and the way he brings critical attention to them. If the man at the Union stones the dog away, Hardy himself does not endorse this act. Fanny's savior fails to achieve anything like protagonicity, but he certainly "goes along" with her and is elevated within the novel as a subject of sympathy.

The novel's human characters now return to their normal procedures, however: as when Troy applies a whip presumably made from leather cowhide to his horse's skin: his "sentence was completed by a smart cut of the whip round Poppet's flank, which caused the animal to start forward at a wild pace. No more was said" (229). Troy does not walk but is pulled by Poppet, whose "wild pace" is at once a substitution for Troy's own locomotion and a proof of Troy's dominance. And Troy's "cut of the whip" seems literally to take the place of language, as a form of articulate violence. The anthropological machine, after a brief cessation, lurches back into operation.

PITYING THE SHEEP

That Hardy is a pastoral author—or an author who adapts and criticizes traditional pastoral conventions—is one of those critical truisms that bears

Figure 6 Thomas Hardy, illustration for "In a Ewelease Near Weatherbury." Reproduced from Thomas Hardy, *Wessex Poems and Other Verses. With 30 Illustrations by the Author* (New York: Harper and Brothers, 1899), 197.

further consideration. When critics discuss the pastoralism of Hardy's work, they address a broad set of topics relating to the contrast between country and city, rural idyll and disenchanted urban scene.[9] But what can be lost when pastoral becomes such a broad category is the specificity of *Far from the Madding Crowd* as a novel about a shepherd, Gabriel Oak, and his sheep and sheepdogs. Although the pastoral plot, by which I mean the shepherd, sheep, and sheepdog plot, is soon combined and complicated by various other modes and comes to one disastrous conclusion quite early on, this mode provides a deep structure and preoccupation for the novel as a whole.

Pastoral has become a major keyword in contemporary theory in large part because of Michel Foucault's arguments about the emergence of this form of power as one of the basic elements of Western modernity. It can be easy to forget how directly Foucault links pastoral power to its origins in the literal occupation of shepherds.

> The essential objective of pastoral power is the salvation of the flock. . . . Pastoral power is a power of care. It looks after the flock, it looks after the individuals of the flock, it sees to it that the sheep do not suffer, it goes in search of those that have strayed off course, and it treats those that are injured. The shepherd is someone who keeps watch . . . above all in the sense of vigilance with regard to any possible misfortune . . . that may threaten the least of his members. He will see to it that things are best for each of the animals of his flock. (126–27)

Foucault cites a rabbinic commentary that "explains how and why Moses was chosen by God to lead the flock of Israel. It was because when Moses was a shepherd in Egypt he knew how to graze his sheep and knew, for example, that when he came to pasture he had to send the youngest sheep first to eat the most tender grass, then those a little older, and then the eldest and most robust who could eat the toughest grass. . . . Yahweh, seeing this, said to him: 'Since you know how to pity the sheep, you will have pity for my people, and I will entrust them to you'" (127).

For Foucault, much of the specificity of our Judeo-Christian inheritance, in contradistinction to Greek-derived models of governance, may be traced to the vocation of the shepherd and his ability to "know how to pity the sheep" and how to turn that cross-species pity or empathy into the action of protective care and governance. *Far from the Madding Crowd* can be understood as an extended thinking through of these very topics, both as literally manifested in the occupation of the shepherd Gabriel Oak and more generally or metaphorically. It teaches its readers, too, to pity and feel for the sheep and to push beyond an exclusively human-centered perspective.[10]

In our early glimpses of Gabriel Oak at work, Hardy emphasizes his labors of caretaking for his sheep, his overseeing of biological or organic life. Part of the "realism" of the novel and its modification of any idealized or conventional pastoralism lies in Hardy's insistence on the sometimes indecorous or bloody bodily life of the sheep in Oak's care. Hardy's sheep are not fluffy baa-lambs but start out as membranous, slightly disgusting beings who must be coaxed to recognize and take hold of their own lives and bodily forms. As in the rabbinic commentary Foucault cites, this caretaking process is most fundamentally or originally based in the supervision of eating and drinking, the consumption of tender grass or, in this case, milk.

> The ring of the sheep-bell, . . . recommenced . . . and continued till Oak withdrew again from the flock. He returned to the hut, bringing in his arms a new-born lamb, consisting of four legs large enough for a full-grown sheep united by an unimportant membrane about half of the substance of the legs collectively, which constituted the animal's entire body at present.
>
> The little speck of life he placed on a wisp of hay before the small stove, over which simmered a can of milk. (11)

We see Oak engaged similarly when he enters Warren's Malthouse with four newborn lambs:

Four lambs hung in various embarrassing attitudes over his shoulders, and the dog George . . . stalked solemnly behind. . . . The genial warmth of the fire now began to stimulate the nearly lifeless lambs to bleat and move their limbs briskly upon the hay—and to recognize for the first time the fact that they were born. . . . Oak pulled the milk can from before the fire, and taking a small teapot from the pocket of his smockfrock, filled it with milk, and taught those of the helpless creatures which were not to be restored to their dams how to drink from the spout—a trick they acquired with astonishing aptitude. . . . The shepherd lifted the sixteen large legs, and four small bodies, he had himself brought, and vanished with them in the direction of the lambing field hard by. (95, 98, 101)

Hardy depicts Gabriel as a caretaker and giver of life. We are perhaps even invited to consider an understated analogy between the activity of a shepherd and that of a novelist or author, who takes on the responsibility of bringing to life and nurturing new creatures in the form of characters. Certainly, as we witness Gabriel continually nursing these infants with warm milk, we see him to be feminized, fulfilling tasks associated with women and filling the place of the absent mothers of these calves; but Hardy is less interested in gender- than species-crossing here. Gabriel, like Moses, knows how to pity the sheep, knows what they need to consume; he takes on the "specks of life" of their infant bodies and transforms these "helpless creatures" into functioning individual animals. Hardy suggests that Gabriel's empathy toward other humans cannot be distinguished from his ability to feel for and with his animals: "Gabriel's fingers alighted on the young woman's wrist. It was beating with a throb of tragic intensity. He had frequently felt the same quick hard beat in the femoral artery of his lambs when overdriven. It suggested a consumption too great of a vitality, which, to judge from her figure and magnitude, was already too little. . . . He fancied that he had felt himself in the penumbra of a very deep sadness when touching that slight and fragile creature" (45–46). Empathy, it is implied, requires a capacity for tactile receptivity to the "throb[bing]" organic life of others, including nonhuman others.

Hardy also emphasizes Gabriel's labors to preserve the life of his adult sheep, as in the memorable scene where he uses a sharpened "small tube" to perform a rapid surgical procedure on more than fifty sheep "with a dexterity that would have graced a hospital surgeon" (124), saving almost all of their lives. It may be useful to consider historical context here. As Joanna Swabe explains, the devastating cattle plague of 1865 marked a turning point in British state administration of the health of cattle and other animals, highlighting "the inefficacy of the existing veterinary regime and the necessity of effective state intervention and control." With the passing of the Contagious Diseases (Animals) Act and Animals Order in 1876, Britain saw a newly modern and centralized approach to the health of animals. Robert Langbaum claims that *Far from the Madding Crowd* "ignores social problems, portraying a timeless rural existence with its natural hardships" (258), but the novel was in fact published, in 1874, in a period marked by a new awareness of the crucial links between animal and human health and of the practical need for not only traditional pastoral but also modernized veterinary care of British animals. The animal body emerged as newly interesting and dangerous, a potential source of disease and other meanings.

Foucault explains that "the shepherd's power is . . . exercised . . . over a flock, and more exactly, over the flock in its movement from one place to another" (125); the shepherd's power concerns itself with movement and transit. At times, this must mean moving for others who cannot move, helping or making them move. Foucault begins his discussion by tracing the origins of the term *to govern* or *gouverner*. "First, we find the purely material, physical, and spatial meaning, of to direct, move forward, or even to move forward oneself on a track, a road. 'To govern' is to follow a path, or put on a path. . . . It also has the material but much wider meaning of supporting by providing means of subsistence. . . . So, 'to govern' in the sense of support, provide for, and give means of subsistence" (121). Gabriel's governance of the sheep involves raising them to the point where they can walk for themselves and, until then, walking for them if necessary, setting out a path for them, "stimulating . . . [them] to move their legs briskly." We recall the visitor to the Hardy home observing the way Hardy and Emma literally made paths (with boards) for their cats, redesigning their human living space to be amenable to feline locomotion. Gabriel, too, "governs" his sheep in the sense of directing them forward, making a path for them.

A culmination of *Far from the Madding Crowd*'s pastoral plot, at least in its most literal form, occurs almost immediately, in chapter 5. In what Hardy terms a "pastoral tragedy," we see Gabriel's utter failure as a pastor or shepherd, judged by the standards Foucault summarized. Or perhaps it is not a complete failure, as Gabriel never fails to know how to sympathize with the sheep, but his governance of his animals culminates in catastrophe as he "puts them on a path" to their death. This scene begins with Hardy continuing his demonstration of Gabriel's cross-species empathy.

Hardy represents the sheepfold or place of pastoral care as a zone of species indistinction where sheep, dogs, and human beings overlap, coinfluence, and sometimes even seem to merge. Gabriel's elder dog George, for example, possesses a kind of gray pelt: "In substance it had originally been hair, but long contact with sheep seemed to be turning it by degrees into wool of a poor quality" (30). The implication is that continued contact with the difference or otherness of creatures of a different species will eventually change or mark one's own identity.[11] A sheepdog becomes literally sheeplike. Gabriel is marked out from the other characters in the novel because of his unusual comfort with the idea of communication with and closeness to animals. We see, for example, a scene of teasing in the pub where Joseph Poorgrass is mocked with a story of how, walking through the wood in the night, he responded to an owl's cry of "whoo-whoo-whoo" with a prompt "Joseph Poorgrass of Weatherby, Sir!" (52) For someone like Poorgrass, certain barriers between the human and animal must be maintained in the name of human dignity. To talk to owls is to invite ridicule; as anthropologist Eduardo Kohn notes of cross-species communications, "People use oblique forms of communication . . . to put brakes on processes that threaten to blur the distinctions among kinds of beings" (144). Gabriel, on the other hand, possesses a "humanity" that is itself defined by a willingness to broach such barriers, in part because his vocation requires him to do so. In the scene I am discussing, Gabriel is awakened by an "abnormal reverberation": "To the shepherd, the note of the sheep-bell, like the ticking of the clock to other people, is a chronic sound that only makes itself noticed by ceasing or altering in some unusual manner from the well-known idle tinkle which signifies to the accustomed ear, however distant, that all is well in the fold. . . . The experienced ear of Oak knew the sound he now heard to be caused by the running of the flock with great velocity" (32). Oak's governance of his charges includes a fine-tuned sensitivity to the sounds of the sheep and the subtle distinctions between normal harmony—all is well in the fold—and any disruption to this equilibrium. To care for the sheep requires listening to them; it is a sensory tuning to the sheep's particular species-being.[12]

Hardy now depicts a shocking undoing of the pastoral ideal of a shepherd who "keeps watch . . . above all in the sense of vigilance with regard to any possible misfortune that may threaten the least of his members." Oak finds two hundred sheep, "the bulk of his flock," seemingly vanished. He soon realizes what has happened: his young dog ("George's son"), "under the impression that, as he was kept for running after sheep, the more he ran after them the better . . . had . . . collected all the ewes into a corner, driven the timid creatures through the hedge, . . . and by main force of worrying had given them momentum enough to break down a portion of the rotten railing, and so hurled them over the edge" (33) of a cliff. They are now "a heap of two hundred mangled carcasses"—no longer individual creatures but flesh or meat, reminiscent of the "heap of dead rabbits" (9) that was one of the first sights to greet Lockwood in *Wuthering Heights*.

This disaster represents a pastoral failure in multiple senses. Oak has, of course, failed the sheep, has been insufficiently vigilant and, rather than governing or guiding them in a straight path forward, has sent them literally off a cliff into an abyss. This is also a failure of training and a pastoral failure for the "poor young dog" who so tragically misunderstood his mandate—and thus, a failure for Oak in his supervision of the dog. Even in this tragedy, however, which also means the end of Oak's hopes to establish himself commercially, he demonstrates the quality of cross-species pity that lies behind the pastoral ideal: "A shadow in his life had always been that his flock ended in mutton—that a day came and found every shepherd an arrant traitor to his defenseless sheep. His first feeling now was one of pity for the untimely fate of these gentle ewes and their unborn lambs" (33). Interestingly, Hardy suggests that one source of the mishap may have been an improper eating of lamb meat. Oak had "left the two dogs on the hill eating a dead lamb (a kind of meat he usually kept from them except when other food ran short)" (31). Hardy suggests that the dog's meal of lamb meat "may have given him additional energy and spirits" (33) to perform his feat of ewe slaughter. In a later poem, "Bags of Meat," Hardy describes a "timid, quivering," sensitive steer who is described as a "fine bag of meat" by the cattle auctioneer selling him to a butcher (*Complete Poems* 809). Hardy does not imply that sheep should never be eaten, but he seems troubled by the pastoral irony that every flock "ends in mutton," with the caregiving shepherd responsible for the transformation of living creature to meat. Here we see an echo of Dickens's disgust at the scene of animal slaughter at Smithfield and other markets in London, with their "cattle-slaughtering, bone-crushing, blood-boiling, . . . and other salubrious proceedings." The transformation of the living animal to mere meat underlines the vulnerability of the nonhuman, its susceptibility to instantaneous transformation into simple matter. Even for authors who may not themselves be vegetarians, this process can be discomfiting; as the adage has it, we do not necessarily enjoy seeing how the sausage is made, how the living beings become mere matter.

The dog's eating of the lamb comes to seem, in this context, a faintly cannibalistic act (recalling Dickens's Mr. Vholes, who "lifts off his tight hat as if he were scalping himself") that reveals a cruel irony within the pastoral scene. As I have mentioned, Catherine Gallagher has suggested that for authors like Eliot and Hardy, the very form of the novel was designed to reproduce the "bioeconomic rituals" of our primitive ancestors "with their underlying logic of forfeiting a life to fertilize the world" (183). In this scene of the senseless death of nearly all of Gabriel Oak's flock, Hardy asks us to consider the ultimately sacrificial, carnivorous logic of the pastoral relationship. The shepherd raises and tenderly cares for every animal in his flock, but this may be, in the end, all in the service of a tender piece of meat.

OMNES ET SINGULATIM

Part of what can seem troubling in this transformation of ewe to mutton is a deindividuating process by which an individual creature becomes a form of undifferentiated matter to be weighed and bagged up. These lambs, ending their lives as mangled carcasses, have in effect reverted to their original state of formless, membranous substance. If one opposite term for *individual* is *multitude,* another could be *meat,* flesh without individuality. Here too Hardy dwells on one of the qualities or problems that Foucault identifies as fundamental to the question of pastoral care.

> [P]astoral power is an individualizing power. That is to say, it is true that the shepherd directs the whole flock, but he can only really direct it insofar as not a single sheep escapes him. The shepherd counts the sheep; he counts them in the morning when he leads them to pasture, and he counts them in the evening to see that they are all there, and he looks after each of them individually. He does everything for the totality of the flock, but he does everything also for each sheep of the flock. . . . [T]he shepherd must keep his eye on all and on each, *omnes et singulatim.* (128)

We might also recognize this as a fundamental problem of the novelist. As we've seen, Alex Woloch has powerfully argued that nineteenth-century realism depends crucially on a set of techniques and methods by which individuality, especially the individuality of the protagonist, or protagonicity, is carved out of or defined in contrast to multiplicity, especially the multiplicity of the crowd, mob, or assemblage of minor characters populating any Victorian novel (its Joseph Poorgrasses). In pastoral terms, this is the problem of the single sheep and the flock, all and each.

Hardy uses his pastoral materials in several ways to press on the problem and irony of the flock and the individual. For one thing, to make an obvious etymological reading, the term *shepherd* incorporates the animal into the human or merges the animal—the sheep—and the human. As Gabriel cares for the four infant lambs in the malthouse and bears their weight on his shoulders, he becomes a kind of multilegged creature, an organism of twenty-two legs consisting of shepherd, his dog, and the four lambs not yet capable of locomotion. In this sense, then, Hardy undermines the self-sufficiency of the human and its distinction from the animal, suggesting that the pastoral scene involves a coexistence of species-being. Hardy also dwells on the processes by which individual creatures are in turn subsumed into collectivities and marked off as distinct from such groups. Hardy often highlights the moment when, to cite one instance from the novel's early pages, "Oak withdrew again from the flock" (11), a phrase that marks a signature action in the novel, that of individuation and the separation of the individual from the mass. The title of the novel comes, of course, from Thomas Gray's poem of pastoral retreat; in its original context, the phrase alludes to an escape from the crowds of urban modernity, but Hardy seems to repurpose it to allude to the processes by which individual creatures become marked off as separate from the crowd or group. The novel is full of observations of small dramas of individuation or deindividuation—as here, for example, where Hardy makes an obscure reference to a form of "transparent, tubular, free-swimming oceanic tunicates found abundantly in all the warmer latitudes" (*Webster's* 1913) whose form conjoins many "individuals" into a single chain acting as one: "A crooked file of men was approaching the back door. The whole string of trailing individuals advanced in the completest balance of intention, like the remarkable creatures known as Chain Salpe, which, distinctly organized in other respects, have one will common to a whole family" (68). In a nod to the tradition of seaside studies popularized in midcentury by the likes of Charles Darwin, George Henry Lewes, and Philip Henry Gosse, Hardy in effect peers into his collecting bucket to learn something new about the strange possibilities and forms taken by organic life in its less developed manifestations.[13] This striking image of a primitive sea creature recalls Hardy's musing in his autobiography on the ethical consequences of understanding all members of a species to be a single mass body: "Altruism . . . will ultimately be brought about I think by the pain we see in others reacting on ourselves, as if we and they were part of one body. Mankind, in fact, may be and possibly will be viewed as members of one corporeal frame" (qtd. in Johnson 272).[14]

In the pastoral context, however, the individual-group distinction is most visible in the opposition between a single sheep and the flock. This pastoral image is powerful for Hardy in part for the ways it evokes individuation and nonindividuation, dramas of flock identity.[15] The flock of sheep is, of course, an emblem of nonindividuation; to call someone a sheep is to deny his individual agency, to suggest that he follows others instead of exerting his own will. Here, Hardy describes how what first appear as "nebulous clouds" become gradually "individually visible" not as individual sheep but somewhat paradoxically *as flocks*: "When the autumn sun slanted over Greenhill this morning and lighted the dewy flat upon its crest, nebulous clouds of dust were to be seen floating between the pairs of hedges which streaked the wide prospects around in all directions. These gradually converged upon the base of the hill, and the flocks became individually visible, climbing the serpentine ways which led to the top. Thus in a slow procession they entered the openings to which the roads wended, multitude after multitude, horned and hornless—blue flocks and red flocks, buff flocks and brown flocks" (295). In this "multiplicity on the move," a shift in the focus of the eye to recognize individual form is less likely to see any specific lamb than the smaller specific group of a certain shepherd's flock.[16] Indeed, for Hardy, herd animals seem defined precisely by their "infinite" multiplicity, as in *Tess* when he describes wooden fence posts "rubbed to a glossy smoothness by the flanks of infinite cows and calves of bygone years" (159).[17] The infinitely extending quality of herd or flock animals does not denigrate or devalue them, but it does subsume individuality in a mass.

Are the sheep of *Far from the Madding Crowd* quintessential minor characters, then, denied any individuality and destined always to be subsumed into large collectivities of crowd or flock? Not necessarily. In fact, the entire novel can be read as a gloss on a scriptural proverb that revolves precisely around the distinction between a single ewe and a collective flock: more precisely, about the special value of a single ewe who is—outrageously—individuated and treated as or like a human member of the family rather than simply as one member of a flock. Hardy first alludes to this proverb somewhat ironically when Troy, flirting with Bathsheba, says reproachfully to her, "I shall not be here long . . . perhaps our regiment will be ordered out soon. And yet you take away the one ewe-lamb of pleasure that I have in this dull life of mine" (153). Troy is citing 2 Samuel 12, which reads as following in the King James version:

And the LORD sent Nathan unto David. And he came unto him, and said unto him, There were two men in one city; the one rich, and the other poor.

The rich man had exceeding many flocks and herds:

But the poor man had nothing, save one little ewe lamb, which he had bought and nourished up: and it grew up together with him, and with his children; it did eat of his own meat, and drank of his own cup, and lay in his bosom, and was unto him as a daughter.

And there came a traveller unto the rich man, and he spared to take of his own flock and of his own herd, to dress for the wayfaring man that was come unto him; but took the poor man's lamb, and dressed it for the man that was come to him.

And David's anger was greatly kindled against the man; and he said to Nathan, As the LORD liveth, the man that hath done this thing shall surely die:

And he shall restore the lamb fourfold, because he did this thing, and because he had no pity.

And Nathan said to David, Thou art the man.

The irony here is that Troy is claiming to Bathsheba that he is the poor man with one poor ewe, and she—by refusing to flirt with him—is the rich man stealing the poor man's lamb, but, in fact, the heedless and charming soldier Troy is anything but the poor man. Troy has promised Fanny Robin, whom he has impregnated, that he will marry her but quickly gives her up when Bathsheba catches his eye. From the perspective of Boldwood, the respectable and very monogamous middle-aged farmer who has fallen madly in love with Bathsheba, Troy is the rich man—rich in female attentions—who has stolen Boldwood's one little ewe lamb of pleasure: "Why did Troy not leave my treasure alone?" (179), he "asks fiercely," and in truth Boldwood's reading of the parable is more persuasive. In the version of the novel that appeared in *Cornhill Magazine*, Hardy alludes to this parable once more in the final chapters. Boldwood's rival Troy, having disappeared and been presumed dead, has returned and enters Boldwood's Christmas Eve party to claim Bathsheba as his wife. Troy is, for the moment, in disguise, and the narrator comments, "Boldwood did not recognize that the impersonator of Heaven's persistent irony toward him, who had once before broken in upon his bliss, scourged him, and snatched his delight away, had come to do these things a second time" (389).

The entire romance plot of the novel, then, can be read as an extrapolation and commentary on the parable of the ewe lamb. Especially interesting, for our purposes, is the way the parable itself obliquely raises the topic of "pity for the sheep." David responds angrily to Nathan's story, saying that the rich man "shall surely die" "because he had no pity." David is, however, a bad interpreter who misapprehends the meaning and object of pity. To read the parable less anthropocentrically is to recognize that the proper object of pity here is not the poor man, or at least not only the poor man, but the ewe lamb itself, taken and killed by the rich man to be served as mutton for the visitor. David's suggestion that the rich man should die and "restore the lamb fourfold" treats the lamb as a commodity, a fungible substance that can be repaid and replaced. But the essence of the parable is this ewe lamb's special status. The lamb was *not* just any member of the flock or a possession of the poor man, but rather a beloved object of pastoral care and a member of the intimate family: "it grew up together with him, and with his children; it did eat of his own meat, and drank of his own cup, and lay in his bosom and was unto him as a daughter." The ewe lamb, paradoxically, was not itself meat to the poor man but "did eat of his own meat." This is a parable about the power of pastoral care, radicalized and literalized to the point that the animal crosses the boundary dividing those creatures that are or can become deindividuated meat and those exempt from such treatment.[18]

Derrida observes that "the 'Thou shalt not kill'—with all its consequences, which are limitless—has never been understood within the Judeo-Christian tradition . . . as a 'Thou shalt not put to death the living in general.' It has become meaningful in religious cultures for which the carnivorous sacrifice is essential" ("Eating Well" 279). What Derrida calls carno-phallogocentrism, in fact, defines the "virile subject" as "the subject [who] does not want just to master and possess nature actively" but who "accepts sacrifice and eats flesh" (281): the rich man, in other words, whose wealth is measured by the abundance of the animal flesh he consumes. As Stephen Webb has demonstrated, early Christianity came to define vegetarianism as "a creed and a lifestyle for outsiders, extremists, and separatists" (32), and to view meat eating as a sign of a faith that had moved beyond the legalistic taboos of Judaism. This parable, then, tells a story of a radical pastoral practice that treats the nonhuman animal as a family member, going to the shocking extreme of considering a ewe lamb akin to a daughter, one's own flesh and blood. The parable—and Hardy's novel—also demonstrate the social marginality and fragility of such an individuating care or love for an animal. The ewe lamb becomes an emblem of a fragile nonhuman subjectivity—fragile because within an anthropocentric society and worldview, it becomes difficult to sustain an understanding of a single ewe lamb as having any value out of the context of a flock raised for profit. Caring for any particular lamb, in this context, seems deeply "sentimental."

This chapter (and, indeed, this book) could be understood as an attempt at producing what Hardy defines, at one point in the novel, as "ovine criticism" (130), meaning literally "analysis of sheep," but more broadly, a literary criticism attuned to the potential meanings of and produced by animals. I hope that I've demonstrated that Hardy's work repays such an approach and that some of its most fundamental concerns, including the process of individuation and the meaning of care for others, are best understood within a less anthropocentric framework than is the norm. To read this novel as an extended gloss on the parable of the ewe lamb reveals its fundamental concern with the problem of pastoral care and the challenges posed to a practice and ethic of care by the numerousness of those to be cared for, the members of the flock. To read the novel this way also reveals its preoccupations with the boundaries of the characterological, of protagonicity. Hardy explores the possibilities for recognizing nonhuman animals—sheep and dogs—within the character space of a realist novel. The novel's title alludes to dramas of human individuation and the distinction between the human individual and the "crowd," but the novel itself pushes beyond such purely human distinctions to think more capaciously, beyond the human, about both individuals and crowds and about the care owed to the weak or minor individual.

CHAPTER SIX

Tracking Animal Agency in
Conan Doyle and Hardy

"Politics supposes livestock," Derrida argues; "There is therefore neither socialization, political constitution, nor politics itself, without the principle of domestication of the wild animal" (*Animal* 96). According to this account, politics, social life, and principles and practices of law, sovereignty, and justice depend on an animal in the place of the other—an animal who itself, crucially, can neither participate in nor benefit from these procedures of jurisprudence and ethics nor manifest any robust agency of its own. Indeed, according to Derrida's account, human personhood and subjectivity themselves depend on an animal object: "Power over the animal is the essence of the 'I' or the 'person,' the essence of the human" (93). I have been trying to demonstrate that a similar logic obtains within both the Victorian novel and the Victorian home: their very structure and self-definition depend on the presence or the trace of an animal, even if that animal is marginalized or even banished.

But why can't an animal itself possess subjectivity or agency, or be, itself, a subject of justice? The history that we have considered of nineteenth-century anticruelty or animal-welfare activism and jurisprudence—and its continuation in the twentieth and twenty-first centuries—would seem to represent, after all, a movement toward such a recognition of the animal as subject to justice. But Derrida's dictum suggests some of the ways that justice as a concept may *depend* on an animal other, a situation that complicates any attempt to open up the concept to nonhuman animals.

The simplest answer to the question of why it is challenging to bring animals into consideration as subjects of justice, according to the most influential modern theories of the concept, is that justice and rights presuppose a social contract and, therefore, require a subject with the capacity to enter into or agree to such a contract. "To make covenants with brute beasts, is impossible," Thomas Hobbes argues in *Leviathan*, "because with beasts, not understanding our speech, they understand not, nor accept of any translation of right; nor can translate any right to another: and without mutual acceptation, there is no covenant" (92). Or as Max Müller strikingly put it in his 1861 *Lectures on the Science of Language*, "the one great barrier between the brute and man is *Language*. Man speaks, and no brute has ever uttered a word. Language is our Rubicon, and no brute will dare to cross it" (367). These brute beasts lack language and accordingly cannot enter into contractual arrangements or enjoy the rights that such arrangements afford.

"It is true, that certain living creatures, as bees, and ants, live sociably one with another, (which are therefore by Aristotle numbered amongst political creatures)." Hobbes admits (113). But, for Hobbes, Aristotle is wrong to consider a bee or an ant as political—because animals lack reason, language, or self-conscious signification and therefore cannot enter into contractual relations or engage in the representational thought necessary for this act. "Lastly, the agreement of these creatures is natural; that of men, is by covenant only, which is artificial" (113). The artificiality of human language, signification, and reason is a prerequisite of the fundamentally unnatural social contract that marks the human social order with its systems of reciprocity and agreement. For Hobbes as for many other social theorists, animals' lack of language is at the root of their exclusion from any social contract or principles of justice; "these creatures, though they have some use of voice, in making known to one another their desires, and other affections" (113), they lack the human "art of Words" to represent and to deceive. Their voice is locked into a single signifying register and cannot translate into others.

Hobbes is just one of many thinkers in the modern Western philosophical tradition who have found in the lack of a rational or developed animal signification the explanation for animals' exclusion from full ethical consideration. As Martha Nussbaum points out, the most influential Western theories of justice from Hobbes, Kant, and Locke through Rawls, whatever their significant differences, are all characterized by what she describes as the "strong rationalism" of a social-contract notion of justice. "The contracting parties—hence, the citizens in the resulting society—are imagined as characterized by rationality, and by roughly equal rationality" (53). For most of these thinkers, an incapacity to be a subject of justice does not imply a total exclusion from humane or kind treatment, but such good treatment will be in effect bestowed as a humanitarian gift of compassion.

As Nussbaum sums up, "Theorists in this tradition typically hold either that we have no direct moral duties to animals (Kant) or that, if we do, they are duties of charity and compassion rather than justice (Rawls)" (21).

In this chapter, I'm in effect following the tracks of Jacques Derrida's analysis of the way such theories of justice and politics have required exacting parsing of why and how animal communication cannot count as agential signification. For Derrida, the problem can be summarized by a supposed lack of animal "response": he argues that in Locke, Descartes, and Hobbes alike—and on to Heidegger, Lacan, and Levinas—animals are seen to be capable of emitting signs and of "reacting" but not of responding or signifying. "No one has ever denied the animal," Derrida argues, the "capacity to track itself, to trace itself or retrace the path of itself. Indeed, the most difficult problem lies in the fact that it has been refused the power to transform those traces into verbal language, to call to itself by means of discursive questions and responses, denied the power to efface its traces" (*Animal* 50). According to most Western philosophy, "the animal neither speaks nor responds, . . . its capacity to produce signs is foreign to language and limited or fixed by a program" (89). Derrida's analysis shares certain preoccupations with a field that has emerged over the last few decades, that of biosemiotics or the consideration of biological or nonhuman signification as coextensive with and not sharply marked off from human signification.[1] In its more radical arguments, biosemiotics considers amoebas and cellular organisms as capable of what should be considered to be meaningful signification, although a term like *meaningful* acquires new valences in this radically nonanthropocentric context.[2]

In the late nineteenth century, we begin to see a new representational concern with the problem of animal signification rooted in an interest in the question of whether animals might possess agency. The gist of my argument here is that these concerns are visible in late nineteenth-century writing in a special focus on the trope of the animal track, trace, or marking as a form of legible signification.

The first place one would naturally think to look in considering British ideas about animal signification in this period would be in the work of Charles Darwin. And, indeed, Darwin's writing, especially the 1872 *The Expression of the Emotions in Man and Animals*, is the single most important source for such ideas in its consideration of the genealogical links between animal expression and higher-order human signifying.[3] I was amazed to discover, in fact, that Darwin commented in his notebook on the apparent fact, which he considered unsurprising, that "Elephants understand contracts."[4] Needless to say, such a claim offers an especially pointed rebuttal to the positioning of animals within the contractual theories of justice of Hobbes, Locke, and others.

Another less-obvious but relevant body of late-century work, however, can be found in the writings of Charles Sanders Peirce, which offer an especially useful origin point for any consideration of ideas about nonhuman signification in this period. One of Peirce's best-known statements asserts that "the universe is perfused by signs," and he means *universe* quite literally: Peirce was the first philosopher strongly to follow up on Darwin's insights to argue that signification and semiotic communication generally are "natural" and in no way limited to the human realm. Claus Emmeche summarizes Peirce as arguing that "even though we are forever thrown upon signs, we share this condition with all living beings" ("A Semiotical Reflection" 332). In an 1892 essay published in *The Monist*, for example, Peirce outright declares that "protoplasm feels"; indeed that "it not only feels but exercises all the functions of mind" (343). But beginning as early as the late 1860s, Peirce began to develop a theory of signs that was fundamentally antianthropocentric (and biosemiotic, if you will) in its vision of a natural universe "perfused" by signs and signifying practices at all levels of the biological web. Peirce has been attracting renewed attention very recently for the opportunities his work opens for reconsidering semiosis as a practice that exists beyond the human; anthropologist Eduardo Kohn draws on Peirce, for example, to develop his argument that "[n]onhuman life forms also represent the world" (8), that "[l]ife is constitutively semiotic," "through and through, the product of sign processes" (9).[5]

If we turn to fiction of this period, we can see a new interest in animal signification that can be understood in relation to Darwin's and Peirce's investigations into nonhuman semiotics. Perhaps the most obvious approach to fictional representation of animal signification is one we could call the sentimental solution (a term that I intend descriptively rather than pejoratively), evident in a text like Anna Sewell's 1877 blockbuster *Black Beauty*, in which animal signification and language is contrived along a highly anthropocentric model. On the one hand, the book takes for granted horses' lack of language. On the other, the entire premise of the novel depends on Beauty's ability to narrate two hundred-odd pages of chatty, musing autobiography.[6] *Black Beauty* does, however, offer a single, fascinating acknowledgment of the impossible status of Beauty's English-language autobiography in a phrase on the novel's title page: "Translated from the original equine by Anna Sewell."

A horse is just like us, in this thinking; if only we could peer into horses' minds, we would surely realize that they possess fully articulate and rational, humanlike subjectivities. Such an approach to the "translation" of animal signification is, however, inherently wishful and incoherent, I would argue, in its fantasy of translation from equine to human, two languages presumed to exist as coeval, on the same plane, as if a horse were simply a speaker of some unknown human language. Later, in the early twentieth century, we begin to see more ambitious attempts to inhabit and imagine animal consciousness without transforming animal subjects into the equivalent of chatty human children. (D. H. Lawrence's *St. Mawr* and Virginia Woolf's *Flush* could both be considered in this light, although the playful *Flush* stays closer to the *Black Beauty* model.) But what this chapter will consider are a few attempts from the end of the nineteenth century, and just into the next, to think about and represent animal signification in a less anthropocentric mode: in the form of animal tracks. My argument here will be that this late-century preoccupation with animal tracks offered an alternative to the *Black Beauty* fantasy of translation from equine to human, instead emphasizing the value of what we could define as an alternate, more epistemologically modest model of what I'll be calling transcription, implying a registration or recording of animal signification without an attempt at translation. One could think about this difference between translation and transcription in relation to the early twentieth-century insights of German biologist Jacob von Uexküll regarding what he described as the *umwelt* or "environment" of every species; von Uexküll's point was that one must not in effect translate the perceptions or even the world of another species into our own human terms but must instead recognize the incommensurable difference between the *umwelt* of, say, a tick and our own. A transcription of animal marks is therefore a recognition of otherness that refrains from a translation into human terms.

Charles Sanders Peirce defined the foot or hoofprint as a quintessential sign: as he wrote in 1906, "That footprint that Robinson Crusoe found in the sand, and which has been stamped in the granite of fame, was an Index to him that some creature was on his island, and at the same time, as a Symbol, called up the idea of a man" ("Prolegomena" 496).[7] Carlo Ginzburg, in an important essay, "Clues: Morelli, Freud, and Sherlock Holmes," argues that twentieth-century semiotic thinking in fact originates specifically in the late nineteenth-century turn toward what Ginzburg characterizes as a "conjectural or semiotic paradigm" based on the analysis of symptoms and "clues" and rooted in ancient practices of animal tracking. "Towards the end of the nineteenth century," he argues, "(more precisely,

in the decade 1870–1880), [the] 'semiotic' approach, a paradigm or model
based on the interpretation of clues, had become increasingly influential
in the field of human sciences." "Its roots, however, were far more ancient." Ginzburg locates these roots in the practical knowledge and interpretive protocols passed down by generations of hunters who "learned to
reconstruct the appearance and movements of an unseen quarry through
its tracks—prints in soft ground, snapped twigs, droppings, snagged hairs
or feathers, smells, puddles, threads of saliva" (87–88).

Ginzburg sees in Doyle's Sherlock Holmes stories and Freud's psychoanalysis alike a distinctly late-century appeal to the symptomatic "clue"
as the basis for thought. This is an approach to interpretation that abandons traditionally more prestigious forms of Platonic or Galilean infer-
ence for what Ginzburg sums up as a conjectural paradigm rooted in an
experiential "low intuition" of the senses and genealogically linked to the
interpretive work of hunters and trackers.

We can witness the centrality of this so-called conjectural turn to late
nineteenth-century writing and thought in Thomas Huxley's 1880 lecture
"On the Method of Zadig: Retrospective Prophecy as a Function of Science," in which he takes the figure of Zadig from Voltaire's 1747 novel
as an embodiment of a new conjectural methodology common to paleontology, geology, and other allied sciences. Zadig was the Babylonian philosopher who withdrew from society to undertake a study of the natural
world. One day he encountered a retinue of the queen's and the king's at-
tendants "who appeared to be in the greatest anxiety," obviously searching for something lost. When they ask Zadig if he has seen the queen's dog,
he replies, oh, of course, "a very small spaniel who has lately had puppies;
she limps with the left foreleg, and has very long ears." "Ah, you have seen
her then," replied the queen's attendant; Zadig says he's seen no dog and
in fact did not even know that the queen owned a spaniel. When a similar exchange occurs about the king's lost horse, which Zadig identifies as
"a first-rate galloper, small-hoofed, five feet high; tail three feet and a half
long" and then denies having seen it, he is thrown in jail and sentenced to
transportation to Siberia for life. Zadig eventually is vindicated when he
explains the deductive method he employed to gain a precise knowledge
of these animals from the traces they've left behind in the sand: "I noticed the tracks of the animal in the sand, and it was easy to see that it
was that of a small dog. Long faint streaks upon the little elevations of
sand between the footmarks convinced me that she must have had puppies not many days since. Other scrapings of the sand, which always lay
close to the marks of the forepaws, indicated that she had very long ears"

and so on (qtd. in Huxley 139–40). Huxley identifies Zadig as an embodiment of "retrospective prophecy," a kind of "carnal common sense" (141)
or reading backward of absent causes from present effects, which Huxley
claims as the model for contemporary science in archeology, paleontology,
and biology. "In no very distant future," Huxley concludes his essay, "the
method of Zadig, applied to a greater body of facts than the present generation is fortunate enough to handle, will enable the biologist to reconstruct the scheme of life from its beginning, and to speak as confidently
of the character of long extinct living beings, no trace of which has been
preserved, as Zadig did of the queen's spaniel and the king's horse" (155).
Zadig's method, then, allows us to grasp the *character* of nonhuman living
creatures who are absent to us; in "reconstructing the scene of life from its
beginning," we write back into history those many creatures of whom "no
trace" now remains.

One could object that Zadig's method as defined by Huxley—and in
turn by Carlo Ginzburg—is simply the method of the hunter in the woods
and as such bears little relationship to any acknowledgment of animal
subjectivity or agency. Rather, this is the methodology used by human
beings since prehistory to hunt down and kill animals. Even so, we may
understand Zadig's method as leading to a greater acknowledgment of
nonhuman beings and their signification, a more robust accounting of the
"traces" and marks rendered but now erased. Retrospective predictions
based on material traces will lead to a fuller recognition of nonhuman histories and agency.[8] Such accounting bears no necessary correlation to any
concept of animal rights or welfare, but it does acknowledge the animal as
a significant forger of signs, or a forger of significant signs. And, of course,
Zadig himself is no hunter but instead a student of nature in all its manifestations and embodiments.

Zadig is, fairly obviously, an ancestor of Sherlock Holmes—who is not
only a keenly insightful retrospective predictor but one whose insights surprisingly often depend on a reading of animal signs. Arthur Conan Doyle's
1904 story "The Adventure of the Priory School" is a striking manifestation of what Ginzburg describes as conjectural or semiotic thinking based
specifically in the reading of horse tracks. The story's plot involves the
disappearance and presumed kidnapping of the young son of the Duke of
Holdernesse from a boarding school. Like so many of Conan Doyle's tales,
the story is "perfused with signs," and is obsessed with communications
and media, beginning with the first introduction of Dr. Huxtable, the
school headmaster, who declares that "I came personally, Mr. Holmes. . . .
I feared that no telegram would convince you of the absolute urgency of

the case." The story is fundamentally preoccupied with different, compet-
ing forms of signification, especially those that take the form of marks on
the ground, tracks of one sort or another: footprints, horse and cow hoofprints, and bicycle tracks.

When Holmes and Watson head out into the wet moors surrounding
the scene of the abduction, they find ground inscribed thoroughly with the
tracks of ruminants but no apparent human tread: "We struck across the
peaty, russet moor, *intersected with a thousand sheep paths. . . .* Certainly,
if the lad had gone homeward, he must have passed this, and he could not
pass it without leaving his traces. But no sign of him or the German could
be seen." (The name of the missing German schoolmaster and presumed
kidnapper happens to be Herr Heidegger, a name that invites anachronistic
analysis of a kind that I will resist!). Holmes scans the ground carefully,
examining "every muddy stain," but: *"Sheep-marks there were in profu-
sion,* and at one place, some miles down, cows had left their tracks. Nothing more." They soon discover a set of bicycle tire tracks, which Holmes
is immediately able to identify as made, unfortunately, by Dunlop tires,
the wrong brand. "Heidegger's tyres were Palmer's, leaving longitudinal
stripes. . . . Therefore, it is not Heidegger's track" (948).

The puzzle of the story, then, lies in the depiction of a territory "perfused by signs" both natural or animal-made and human, but the *wrong
signs.* Holmes's breakthrough comes when he realizes that he has miscat-
egorized both the animal (cow) tracks and the human (bicycle tire) tracks.

> "Strange, Watson, that we should see tracks all along our line, but never
> a cow on the whole moor; very strange. . . . Can you recall that the
> tracks were sometimes like that, Watson"—he arranged a number of
> bread-crumbs in this fashion—::::—"and sometimes like this"—:.:.:.:.—
> "and occasionally like this"—.-.-. "Can you remember that?" (957)

"What is your conclusion?" Watson asks dimly, not getting it, as usual—to
which Holmes replies, "Only that it is a remarkable cow which walks,
canters, and gallops." What Holmes has realized is that the criminal has
masked the tracks of his horse with trick horseshoes designed to appear as
the tracks of a cow. We learn at the end of the story that these shoes "were
dug up in the moat of Holdernesse Hall. They are for the use of horses, but
they are shaped below with a cloven foot of iron, so as to throw pursuers
off the track. They are supposed to have belonged to some of the maraud-
ing Barons of Holdernesse in the Middle Ages" (971).

"The Adventure of the Priory School" thus perfectly embodies Ginzburg's claims for the emergence around the turn of the twentieth century of a new kind of semiotic, conjectural thought and, even more specifically, his claim that such semiotic thinking inherits a long human tradition of analyzing and interpreting animal tracks as signs. Is the story at all concerned with animal agency or subjectivity in relation to sign making, however? Seemingly not. If anything, it can be read as an allegory of animal signification's routine manipulation for human, cultural purposes. The *natural* signs of cows, horses, and sheep here merely offer material for the sophisticated, devious plottings and interpretations of human criminals and detectives. For Hobbes and many other subsequent thinkers in the Western tradition, animal communication is fundamentally limited by its inability to deceive; the animal has, in Derrida's words, "been denied the power to efface its traces." "The Adventure of the Priory School" seems almost to revolve around this insight in its depiction of the *effacing of tracks in order to deceive* as a distinctly human practice.

I would argue, however, that Conan Doyle does signal an implicit awareness of a problem of animal subjectivity, agency, or ethical standing in such a scene of semiotic activity. We can see this more clearly in his 1902 novel *The Hound of the Baskervilles*, which is equally concerned with the track or footprint as a key semiotic code. Consider a famous passage from the book's second chapter:

> "But one false statement was made by Barrymore at the inquest. He said that there were no traces upon the ground round the body. He did not observe any. But I did—some little distance off, but fresh and clear."
>
> "Footprints?"
>
> "Footprints."
>
> "A man's or a woman's?"
>
> Dr. Mortimer looked strangely at us for an instant, and his voice sank almost to a whisper as he answered.
>
> "Mr. Holmes, they were the footprints of a gigantic hound!" (32)

This footprint functions throughout much of the novel as an ominously mysterious sign, one implying an otherworldly origin for the novel's crimes and their link to ancestral, premodern family legends of crime and haunting. That Dr. Mortimer refers to a "footprint" as opposed to a "pawprint" might be read as evidence that signification as such tends to be associated with the human—a tendency that Conan Doyle may be questioning. As in "The Adventure of the Priory School," distinctions between dry,

hard ground on which no tracks will be left, damp ground that will easily take tracks, and wet boggy marshland that (here) will swallow a body
entirely play a crucial role in the plot; Conan Doyle seems to figure the
earth's surface as a textual surface possessing varying degrees of receptivity to imprinting.

A crucial marker of animal agency and even perhaps an inarticulate
claim to recognition or ethical standing in the novel can be found in the
hound's mysteriously melancholy howl: "A long, low moan, indescribably
sad, swept over the moor. It filled the whole air, and yet it was impossible
to say whence it came. From a dull murmur it swelled into a deep roar
and then sank back into a melancholy, throbbing murmur once again" (83).
Why, indeed, is the hound of the Baskervilles melancholy? We learn in
the end that he has been kept locked up by Stapleton, the novel's villain,
so there is ultimately an explanation within the plot. But I'd argue that
Conan Doyle's novel contains a signifying residue of animal affect that
goes beyond any diegetic explanation, a residue most clearly manifested
in this moaning howl. We can also hear it in the "dreadful cries" of the
"miserable" ponies who are regularly sucked into the boggy swamp of the
moor and disappear into it:

> "Only yesterday I saw one of the moor ponies wander into it. He never
> came out. I saw his head for quite a long time craning out of the bog-
> hole, but it sucked him down at last. . . . By George, there is another of
> those miserable ponies!"
>
> Something brown was rolling and tossing among the green sedges.
> Then a long, agonized, writhing neck shot upward and a dreadful cry
> echoed over the moor. It turned me cold with horror, but my compan-
> ion's nerves seemed to be stronger than mine.
>
> "It's gone!" said he. "The Mire has him." (82)

The animal cry, allied with the animal print, constitute in the novel the
articulations of a creature whose signification, as we saw in "The Adventure of the Priory School," cannot really be properly read or understood in
writing.[9] Conan Doyle's hound possesses a drive to signify within a form
that offers little opportunity (outside a novel like *Black Beauty*) for any effective nonhuman articulation. The cries and prints of dogs, cows, horses,
and ponies matter only insofar as they can be manipulated and read by
human beings for human purposes. The hound's cries remain to some degree unaccountable, "indescribable"—that is, not capable of reinscription.

Their "melancholy," then, articulates the sorrow of the animal's failure to signify effectively—and its description (by Conan Doyle) at least signals a recognition of this as a problem.

Returning to "The Adventure of the Priory School," let's further consider the moment in the text when Holmes arranges bread crumbs in the patterns left by the hoofprints: "'Can you recall that the tracks were sometimes like that, Watson'—he arranged a number of bread-crumbs in this fashion—:::::—'and sometimes like this'—:.:.:.:.—'and occasionally like this'—.-.-." These bread crumbs are represented, of course, by typographical marks: periods and colons. In this odd textual representation of a horse track, simulating a cow track, represented in bread crumbs, refigured as typeset punctuation marks, we can read a concise and overdetermined allegory of the fate of animal signification within print culture. These punctuation marks are obviously not the sign making of any actual animal, but they do offer an intriguing experiment in the fictional representation of animal marks or signs. Conan Doyle's dogs, horses, and cows are creatures that embody the animal fate Hobbes described: they can make signs and call out but lack any higher-order representational capacity that would render their "limited" signs capable of meaning within communicative networks. Instead, these animals are effectively mute and dumb and therefore necessarily outside of politics or justice. In these crime scenes they may constitute clues or offer red herrings, but they can never be victims due any redress. The hound dies, "with a last howl of agony and a vicious snap in the air," unmourned and to some degree uninscribed. Conan Doyle both does and does not, then, transcribe nonhuman signs in this story; we can read the tracks over Holmes's shoulder and decode his breadcrumb mimicry of their marks, but the logic of the tale leads toward a blocked or only second-order registration of any nonhuman signification, a kind of acknowledgment of that which cannot be truly or fully represented.

I now turn once again to the work of Thomas Hardy, who, as we have seen, throughout his writing experimented with new ways to represent and acknowledge animal or nonhuman consciousness, agency, and being, and whose work resembles Conan Doyle's in its vision of sign making and signification as practices of all living creatures rather than as distinctly human. Hardy goes further than Conan Doyle (in an earlier work), however, in his attempt to move beyond translation toward a transcription of animal marks.

I've discussed Anna Sewell's claim, on the title page of *Black Beauty*, to be not an author but a translator "from the equine" and the ways Conan

Doyle's representations of animal marks and signs can be understood as an ambivalent, partial attempt to transcribe rather than to translate animal signs (that is, to record nonhuman agency without revising it into some version of human agency). More radically than either Sewell or Conan Doyle, Hardy can be understood as trying to create a novelistic form that might more satisfactorily transcribe nonhuman agency or sign making—recognizing it *as* signification—while still respecting or acknowledging its nonhuman difference.

Many of his novels contain memorable representations of animal signification, marking, or imprints. Take as typical, for example, this beautiful description from *Tess of the D'Urbervilles* (1891) of the way a cow's body imprints itself on the meadow: "On the gray moisture of the grass were marks where the cows had lain through the night—dark-green islands of dry herbage the size of their carcasses, in the general sea of dew. From each island proceeded a serpentine trail, by which the cow had rambled away to feed after getting up, at the end of which trail they found her" (131). Hardy is explicitly interested in how such markings represent animal agency and in how the making of marks, tracks, and trails is a transspecies practice—a practice of the living rather than of the human.

That human histories and activities are historical and geological is a key presumption of Hardy's. Every step we take, every mark we inscribe is written over previous marks and tracks by other beings.[10] Hardy's work offers persuasive evidence for Ginzburg's hypothesis that "perhaps indeed the idea of a narrative, as opposed to spell or exorcism or invocation, originated in a hunting society, from the experience of interpreting tracks" (89). I cite from *The Return of the Native* (1878):

> He frequently walked the heath alone, when the past seized upon him with its shadowy hand, and held him there to listen to its tale. His imagination would then people the spot with its ancient inhabitants—forgotten Celtic tribes trod their tracks about him, and he could almost live among them, look in their faces, and see them standing beside the barrows which swelled around, untouched and perfect as at the time of their erection. Those of the dyed barbarians who had chosen the cultivable tracts were, in comparison with those who had left their marks here, as writers on paper beside writers on parchment. Their records had perished long ago by the plough, while the works of these remained. Yet they all had lived and died unconscious of the different fates awaiting their works. It reminded him that unforeseen factors operate in the production of immortality. (387)

That Hardy's work is saturated by geological historicism is a truism, but it's less often acknowledged that Hardy pushes this tendency to the point where human/nonhuman distinctions break down as surely as modern/premodern ones do. Early in *The Trumpet-Major* (1880), for example, we see a palimpsest of tracks and marks in the ground, created by multiple species: "The dry hard mud of the opening was marked with several horse and cow tracks, that had been half obliterated by fifty score sheep tracks, surcharged with the tracks of a man and a dog. Beyond this geological record appeared a carriage-road nearly grown over with grass" (46). When you travel far enough back into English prehistory, all marks, signs, paths, and roads become comparatively "dehumanized," or at least opened to nonhuman markings. To walk or to make a path as a human being is not to create original markings but to "surcharge" preexisting nonhuman ones.

In *Jude the Obscure* (1895), we see itinerant peddlers and proprietors of fairground shows as akin to "strange wild birds": "As strange wild birds are seen assembled on some lofty promontory, meditatively pausing for longer flights, or to return by the course they followed thither, so here, in this cliff-town, stood in stultified silence the yellow and green caravans bearing names not local, as if surprised by a change in the landscape so violent as to hinder their further progress; and here they usually remained all the winter till they turned to seek again their old tracks in the following spring" (192). Hardy depicts human history as itself a process of seeking "old tracks," marking over the marks of beings who have walked before us. One might describe Hardy as Peircean in this respect; consider Peirce's remarks from 1892 about the "taking [of] habits" on the part of protoplasm: "Another physical property of protoplasm is that of taking habits. The course which the spread of liquefaction has taken in the past is rendered thereby more likely to be taken in the future; although there is no absolute certainty that the same path will be followed again" ("Man's Glassy" 343). As Claus Emmeche observes, for Peirce "subjectivity as a mode of being is not just a property of the human subject, but exists 'dissolved' in a small dose in all living cells" ("A Semiotical Reflection" 332). For Peirce and, I would argue, for Hardy as well, life is defined by the taking of habits, the following of paths, and the making of marks. The earth becomes a vast sheet of paper (or parchment) on which all creatures inscribe signs. Hardy's aim, then, seems to be at once to recognize sign making as a transspecies practice (not one on which humans have a monopoly) and to acknowledge the impossibility of translating the signs of, say, horses or cows directly into human terms, in the mode of a *Black Beauty*.

The publication history of Hardy's *Far from the Madding Crowd* offers

one especially fascinating early example of the literal editing out—as not
proper to the form of the novel—of an impulse to register animal signification in prose. In the passages I'll now discuss, we can see a tension between
Hardy's own impulse to write into the form of the novel a fuller record of
a transspecies history of signification and his editor's sense that what is
proper to the novel—or perhaps to print generally—must be solely human,
with any animal signs "translated" fully into proper print English.

The chapter "Night—Horses Tramping" describes the attempts by the
novel's protagonist Gabriel and two helpers to retrieve a horse whom they
believe has been stolen by gypsies. In the dark and out of earshot of the
horse and her thieves Gabriel must find a way to interpret the signs left by
the horse—to perform an act of conjectural tracking or reading of animal
signification. "The footprints forming this recent impression were full of
information as to pace . . . being difficult to describe in words they are
given in the following diagram." The subsequent passage features hoofprint diagrams sketched by Hardy:

> He lighted another match and examined the ground again.
> [diagram]
> "Tis a canter now," he said, throwing away the light. "A twisty
> rickety pace." (185)

Hardy's original sketches (reproduced in the Penguin Classics edition
of the novel) are not, of course, literal hoofprints, and they are no less written by Hardy than the words, but they constitute an attempt to register on
the page the sign making of a horse. They represent, that is, an attempt
at the inscription of a nonhuman signification into the novel. Gabriel is
trained in veterinary science, and so to him the hoofprints are "full of
information." In a novel rendered in type, it is difficult fully to convey
the same "information" to the reader: the hoofprints are akin to human
handwriting. Hardy's goal might be to nudge his reader to acknowledge
the signifying fullness of these prints—without translating them into human language. The point is to recognize the hoofprints as signs inscribed
by a nonhuman agency.

Hardy's drawing of the tracks, inserted in the text, attempts physically
to reproduce the animal marks in his own hand—thus coming closer
than the typeface transcription does to the embodied but not mechanized
marking that the animal makes on the ground with its hooves. But Hardy's editor found these hoofprints to be unsuitable—in need, precisely,
of being translated into a more typical prose. The editor to the contem-

porary Penguin edition of the novel, Rosemarie Morgan, glosses: "[Leslie] Stephen's pencil has gone through most of Hardy's footprint diagrams in this episode. . . . Instead, [the *Cornhill Magazine* first publication of the novel] has descriptive accounts such as: 'they were in equidistant pairs, three or four feet apart, the right and left foot of each pair being exactly opposite one another'" (377). Leslie Stephen, that is, in effect translated Hardy's diagrams *back from equine* into the usual human prose—in doing so, excising one of Hardy's most interesting experiments in dehumanizing (or at least opening to the nonhuman) the form of the novel.

This editorial interference asserts the intransigent anthropocentrism of the realist novel. We can find animal life in all its diversity in its pages but most often in the margins or corners, owning a fragile or uncertain claim on the structures of plot and narrative. I'll conclude with just one more moment from *Far from the Madding Crowd*. "Gabriel proceeded towards his house. In approaching the door his toe kicked something which felt and sounded soft, leathery and distended, like a small boxing-glove. It was a large toad humbly traveling across the path" (212). Gabriel "finding it uninjured . . . placed it again among the grass." Hardy explains that the toad is a signal of an approaching storm, a signal Gabriel well knows how to read: he is a diviner, deeply skilled in the forms of "low intuition" Ginzburg ascribes to the conjectural paradigm. (He also checks his flock: "if there was one class of manifestation on this matter that he thoroughly understood, it was the instincts of sheep" [212].) The toad here is a sign in spite of itself and a sign of something other than itself. Hardy's intention here is not to translate the marks or movements of the toad, to put them into human language, but instead—and more simply—to transcribe them, to record their marks in as close to their original form as is possible within print. Part of the toad's function in the novel may be simply to stand as a record or trace of this particular species-being—as a reminder that, along with human beings, sheep, and sheepdogs, toads also lived here, on these roads and also in the print world of the novel itself, crossing human paths with their own itineraries, marks, and signs.

"Infinite Compassion": Nonhuman Life in Schreiner's *The Story of an African Farm*

Olive Schreiner joins Hardy, in my account, as a second later-Victorian novelist who sought to move beyond some of the anthropocentric strictures of the Victorian novel—to push the limits of how animal life, consciousness, or personhood might be represented in fiction. In her preface to *The Story of an African Farm* (1883), Schreiner contrasts two methods of fiction writing: first, the "stage method," allied with conventional realist approaches and, second, "the method of the life we all lead," characterized by uncertainty, discontinuity, and "a strange coming and going of feet" (xxxix). She continues by observing that "[i]t has been suggested by a kind critic that he would better have liked the little book if it had been a history of wild adventure; of cattle driven into inaccessible 'kranzes' by Bushmen; 'of encounters with ravening lions, and hair-breadth escape.' This could not be. Such works are best written in Piccadilly or the Strand" (xxxix–xl).[1] Schreiner thus defines her own chosen method against both conventional realism (think Trollope or Eliot) and against colonial "wild adventure" novels intended for English readers (think Rider Haggard). Schreiner associates such novels of adventure that she does not wish to write with figures of animal life: the cattle herds and lions of African cliché. But the artist must paint not the "brilliant phases and shapes" of imagination but "what lies before him." The implication would seem to be that this artist of South African reality, of Schreiner's revised realism, must keep a focus exclusively on the human world in order to avoid those colonialist clichés and fantasies drawing on colorful images of animals.[2] Yet, perhaps surprisingly, given these opening claims, when we continue from the preface to the novel itself, we discover that Schreiner's farm and its "strange coming and going of feet" in fact include many nonhuman hooves and feet (a significant lion's paw even makes a late appearance)—

and, indeed, that her vision of South African life and of her own experimental realism seems to depend, quite crucially, on a broadening of horizons beyond a traditionally anthropocentric frame.

Elaine Showalter's oft-cited declaration that Lyndall, a protagonist of *The Story of an African Farm*, was "the first wholly serious feminist heroine in the English novel" (199) placed the novel on the map as a central text for feminism in the 1970s. In the subsequent decades, many other critics—such as Laura Chrisman, Anne McClintock, and J. M. Coetzee—have rendered Schreiner's text also crucial for any consideration of late-Victorian fiction's relationship to colonialism and race. Here I argue that, notwithstanding one critic's recent description of the novel as an "odd duck" and a "literary platypus" (Esty 407), scholars have by and large neglected a thread of meanings within the novel no less fundamental to Schreiner's intentions and achievement: namely, one relating to a discourse of species, animality, and human-animal relation. By ignoring animals and animality in *The Story of an African Farm*, we also incompletely account for those more familiar contexts for the novel because for Schreiner gender, sexuality, and race all operate in part by means of shifting procedures of humanization and animalization. For Schreiner identity as a woman or a man, a Boer, a native African, or an Englishman, is shaped by relationships to animals. Animals themselves "matter" in the novel as figures of identity and being that reach beyond realist, humanist, or anthropocentric frames of characterization, representation, and ethics.

Jed Esty describes *The Story of an African Farm* as one of a group of late nineteenth- and early twentieth-century texts that "disrupt the bildungsroman and its humanist ideals" (407). A fuller consideration of Schreiner's engagement with tropes and figures of nonhuman life can usefully contribute to our understanding of what Esty describes as the novel's "odd duck" elements "in terms of genre and style," its "ungainly combination of parts and functions [that] seems to flummox both classification and periodization" and that "seems to anticipate a number of modernist fictional techniques" (407). Esty argues that in Schreiner's novel, as in other "modernist fiction[s] of unseasonable youth" of the period 1880–1920, "temporal experimentation scrambles biographical time" (415), and we find "a nonteleological model of subject formation . . . and narrative distension" (416). He reads both Waldo and Lyndall as in effect stunted "protagonists who cannot mature" (423), who operate as analogs for "colonies that cannot modernize" (423), and whose life narratives also become stunted, strange, nonlinear. Here I concur with many of Esty's claims but reorient them in relation to human/nonhuman distinctions.[3] Where Esty reads Waldo as unable to develop and stuck in "endless youth," I see (in perhaps more positive or recuperative ways) his failure or refusal to inhabit norms of fully developed subjectivity—what Esty describes as "the full human norm of the Goethian mode" (417) of the classic bildungsroman—as a corollary to his unusual openness and receptiveness to the nonhuman, such that his own identity and subjectivity become in crucial ways dehumanized or animalized.

The disrupted humanism Esty addresses is, then, among other things, a species category that Schreiner opens into a broader frame. In disrupting humanist ideals and failing to produce a complete subject-citizen in the manner of a classic bildungsroman, she also questions more traditionally anthropocentric understandings of personhood and agency. "Nothing is despicable—all is meaning-full" (118) emerges as a keynote of this novel, in which to possess or create meaning is never a solely human prerogative—although *possess* strikes the wrong note here, for the "meaning" Schreiner so defines is pointedly nonindividualistic, not something produced by a single powerful agent or actor.[4] Ultimately the novel foils Lyndall's early strivings for powerful (humanist as well as feminist) agency and concludes with Waldo's (but Lyndall's as well) passivity, openness to experience and to suffering, and a version of what Anne-Lise François has called "recessive" (173) action or noninstrumental agency that abandons some of the prerogatives of human identity for a more receptive proximity to what Jacques Derrida calls the "living in general" (*Animal* 12).[5]

I read Schreiner's novel through a lens informed by a number of theorists and critics but especially by François's *Open Secrets: The Literature of Uncounted Experience* and Derrida's late work on species and animality. Their ideas are of course not interchangeable but share a number of overlapping concerns and emphases. My approach (and my title) in this chapter are particularly informed by Derrida's late writings about an unconditional or "hyperbolic" posthumanist ethics that would cease to put "the animal outside the ethical circuit" (*Animal* 106).[6] For her part, François explores the possibilities of an ethics and aesthetics of renunciation and passivity that she finds in romantic literature (broadly construed), one characterized by "instances of a type of strangely immaterial, virginal, negative or renunciatory 'act' of desistance or leaving untouched" (34) and by "an accepted satisfaction oddly indistinguishable from a willingness to let fade or pass by" (53). François explains that our customary habits of interpretation have difficulty with such renunciatory aesthetics or actions, which can so easily seem alternately ineffective, meaningless, empty, or (affectively) depressive. Her set of terms and approaches prove a good fit for Schreiner's strange novel, which can be easily misconstrued as simply pessimistic or despairing in a naturalist mode when it pursues a logic that I see as containing more affirmative implications.

MIERKAT ETHICS

In her posthumously published novel *From Man to Man*, Schreiner (in the speech of her protagonist Rebekah) hails the native South African mierkat as an exemplum and model of "passionate love for one another" and "endless self-sacrifice of all" as well as a form of unexpected strength in vulnerability:

> The survival of the mierkat, so small and defenceless on the barren plains where so many other creatures become extinct in the presence of danger and of enemies, is accountable only when you know that each mierkat acts for all; not for their own young only, but for each other, and for the younger and more helpless, all labor and sacrifice themselves. When the hawk approaches, if the older males and females be gone out far to look for food, tiny creatures, themselves hardly weaned, will seize all the tinier ones half an inch shorter than themselves and in desperate anguish strive to carry them off to the hole, forgetting all fear for themselves in their passionate attempt to save those who may have no blood relationship with themselves, while the older males and females grow gaunt and thin in the breeding-time, because almost all food they find is brought to lay at the feet of the young. (211)

We've already seen Schreiner disavow the "ravening lion" as a figure for fiction because of its associations with adventure clichés. Now she positions the mierkat as a creature much better suited than a lion to modernity (and to coexistence with human beings): "It is this passionate love for one another, this endless self-sacrifice of all, this devotion to the weaker by the stronger, which makes it possible for these little delicate furry creatures with their beautiful eyes and small powers of defence to survive in our terrible barren enemy-filled plains. The panther and the lion have vanished in the terrible presence of man, and many other forms of life grow very scarce, but these tiny creatures are still surviving, aided by their passionate devotion and self-sacrifice" (211). The lion seems initially to figure here as the menacing predator who would devour the "delicate furry" mierkat, but Schreiner's point is that the lion faces extinction *because* of its incapacity for the selfless "act[ing] for all" of the physically weaker but evolutionarily hardier mierkat. Schreiner develops these points into a broadly ranging, Darwinian-Spencerian argument that human ethics, love, and cooperation are rooted in principles shared throughout the living world "from the mysterious drawing together of amoeba to amoeba . . . on through all the forms of sentient life" (213).[7] In its vulnerability, weakness, and susceptibility—its smallness (in this context "tiny creatures" are large in comparison with the "tinier") and "small powers of defence"—in fact lies the mierkat's virtue and strength.

Schreiner's lesson in mierkat ethics serves as a good introduction to the crucial role nonhuman creatures played in her thinking about what she considered to be the most important problems of human experience. When she associates a character with nonhuman life or seems to trouble his or her claim to fully human status, therefore, one cannot assume the link as necessarily denigrating; *The Story of an African Farm* enacts a dehumanizing of its protagonists that is misunderstood if it is seen only as negative or prejudicial. In revising the form of the realist bildungsroman, Schreiner opens the possibility of a form of human experience that would, at the cost of an extreme vulnerability and openness to suffering (it is not easy to be a mierkat), gain a wider sense of fellowship and empathy with the lives of others—including nonhuman others—and an escape from the fundamental "intense loneliness" (9) to which human existence is prone. This dehumanizing tendency, which could also be described as animalizing, has been difficult for critics adequately to recognize, I believe, because of the immense gravitational pull exerted by issues of race, ethnicity, and racism on Schreiner criticism. For good reason, scholars have been preoccupied for several decades with the question of how to understand and position Schreiner in relation to South African's painful racial history. John Kucich suggests that Schreiner criticism has shifted from previously associating her with "submission" (in the feminist criticism of the 1970s and 1980s) to now seeing her as more culpable in practices of "mastery" in relation to racism and colonialism ("Olive Schreiner" 81). Like Kucich, I believe that analysis of Schreiner's culpability or flaws as a complexly ambivalent thinker on race and colonialism, however salutary and necessary such analysis has been, can now become limiting if it rules out alternate or complementary approaches to her work.

A problem that must be faced in thinking about questions of species and dehumanization in Schreiner's work is that, in it, tropes or images of species overlap with those of race in sometimes disturbingly racist ways. There is not much one can say to defend a description of a "little wooly-headed Kaffir" as presenting the appearance "of an ill-conditioned young buffalo" (70). As Anne McClintock puts it, among Schreiner's many contradictions, "[s]tartlingly advanced in her anti-racism and political analysis, she could fall on occasion into the most familiar racist stereotypes" (259). But if Schreiner does sometimes dehumanize her native African characters in troubling ways, my emphasis here will be on her gestures of dehumanizing or animalizing that seem more complex in their pushing beyond a humanist and anthropocentric worldview. This dehumanizing strain of her work, notwithstanding certain dismaying moments, is one part of a logic that ultimately challenges European—and, indeed, human—claims of evolutionary preeminence and dominance. And it should also be stressed that the novel clearly defines those characters who are most racist as the novel's most ignorant and benighted; for example, in this description of a Sunday service: "The Kaffir servants were not there, because Tant' Sannie held they were descended from apes, and needed no salvation" (35).

Issues of species, animality, and human-animal relations, when they are considered at all in reference to Schreiner (and indeed in literary studies more generally), have in the past often tended to occupy a position as part of a taken-for-granted ground against which other more prominent figures, such as race and colonialism, are examined—such that dehumanization can appear to be virtually a corollary or effect of, or indistinguishable from, a more basic racism. Here, however, I aim provisionally to shift that ground or background to the status of figure at the center of our reading of the novel, so that we might see racism itself as simply *one* of various possible forms of dehumanizing, or a redefinition of the meaning of the human: potentially pejorative or stigmatizing but also potentially less so. To be compared to an animal need not always be an insult, that is, even if it sometimes is. Schreiner's representations of gender, too, like those of race, can be rethought in relation to a discourse of species and animality. Such a reconsideration allows us to see that, for example, Lyndall's suffering, even as she herself often defines it as a specifically female experience, is matched by Waldo's in ways that draw both characters into a logic of dehumanization, in relation to which I would argue that human-animal distinctions ultimately shape identity even more fundamentally than do either gender *or* race.[8] I certainly have no wish to dethrone Schreiner's text as a key feminist novel (without question, it is that), but I do think that any exclusive focus on gender—as on race—can lead to an underestimation of the fundamental importance for Schreiner of categories of species and the "living in general"—and that the working of both race and gender in the novel can in fact be usefully reconsidered from this perspective.[9]

In a long 1892 letter to a Congregational minister who had written her
for advice about his growing theological doubts (he later left the church),
Schreiner wrote of the limitations she sees in orthodox Christianity because of its "scorn for the animal world."

> I think among great religious teachers he [Jesus] does not quite draw
> me as Buddha and others, because his teaching stops short with the
> human world; it is to me doubtful whether he ever caught sight of that
> larger unity; whether he ever realized the divinity in plant and animal,
> as well as man. . . . You see, my dear friend, how absolutely close we
> are, and yet I *cannot* stop in the thought of "God" as the father of man;
> and men as brothers; *I have to go further.* Nothing tortured me so in
> Christian teaching as the scorn for the animal world, and the hatred of
> matter. But if we really knew what the beautiful soul of Jesus thought
> and felt, we should find it loved wider and deeper than its followers left
> us any record of. (214)[10]

Perhaps in concession to her addressee, she distinguishes between conventional Christian teaching and the (possible) true beliefs of Jesus himself, whose "wider and deeper" love for the creaturely world she posits as
a model for her own drive to reimagine the human beyond an exclusive
species frame. *The Story of an African Farm* "goes further" in this direction, aiming to recognize or at least acknowledge a natural "divinity" to
be found in an unrestricted understanding of life. Schreiner's Waldo discovers that there is "no God; not anywhere!" (69)—but the novel offers a
substitute of sorts in a vision, adapted in part from her reading of Herbert
Spencer, of a living world saturated with divinity.[11]

Schreiner destabilizes conventional distinctions between human and
animal and between the living and the nonliving, the sentient and insen-
tient. One could think about the meanings and significance of animals or
nonhuman creatures in the novel in various ways; among the most important, I would include: animals as meat, flesh, and objects of consumption; as figures of indigeneity or nativity with a special relationship to the
"land," sometimes figured very literally as soil or dirt, complicating national and racial imaginings of these categories; as objects or victims of
abuse—beaten, killed, hunted, and enclosed; as figures of sufficiency and
totality or natural "harmony" that is linked to a vision of a perpetually
recycling organic matter; and as companions to human beings, adjacent
fellow creatures or "brother life" (269), potential objects of sympathy offering an alternative to the atomization of individualist human subjectivity.

INDIGENEITY: PLAIN, FARM, KRAAL, DIRT

Indigeneity or nativity is a key concept for Schreiner. Who among the novel's cast of characters, with their various ethnic and national affiliations—the Dutch owner of the farm, Tant' Sannie, and her daughter Em; the farm overseer, the German Otto; the South Africans of European descent, Otto's son Waldo and the orphan Lyndall; the Irish confidence man Bonaparte Blenkins; the marginalized and mostly nameless African or "Kaffir" servants and farmworkers—belongs to and on this South African land? Deborah Shapple defines Waldo, the novel's male protagonist, as "a kind of colonial indigene" possessing "a rather paradoxical relationship to his native precursors" (81) who "must confront the alterity of another, more original, indigenous South African society" (82). Shapple's focus is primarily on Waldo's complex relationship to a native San or "Bushman" presence that the novel represents as "relegated to a remote past" (90). She observes that "Waldo's right to the land, while officially denied, emerges through his formation within this land and his ability to interpret its natural-historical significance. It is therefore appropriate that Lyndall compares Waldo to a thorn tree, an indigenous plant whose roots delve into the red soil of the predominantly arid Karoo" (84). Here I want to extend this insight—about Waldo's relationship to an indigenous nature—more fully into questions of animality and species-being. Waldo's status as "a colonial indigene" acquires new valences if we are willing to take seriously the possibility that the nonhuman creatures of this novel are also, themselves, in some sense "native indigenes" "full" of meanings.

By defining her setting as an African farm, Schreiner immediately locates her narrative along an overlap between human culture and nonhuman nature or wildness. Her farm has some things in common with earlier examples of rural nature-culture we've considered by the likes of Emily Brontë and Hardy: settings where domestic space is only ambiguously and imperfectly set off from a surrounding natural world. Schreiner also places her text in relation to a national subgenre, however, that of the South African farm novel or *plaasroman*.[12] The farm, a site defined by its mastery and enclosure of the surrounding landscape and earth, offers an occasion for thinking about what Donna Haraway sums up as the "relation between what counts as nature and what counts as culture" (*Companion Species* 27) in any given culture. The question of who and what counts as "natural" or indigenous is partly a matter of a literal relationship to the land and soil; to be part of or to belong to the world of the farm, for Schreiner, means to be in some sense literally part of and constituted by soil and, therefore, to straddle the natural and cultural. A striving, agential form of humanness measures its worth by the degree to which is rises above and walks firmly upon the ground.[13] In this normative South African context, to rise above the earth is especially crucial; the local ruling nonnative class, after all, were named *diggers*, a term referring "to the Europeans who went to the Fields to make diamond claims, although they hired Africans to do the manual work of the claim" (First and Scott 64). Power and prestige here reside with the group whose very name associates them with a labor of digging soil, which they in fact delegate to a servant class. But Schreiner, rather, celebrates a way of being that tends to be "dusty" and even to sink into and become indistinguishable from earth, dirt, and animal: "Waldo his son herded the ewes and lambs—a small and dusty herd—powdered all over from head to foot with red sand" (5). Waldo, not unlike Hardy's Gabriel Oak, places himself with and among the sheep, lacking any forceful human distinction that would mark him as separate.[14] Note the grammatical ambiguity about whether Waldo, the lambs, or both are "powdered all over" with sand. In this "small and dusty herd," who is natural, who cultural or human? Waldo and his charges achieve a creaturely indistinction.

J. M. Coetzee defines Schreiner's farm as "an unnatural and arbitrary imposition on a doggedly ahistorical landscape" (66), summing up the choices faced by the novel's characters:

> Either one lives on the inhospitable land (as Waldo tries to do) and perishes or one lives in the farmhouse and succumbs at last to adulthood, becoming another Tant' Sannie, counting one's money, counting one's sheep. For the farmhouse is at war with nature. The children who bring the germ of nature into the house (Waldo, Lyndall) have it thrashed out of them. . . . Insofar as there is life in the veld, it is not the life of sheep—which stand about sluggish and heat-stunned—but the life of insects. . . . To accept the farm as home is to accept a living death. (*White Writing* 65–66)

Coetzee describes the farm as engaged in a struggle to the death with the living itself. He equates the counting of money and of sheep by the Boer farm owner Tant' Sannie, for the sheep are, in this context, a commodity and a resource, instrumental material (for meat or wool, or perhaps even for that parchment into which we're told sheep are turned in *Bleak House*) for profit more than living creatures. Coetzee helps us see how much pressure the novel puts on the categories of the living versus the nonliving, the sentient and lively versus the "sluggish and heat-stunned," the cultural and the natural.[15] Derrida suggests that one legacy of Cartesian thought is a belief that "thinking" or rationality "excludes everything detachable constituted by life, the living body, animal life" (*Animal* 72). For Schreiner, very differently, humanity or human identity is always defined in various ways by one or another relationship to "the living," to natural life or nonhuman creatures; humanness inevitably contains a supplement of nonhuman living, which will be either acknowledged or disavowed.

Schreiner first begins to raise questions of the relation of human and animal in definitions of nature-culture in some of the novel's early considerations of animals as living creatures subject to use—primarily domestication, enclosure, and consumption—by human beings. To be *enclosed* is here a form of domestication that defines its objects as creaturely. The homestead is organized according to a hierarchized structure of enclosure: "First, the stone-walled 'sheep-kraals' and Kaffir huts: beyond them the dwelling house." The architecture organizes life-forms into those who *dwell*, who live in a cultural interior, a house, and those who are *enclosed* in kraals or huts, namely the sheep and the "Kaffirs" or native Africans. Joseph Bristow tells us in the novel's editorial notes that "the word kraal may refer to either a pen for keeping herded animals or a black-African encampment" (272); this term, *kraal*, spatializes a designation of creaturely nonhumanness that is ambiguously a matter of race and species. To be enclosed and to live in a kraal is to live in ambiguous territory on the animal/nonanimal border.

So, to be human, a character or protagonist is to dwell in a dwelling, an exclusionary space or structure—and one that does not confine—conjoined to a kraal, a space that encloses the nonhuman sheep or the ambiguously human, racialized Kaffirs. The value system governing here divides all the living into the separate spaces of the dwelling, the kraal, and the "solemn monotony" of the unenclosed "wide, lonely plain."[16] That is, from the perspective of the farm, to live fully as human is to dwell and to distinguish oneself from the openness of plain and the intermediate enclosure of the kraal. The plain is unmediated, unbroken, undifferentiated; it is broken in order to impose space and to define the hierarchies of living space. Derrida observes that divisions marking out the human-animal border operate both linguistically and in terms of spatial geography: "Confined within this catch-all concept, within this vast encampment of the animal, in this general singular, within the strict enclosure of this definite article ("the Animal" and not "animals"), as in a virgin forest, a zoo, a hunting or fishing ground, a paddock or an abattoir, a space of domestication, are all the living things that man does not recognize as his fellows, his neighbors, or his brothers" (*Animal* 34). The geography of Schreiner's farm, kraal and plain enacts a similar hierarchical sorting of different kinds of living and different relations to the cultural or domestic.

The ambiguity of *kraal* suggests, of course, the novel's (or its depicted world's) entanglement in racist and racial systems of meaning, but there may be an interpretive loss in viewing the "sheep-" of "sheep-kraal" as *only* or simply enacting a dehumanization of the native Africans. That a kraal can be both a pen for sheep or a "black-African encampment" certainly signals a racist system that associates native Africans with animals, but this kraal is also an element in a broader set of meanings in which the sheep are also actors and not only figures for dehumanization. (The problem with that term—*dehumanize*—as it's generally understood, as I've been suggesting, is the way it presumes that to take anything away from a fully or exclusively human status must be to condemn or insult.) The difference could be understood as one between a view of the sheep as *matter* or secondary substance and as themselves *mattering* or meaning. The sheep and other animals are important—matter and signify—in the novel, even if by virtue of their unimportance and their unfreedom; for example, in this case, because of their enclosure in kraals. They produce meanings but only what might be understood as "recessive" or "reticent" meanings in Anne-Lise François's terms (e.g., xvi): minor, ephemeral, leaving little permanent trace, falling well short of protagonicity but still signifying.

SUPERSEDED AND EPHEMERAL LIFE: "SOME GIANT'S GRAVE"

Coetzee insists that "to accept the farm as home is to accept a living death," and one could say more generally that the farm's own "life" is defined in relation to the death or nonlife of other forms of the living. The novel's first paragraphs describe the "solemn monotony" of the South African landscape as it is "broken" by a "kopje" or hill and the homestead: "Alone it lay there, a heap of round iron-stones piled one upon another, as over some giant's grave" (Schreiner, *The Story* 1). Here Schreiner immediately implies that the current life of the farm is metaphorically situated on or over another, superseded life. The present-day living erects itself on the grave of the displaced or vanished formerly living, as if the operations of the human as culturally defined necessitate the killing off of some previous life-form, one possessing the mythic resonance of "some giant." The native San or "Bushmen" are the closest literal referent for that giant, but the figure also invokes a broader life that has been incorporated, appropriated, and displaced, as Schreiner makes clear in Waldo's early discussion of the "Bushman paintings." He, and Lyndall and Em "sit under a shelving rock, on the surface of which were visible some old Bushman-paintings . . . grotesque oxen, elephants, rhinoceroses, and a one-horned beast, such as no man ever has seen or ever shall" (10). These "grotesque" animals are all to various degrees imaginary, aesthetic, and/or vanished from the current South African land. These "non-anthropomorphic" (Shapple 82) paintings are certainly "the sign of a repressed precolonial history" (Shapple 79), but what has been little noted are the ways this repressed history, left in traces on the rock in "red and black pigments" (Schreiner, *The Story* 10)—pigments made of "juice" (16) presumably from berries—is more fundamentally a nonanthropocentric history, one of a displaced South African people who lived with and among the nonhuman in a manner that now seems archaic. (Remember Hardy's ancient sheep paths; one sign of premodernity is a less exclusively human-centered relationship to the land.) The "one-horned beast" depicted—"such as no man ever has seen or ever shall"—becomes, in this context, a figure not just for the power of imagination to create aesthetic fictions but for a pushing beyond humanist frames toward a (perhaps impossible) encounter with an animality or life existing outside a modern human vision. The paintings also become models and objects of aesthetic longing for Schreiner's own fiction, as she seeks to push it away from the thoroughgoing anthropocentrism of Victorian realism.

Lying under the paintings, Waldo imaginatively revives them:

> Sometimes . . . I lie under there with my sheep, and it seems that the stones are really speaking—speaking of the old things, of the time when the strange fishes and animals lived that are turned to stone now, and the lakes were here; and then of the time when the little Bushmen lived here, so small and so ugly, and used to sleep in the wild dog holes, and in the "sloots," and eat snakes, and shot the bucks with their poisoned arrows. . . . Now the Boers have shot them all, so that we never see a little yellow face peeping out among the stones. . . . And the wild bucks have gone, and those days, and we are here. . . . I know that it is I who am thinking . . . but it seems as though it were they who are talking. (15–16)

Waldo here ventriloquizes Schreiner's own recollections of her childhood perceptions of nature: "When I was a little child of five and sat alone among the tall weeds at the back of our house, this perception of the unity of all things, and that they were alive, and that I was a part of them, was as clear and overpowering to me as it is today. It is the one thing I am never able to doubt" (*Letters* 212). Waldo's visions seem enabled by his lying "with my sheep"—as "dusty" shepherd, he gives up some of the privileges of the modern human subject; like the "little Bushmen" who "used to sleep in the wild dog holes" or like Gabriel Oak, Waldo is down in the dirt with the animals. Waldo's experience leads to an odd splitting of subjectivity or disassociation in his perception of his own "thinking" producing the "talking" of these vanished beings. These paintings induce something resembling Deleuze and Guattari's "becoming-animal," a pushing beyond the frames of the human and of the individualized subject into a subjectivity and utterance that is split, nonindividual, diffuse.[17] Schreiner recalled her feelings of being "part of" the unity of "all things" as she "sat alone among the tall weeds"; Waldo lies with his sheep under the stone, recalling the now-vanished inhabitants of the land who once slept "in the little dog holes." Schreiner sketches an implicit history—one that she seeks, if inconsistently, to reimagine or undo—in which the human lifts itself from the dirt, dust, grounds, and weeds, murders off or displaces the nonhuman and the non-European, and attains a modern possessive individualism.

A simple fact worth emphasizing is that those "bucks" and the other "strange fish and animals"—"turned to stone" and memorialized in paint made of juices—are as much a part of this scene as either Waldo or the "Bushmen" he recalls and as such should be considered in any accounting of Schreiner's representation of indigenous life. That is, although they may seem to occupy a second- or third-order status as representations of vanished life-forms, they should by Schreiner's logic be understood as present within the scene. These are forms of life that have been superseded, overcome, replaced, yet still bear meaning; one lesson here is that any current life-form or way of life is constituted by that it has replaced, such that all life is following different forms of the living, with none possessing necessary precedence. In Derrida's reading of Kant's *Anthropology*, the animal, in its sheer natural or physical power, possesses a "being-before" while "man is after the animal" (*Beast* 1: 96); that disconcerting "priority or superiority" of the animal is "reversed only when a weakening . . . on the part of the animal makes it submit to man and to the domestication that makes it more useful to humans than the wild beast." Human identity bears an anxious relationship to an animality that threatens to "precede" it as more powerful. Domestication itself serves to undo this anxiety by insisting that the human can dominate, control, and even (through breeding) alter the animal. With the wall paintings, Schreiner fantasizes an era when human and nonhuman were embedded in shared environments, a coexistence that did not of course preclude violence (shooting with poisoned arrows) but that lacked the modern abjection or "disanimalizing" (Derrida, *Animal* 80) of the animal from the human. Waldo's experience of the stones and paintings as "really speaking" and "talking" also implies the living force of representations and inert things, which should not (and will not) be confined to a second-order status of nonliving objects. This implication also bears upon the status of Schreiner's own representations; she suggests that imaginative creations and dreams are, like rock paintings, themselves alive or organic. One thinks of Schreiner's childhood Bible, which "was her companion all through childhood: she pressed flowers in it and hid it in a hollow tree in the bush" (First and Scott 54): for her, it would seem, a book's value derived in part from its closeness, as paper, to the natural forms of flowers and trees. Her novel implicitly takes the rock paintings as an aesthetic model for a form of creation that could be "dusty," of the earth, and not cut off from organic life.

Schreiner's vision of life-forms coembedded in shared environments deemphasizes the sovereignty or autonomy of the individual person or creature and emphasizes the transitoriness of individual life. The novel invests value or meaning in life that is ephemeral—that accepts its own status as temporary or fleeting and replaceable. Later in the book, Lyndall abandons her earlier quest for a "power" capable of meeting a tyrant like Bonaparte on his own terms and moves closer to what we could call Waldo's more passive and reticent mode of acceptance and openness. She now describes the "marks" and "traces" left by human beings in terms that recall the faint juice stone paintings, almost washed away: "Men have set their mark on mankind for ever, as they thought; but time has washed it out as it has washed out mountains and continents. . . . Mankind is only an ephemeral blossom on the tree of time; there were others before it opened; there will be others after it has fallen. Where was man in the time of the dicynodont, and when hoary monsters wallowed in the mud? . . . We are sparks, we are shadows, we are pollen, which the next wind will carry away" (*The Story* 184). Schreiner's emphasis lies on the ephemerality of such marks or traces, their precariousness, typical of organic life (and somewhat reminiscent of Hardy's and Conan Doyle's foot and hoofprints). The berry-juice paintings are "still visible" (10), possessing a somewhat paradoxical permanent ephemerality. The prehistoric "hoary monsters" "wallowed in the mud," thoroughly of the ground and earth; Lyndall now defines the human, too, as earthy and organic, natural matter, which is always framed by the knowledge of its future erasure or dispersal. We might recall Schreiner's discussion, in her preface, of some readers' questions about (and objection to) the "Stranger" who appears early in the novel and then simply disappears, having given Waldo a book that seems a proxy for the copy of Spencer's *First Principles* a visitor left with a teenage Schreiner herself. There seems to be "a feeling," she writes, that "a man should not appear on the scene and then disappear, leaving behind him no more substantial trace than a mere book" (xxxix). But within Schreiner's chosen "method," "men appear, act and re-act upon each other, and pass away"; the commitment is not only to aesthetic discontinuity but to a more basic principle of organic ephemerality. That which is most valued may be that which most thoroughly "pass[es] away" or is "carr[ied] away" or "washed out," that which vanishes utterly. The most powerful books, in particular, are in an important sense "mere traces."

COMPOSTING LIFE: DEAD BIRDS, SHEEP'S TROTTERS, ROTTEN PUMPKIN

In an 1887 letter to her friend Edward Carpenter, Schreiner wrote of her desire to move to a "tiny cottage in Switzerland with a garden. . . . In such a life one almost *has* to give up animal food because one can't kill the things!" (125). She was not herself a vegetarian—as Carpenter was—but like certain other Victorian authors and intellectuals with strong feelings for animals she seems to have been somewhat troubled by the reliance of human life on the flesh of animals. In our first introduction to the character, Tant' Sannie dreams of an incomplete or failed incorporation of animal flesh: "[S]he dreamed bad dreams. Not of the ghosts and devils that so haunted her waking thoughts; not of her second husband, the consumptive Englishman, whose grave lay away beyond the ostrich-camps; nor of her first, the young Boer; but only of the sheep's trotters she had eaten for supper that night. She dreamed that one stuck fast in her throat, and she rolled her huge form from side to side, and snorted horribly" (2). We have seen that the farm is erected "as over some giant's grave" as if enacting a superseding of some preceding life-form. Tant' Sannie embodies this superseding literally in her history of now-deceased husbands. Yet, if she is "husband-haunted," what presently haunts her dreams is sheep flesh, "sheep's trotters," which seem to block her throat as if the sheep has its hoof on her neck (this is one of those nonhuman feet to which I've alluded). The farm was built as if on the grave of a giant and adjoins the kraal for the sheep, and, similarly, the Boer woman's own "huge form" has incorporated the sheep such that her body is, in a sense, a grave or kraal for the animal. In her carnivorous greed—the novel, sometimes rather cruelly, dwells on her eating and fatness—she typifies the farm way of living insofar as its life is made up of other displaced, marginalized, and consumed life-forms. Judging by her dreams, her unconscious features a nearly continual loop of woman vs. sheep struggles: "Didn't I tell you this morning that I dreamed of a great beast like a sheep, with red eyes, and I killed it?" (168). She resembles Rousseau's prehistoric "chief," in Derrida's analysis, who "does not keep the beast *by devouring* it, he does not first keep the cattle and then, subsequently, devour said cattle, no, he keeps the cattle *with a view to devouring it*, he only keeps the cattle *in order to* devour it, so as to devour it savagely and gluttonously, tearing at it with his teeth, violently" (*Beast* 1: 32).[18] An ethic of aggressively violent consumption of other beings is also summed up neatly by the novel's early villain, Bonaparte: "When the worms come out then the blackbirds feed. Ha, ha, ha!" (52) The point is not so much that Schreiner implies a critique of meat eating generally but that Tant' Sannie's relationship to animal flesh is particularly exemplary of the farm's status as a culture defined in relation to a violently appropriated animal life. In her dreams of sheep flesh choking her that make her roll and "snort horribly," Tant' Sannie embodies the troubled bad faith of the farm's appropriative relationship to the nonhuman.[19]

Just following this scene, we see Waldo conducting an impromptu, unorthodox ritual sacrifice of a piece of mutton on a homemade altar: "Oh, God, my Father, I have made Thee a sacrifice. I have only twopence, so I cannot buy a lamb. If the lambs were mine I would give Thee one; but now I have only this meat; it is my dinner-meat. Please, my Father, send fire down from heaven to burn it" (6). The young Waldo is no less carnivorous than Tant' Sannie—everyone in the novel eats mutton—but the difference lies in the solemnity and respect he brings to the scene of animal consumption. He seems to view the flesh of the animals he tends as a potential—if unrealized—conduit to something resembling divinity. The piece of meat tends toward reincorporation with the earth: "the sun had melted the fat of the little mutton-chop, and it ran down upon the stones . . . some ants had come to the meat on the altar" (7). Waldo's attempted sacrifice seems futile in part because the piece of meat, in this hot landscape, will inevitably break down and "melt" into the landscape (rather than ascend upward as a divine sacrifice). This incident was apparently based on Schreiner's own experience: "on an altar of twelve flat stones she offered up a fat lamb chop and waited in the sacrificial heat for the torch of God. But the conflagration never came and in a paroxysm of disbelief, she smeared her body with dung" (McClintock 264). The failure of the sacrifice points not only to Schreiner's atheism—Waldo's belief in a monotheistic God is an early phase that he must move beyond—but also to her post-Darwinian, deistic natural theology that sees a kind of divinity in life itself. Schreiner's dung smearing could plausibly be understood as not only a gesture of masochistic abjection but also a ceremonial bringing of the body closer to the earth. The novel also contains a memorable dung beetle: "The beetle was hard at work trying to roll home a great ball of dung it had been collecting all the morning; but Doss broke the ball, and ate the beetle's hind legs, and then bit off its head. . . . A striving, and a striving, and an ending in nothing" (74). Such images reveal the tendency of images of dust, dirt, and organic matter for Schreiner to bear, alternately and ambivalently, meanings both negative (linked to abjection and meaninglessness) as well as more affirmative, when associated with recurring, fecund life cycles.

Schreiner often emphasizes the tendency of flesh to decay or rot in a kind of composting process of becoming earth. This emphasis probably derives in part from her fervent reading of Spencer's *First Principles*, which offers a vision of all things and beings on earth as continually "growing or decaying, accumulating matter or wearing away, integrating or disintegrating" (Spencer 285); all matter is "in process of decay" (282), a claim that to Spencer implies not pessimism but a belief in life as a cyclical, self-renewing process.[20] Schreiner writes in a letter, "I used to love the birds and animals and inanimate nature better after she was dead; the whole of existence seemed to me more beautiful because it had brought forth and taken back to itself such a beautiful thing as she was to me" (213). In a letter of March 5, 1886, to Karl Pearson, she reports on her visit to Percy Shelley's monument in the priory in Christchurch, Hampshire, citing his poem "The Daemon of the World": "Shelley couldn't die: he never died. 'I change, but cannot die.' He was like one of his little skylarks. I picked up a little dead one this morning, just decaying and passing back into the dear old earth and grass" (74). These comments, which recall Spencer's discussion of every man's fate to find "his body resolved into the gaseous products of decomposition" (282), suggest a vision of a world of life-forms not dying definitively but "just decaying and passing back" into earth or soil—such that we might interpret Tant' Sannie's dream of the sheep trotter "stuck fast in her throat" as an image of a blockage or thwarting of the natural process of incorporation and digestion. Schreiner's observations about the skylark remind us that dirt or soil is in fact decayed animal life.[21] The "dear old earth and grass" contains and in some sense *is* the bodies of generations of creatures who died on or were buried within it. The novel frequently reveals a vision of a world in which "nothing is despicable—all is meaning-full; nothing is small—all is part of a whole" (118), a declaration sometimes literalized in images of recycling and re-incorporation of life-forms. As we've see in the despairing image of the dung beetle whose work is destroyed in a snap by Doss, dung and dirt may be associated with a death perceived as empty and unrewarded, but they ultimately tend in the novel to lead toward more affirmative images of life processes and indigeneity. And her comments on Shelley suggest that, for Schreiner, literary and aesthetic power itself were linked to this compost-ing, decomposing potential of organic life: as if the literary text itself, lit-eralized in its status as paper made from tree pulp, and having rejected its anthropomorphic literary heritage, becomes charged with the living force of meat, flesh, and soil.

When Waldo stares at the farm's pigs in their sty, he muses on "why they were pleasant to look at." "Taken singly they were not beautiful; taken together they were." This nonindividual beauty is in part a matter of harmony, of individual life-forms constituting a totality. But the harmony also seems to relate to a sense of sufficiency based in what I'm describing as a vision of life processes as, in Spencer's terms, always decomposing or disintegrating, a cycling through of life through earth to living creatures and back again.

> Half of the sty was dry, but the lower half was a pool of mud, on the edge of which the mother sow lay with closed eyes, her ten little ones sucking; the father pig, knee-deep in the mud, stood running his snout into a rotten pumpkin and wriggling his curled tail. . . . The old sow was suited to the little pigs, and the little pigs to their mother; the old boar to the rotten pumpkin, and all to the mud. They suggested the thought of nothing that should be added, of nothing that should be taken away. (78)

This harmony and sufficiency originates, ultimately, in the rotting pump-kin and the mud; Waldo's perception of "nothing that should be added" or "taken away" points to a vision of the natural world as a self-defining and indeed self-composting system, with no true waste, all reincorporated. "It is impossible to think of something becoming nothing," Spencer writes; "[t]he annihilation of Matter is unthinkable" (182); "matter is indestruc-tible" (177). The pigs' devouring of the rotten pumpkin is an antithesis to Tant' Sannie's sheep trotter: where the trotter was "stuck fast" as block-

age, the pumpkin is on its way to breaking down into mud and pig flesh, a
kind of animated stew of organic life.

The scene in which Gregory Rose, in order to care for Lyndall unrecog-
nized by her, shaves his beard and puts on the costume of a female nurse,
is generally—for obvious reasons—read in terms of its destabilizing of
gender identity, but this transformation also reveals just such a reincorporation and a transformation of culture or the human into a nature-culture:
"Then he took out a razor. Tuft by tuft the soft brown beard fell down into
the sand, and the little ants took it to line their nests with" (238). These
ants are a perfect instance of Schreiner's mantra that nothing can be either
small or despicable or without meaning: they are physically tiny, but they
begin the crucial work of the process of transforming Gregory Rose into
earth. They could even be said to indigenize him: he has previously been
defined as thoroughly artificial and altogether foreign to the local South
African landscape, with his bedroom walls "profusely covered with prints
cut from the 'Illustrated London News'" (139), like Dickens's Tony Jobling
from *Bleak House*, but now the ants begin the work of incorporating his
body into the ground. For Schreiner, the earth itself also is or becomes
animal and human—becomes creaturely—through organic processes of
life and death, as here manifested in a swarm of busy insects. Shaving
as a cultural practice can plausibly be understood as an instance of disanimalization, by which the human defines itself via the rejection and
abjection of waste defined as nonhuman and animal—according to which
logic Rose could be understood to be not only making himself a woman
but also making or emphasizing himself as a nonanimal, domesticating
himself. Yet Schreiner in effect redeems this waste matter of Rose's hair,
as she did with Waldo's piece of mutton, by depicting its reincorporation
into a nonhuman natural world. Agamben turns, as one possible way out
of his "anthropological machine," to the early twentieth-century work
of the biologist and ethologist Jacob von Uexküll, whose writings, in his
words, "contain illustrations that try to suggest how a segment of the human world would appear from the point of view of a hedgehog, a bee, a fly
or a dog" (45). This scene attains something like von Uexküll's goal in its
focus on the little ants' adapting of the hairs as nest lining—and, indeed,
this is a typical move on Schreiner's part, to zoom out of a human perspective into a nonhuman one, striating her prose with fleeting animal points
of view.

Schreiner in this regard recalls the experiments by Thomas Hardy
with nonhuman, animal perspective; both Schreiner and Hardy literalize,
in a sense, George Eliot's metaphor from *Middlemarch* about the effects

of "hearing the grass grow and the squirrel's heart beat" (124). With this image, Eliot addresses the limits of human sympathy, with sympathy for animals serving as a metaphorical outer limit suggesting a fall into sheer, inhuman sensory overload. In her work, to be unable to care for animals whatsoever (to banish the puppy, as Dorothea does) represents a failure of sympathy, but animals are by and large presumed to lie outside the boundaries of ordinary human sympathy, as not beings with whom one can "go along" in sympathetic understanding. As in Victorian culture more broadly, love for the animal operates as a kind of exceptional excess, confined to certain chosen pets.

But Schreiner, like Hardy, truly seems to want to hear or at least to listen for that animal heartbeat. Eliot's squirrel heartbeat, in fact, with its "roar on the other side of silence," has some similarity as a figure (although differently deployed) to Schreiner's "one-horned beast, such as no man ever has seen or ever shall" (10); both are animal figurations suggesting some insight beyond the normal human capacity for perception or sympathy. Another example of Schreiner's shift into a nonhuman perspective would be the moment when Bonaparte moans theatrically: "He howled, till the tarantulas, who lived between the rafters and the zinc roof, felt the unusual vibration, and looked out with their wicked bright eyes, to see what was going on" (45). These invocations of animal or nonhuman (here insect) life punctuate the novel as reminders that a multitude of beings inhabit the world depicted—there will always be tarantulas under the rafters, so to speak—and that the events described from a primarily human perspective may always be reenvisioned from the perspective of, alternately, an ant, tarantulas, dog, chicken, or cow, one from which the most pressing human event may not matter very much: "the cows, busy with their calves, took no notice of the little human farce" (144).[22]

UNLIKE LIVES/UNLIKE NARRATIVES

In 1884 Schreiner wrote Ellis of her reading of Thomas Hardy's *A Pair of Blue Eyes*, in which she found "a certain shallowness and unrealness"; "no, that's putting it too strongly; it seems to me as though he was only fingering his characters with his hands, not pressing them up against him till he felt their hearts beat" (*Letters* 35). Schreiner, whose early career ambition was to become a nurse, here articulates a basic aim of her fiction, which draws on her childhood interest in physiology and dissection to push toward a radical closeness or intimacy with—along with knowledge of—both the human and nonhuman body, an intimacy that impels

Schreiner beyond the norms of Victorian realist form. "I used to dissect ostriches' and sheep's hearts and livers, and almost the first book I ever bought myself was an elementary physiology" (*Letters* 39); "Yesterday I was reading in my *Zoology* (that fertile source of ideas) and looking at the diagram of the nervous system in vertebrates and invertebrates" (*Letters* 150). Lyndall implies that full knowledge of any being may only be attainable in self-scrutiny, figured as self-dissection: "We shall find nothing new in human nature after we have once carefully dissected and analyzed the one being we ever shall truly know—ourself" (164). But it is necessary to move outward from such self-knowledge to comprehend other beings. In a long passage from the poetic "Times and Seasons" chapter, the section of the book that most clearly shifts into protomodernist form, Schreiner locates in Waldo's childhood dissection of a drowned duck an insight into a fundamental unity of living things:

> We look into dead ducks and lambs. In the evening we carry them home, spread newspapers on the floor, and lie working with them till midnight. With a startled feeling near akin to ecstasy we open the lump of flesh called a heart, and find little doors and strings inside. We feel them, and put the heart away; but every now and then return to look, and to feel them again. Why we like them so we can hardly tell. . . . Each branch of the blood-vessels is comprised of a trunk, bifurcating and rebifurcating into the most delicate, hair-like threads, symmetrically arranged. We are struck with its singular beauty. And, moreover—and here we drop from our kneeling into a sitting posture— this also we remark: of that same exact shape and outline is our thorn- tree seen against the sky in mid-winter: of that shape also is delicate metallic tracery between our rocks; in that exact path does our water flow when without a furrow we lead it from the dam; so shaped are the antlers of the horned beetle. How are these things related that such deep union should exist between them all? Is it chance? Or, are they not all the fine branches of one trunk, whose sap flows through us all? That would explain it. (117–18)

This Bergsonian reverie sees a vitalist commonality in all life-forms, which cluster into parallel or recurring shapes and forms—forms that may serve as an implicit model for Schreiner's sense of literary form itself: the innovative, protomodernist experiments of "Times and Seasons" seems to grant to fictional prose an expansive, organicist form modeled on the flow of life force through bodies. We've seen Esty emphasize the roots of

Schreiner's modernist experimentation in a failure of her protagonists to achieve the classically "full human" (Esty 417) telos of the subject of a bildungsroman; here is a good example of how this failure might be reframed as a more positive dehumanization or at least a decentering of the human subject. This is a subject who embraces and literally plunges into nonhuman bodies in a search for new understanding of the links joining all organic life and who, as a result, can occupy new kinds of narratives that develop and flow in unpredictable ways, organized by what Spencer defined as a world in which "[a]ll things are growing or decaying, accumulating matter or wearing away, integrating or disintegrating" (285).

Of course, to dissect can be to "murder" (as Wordsworth puts it), and it can also be to "only finger . . . with [one's] hands" and so to fail fully to apprehend; to dissect in the way Schreiner calls for, the experimenter must in effect press the strange bodies "up against him till he felt their hearts beat," literally to grasp the others' heart in one's hand. This is not a cold or impersonal science but rather a form of radical intimacy that conjoins dissection with a love of (nonhuman) organic life. These dissection scenes can be read not only in relation to Hardy but as, in effect, revisions and rethinkings of Lydgate's dissections and anatomical research in *Middlemarch* and, as such, offering a critique of the high realist mode of Victorian fiction (compare Schreiner's comments in the preface of the "stage method"). For Eliot's Lydgate, "[t]he moment of vocation had come" when he stumbled on an anatomy book in a library:

> the first passage that drew his eyes was on the valves of the heart. He was not much acquainted with valves of any sort, but he knew that valvae were folding-doors, and through this crevice came a sudden light startling him with his first vivid notion of finely adjusted mechanism in the human frame. . . . [T]he world was made new to him by a presentiment of endless processes filling the vast spaces planked out of his sight by that wordy ignorance which he had supposed to be knowledge. From that hour Lydgate felt the growth of an intellectual passion. (142)

Eliot emphasizes that Lydgate's passion originates in the pages of a book and in response to a diagram of a heart rather than an actual organ—and, later, that he never does gain a satisfactory understanding of the basic structure of organic life. Richard Menke has also convincingly argued that Lydgate, even as he moves to actual animal experiments, fails to bring the possible lessons of his anatomy work to his personal relationships; he "scarcely attends to the inner workings of Laure's or Rosamond's mind at all," and it is Eliot herself, not her scientist character, who "applies the imaginative 'eye of research' to the 'minute processes' of the mind" (634). Schreiner's description of Waldo's own anatomical investigations seems to offer a reflection on and critique of Lydgate—and perhaps also of Eliot and of Victorian realism more broadly. Schreiner's child anatomist gets his hands bloody from the insides of animals and develops his knowledge in reference to a local natural world already well understood as vividly experienced sensations ("of that same exact shape and outline is our thorn-tree seen against the sky in mid-winter"). Schreiner seems to be announcing what she will do differently than her Victorian predecessors: offering visceral, tactile sensation in the place of a more coolly objective vision or knowledge (Lydate's reading) and in place of the Adam Smithian sympathy that tends to operate in Victorian realist fiction as a mode of estrangement and distancing (see Greiner)—as in, at least by Schreiner's account, Hardy's too-dainty or distanced "fingering" of his characters.

Lyndall possesses the novelistic capacity she herself describes as "the rare power of entering into other lives unlike her own, and intuitively reading them aright" (183). Schreiner associates this power—one to be distinguished from an Eliotian sympathy—with what she later refers to as an ideal of "infinite compassion for others," a form of post-Christian "holiness" (249) that must operate via a sensory immersion and openness, an embrace of the potentially maddening sound of the squirrel's heartbeat. We might relate this notion of holy "infinite compassion" to Derrida's recurring gestures toward "hyperbolic" conceptions of ethical responsibility as "absolute, unconditional, hyperbolical hospitality" (Of Hospitality 75)—a form of hospitality that would welcome "who or what turns up, . . . before any identification . . . whether or not the new arrival is the citizen of another country, a human, animal, or divine creature" (77), an "absolute, anonymous, unknown other" (25). As Lyndall and Waldo lie in an empty horse cart late at night on Tant' Sannie's wedding celebration, she observes, "It is so nice to lie here and hear that noise." The noise is the "twanging of the fiddles" and the "thud of the dancers," but in her description she abstracts outward from these particulars to a broader sense of "life itself," the life of other beings, as something alien into which one can nevertheless enter into a relationship of intimacy: "I like to feel that strange life beating up against me. I like to realize forms of life utterly unlike mine" (181). Lyndall's own tendencies, at least initially, tend to be human focused; when nonhuman creatures enter her evocation of "strange life," they are peripheral: "A Kaffir witch-doctor seeking for herbs by moonlight, while from the huts on the hill-side come the sound of dogs barking, and the voices of women and children" (182). After she gives birth to a child who dies in delivery, however, she achieves a rather startling form of physical intimacy with a creature altogether unlike her: the dog Doss.

Doss is an important (semi-)character throughout the novel. In some ways he may appear to be a classic Victorian novelistic nonhuman companion or pet figure, one who is often present but generally peripheral to the main, human-centered events of the plot. He seems allotted some but not all the prerogatives of the category of the *character* or the *person*. He often simply "follows" the human characters—first Waldo, later Lyndall—in the supplemental companion mode of the domestic pet: "the boy shuffled away to rejoin his flock, while Doss ran at his heels, snapping at the ends of the torn trousers as they fluttered in the wind" (16); "Doss, finding he could not follow his master up the round bars, sat patiently at the foot of the ladder. Presently he looked up longingly" (75); "It is Lyndall, followed by Doss" (202).[23] As with the tarantulas and the cattle, however, he also offers a recurring nonhuman perspective on the "human farce" of the novel's plot by manifesting his own canine preoccupations, which Schreiner occasionally mentions in passing as if to hint at an entire world of nonhuman perspectives and priorities: "the dog, who was endeavouring to unearth a mole, an occupation to which he had been zealously addicted from the third month, but in which he had never on any single occasion proved successful" (162); "Doss was engaged in howling imploringly to a lizard who had crept between two stones, and who had not the slightest intention of re-sunning himself at that particular moment" (193). Doss is, then, at once aligned with the human as subordinated companion pet but also alien or other, occupying a different life world.

Lyndall in effect takes Doss over as companion from Waldo. For much of her time as Doss's master, she seems to define her relationship to him as one of "love" within certain clear, implicitly species-defined limits. "Do you see this dog? He licks my hand because I love him; and I allow him to" (199). Shortly after this comment she declares, "One day I will love something utterly, and then I will be better" (210). Her feeling for Doss is love, then, but not utter love; finite compassion, we could say. (Perhaps one purpose of the animal-human border—as Barbara Herrnstein Smith ["Animal Relatives"] suggests—is to erect a somewhat arbitrary limit to a compassion that might otherwise threaten to become, in the manner Eliot suggested, overwhelming in its potential unboundedness?) Something resembling this implied boundary between a finite and a more open-ended compassion seems to be broached later, however, after Lyndall's childbirth.

One of the novel's most famous scenes is that of Gregory Rose taking on the disguise of a woman in order to serve as nurse for the dying Lyndall, but just as surprising and radical within a late nineteenth-century novel as this gender-crossing, I would argue, is the species-crossing scene where Lyndall enacts something like the nursing of the dog Doss as a substitute for her lost child.

We've earlier seen Em marveling at a cow's loving adoptive parenting: "I always come to watch the milking. That red cow with the short horns is bringing up the calf of the white cow that died. She loves it so—just as if it were her own. It is so nice to see her lick its little ears. Just look!" (143) In an 1896 letter, Schreiner wrote approvingly of the way a male ostrich will nurse a female's eggs: "I do think the husband and wife should share equally or almost so the care of the children: but ostriches are the ideal creatures for me in this respect—the way in which the male watches over the eggs and the young with as much tender solicitude as the female" (*Letters* 291). And we've seen Schreiner's admiration for the way "each mierkat acts for all; not for their own young only." Schreiner worked for years as a governess and did not have children of her own, and she seems interested in the possibilities of parental or maternal "solicitude," outside biological lineage, as one model of a compassion pushing beyond at least certain conventional limits. (She was also in the habit of referring to her fictional characters as her "children" whom she "loved too much" [First and Scott 83].) In this scene, as Lyndall lies on her deathbed, she seems to come closer to that "infinite compassion" by way of a species-crossing act of maternal love.

> "Can I do anything for you?"
> "No, nothing."
> She still drew her lips together, and motioned with her fingers toward the dog who lay sleeping at her feet. Gregory lifted him and laid him at her side. She made Gregory turn open the bosom of her nightdress, that the dog might put his black muzzle between her breasts. She crossed her arms over him. Gregory left them lying there together.
> Next day, when they asked her how she was, she answered "Better." (243)

She subsequently requests a breakfast of toast, eggs, and meat, and "cut the toast into long strips, broke open both eggs, put a tiny morsel of bread into her own mouth, and fed the dog with pieces of meat put into his jaws with her fingers" (243). She has recently buried her infant baby, of whom she comments, "It crept close to me; it wanted to drink, it wanted to be warm" (246). Now she feeds Doss eggs and meat in what resembles an act of substitute or cross-species nursing. In these her final hours, she engages in something like a "becoming-animal," allowing a new intimacy with Doss, whom she also curiously comes to resemble in certain respects. Doss had earlier hurt his paw: "Lyndall was softly touching the little sore foot as she read, and Doss, to show he liked it, licked her hand." Now in her final hours, she finds herself staring at a "massive lion's paw on which the wardrobe rested," commenting in irritation at it, "Always that lion's paw!" and then asking Gregory to help her dress: "Gregory knelt on the floor before her, and tried to draw on one stocking, but the little swollen foot refused to be covered." The line of imagery linking Doss's paw, the dead lion's paw, and Lyndall's own sore foot links to Lyndall's earlier image of a Chinese woman's bound feet as a symbol of female domination— "We fit our sphere as a Chinese woman's foot fits her shoe, exactly"—with a suggestion that the domination of women parallels the domination of the nonhuman and with Lyndall feeling herself as defeated as the big game trophy on the ground.[24] Given Schreiner's characterization in her preface of the kind of novel she believes certain readers would have preferred she write as one filled with "encounters with ravening lions" (xl), the paw also seems to make a defiant gesture in the direction of any reader disappointed to find themselves reading an experimental philosophical novel rather than an Haggardesque tale of African adventure. In any case, this chain of images seems further to align Lyndall with Doss on her deathbed and, perhaps, to allow her to "realize" a form of "life utterly unlike" (181) her own at her death.

THE NONPOWER OF SUFFERING

Derrida writes, in his reading of Jeremy Bentham's comments on animal suffering, that "[b]eing able to suffer is no longer a power, it is a possibility without power, a possibility of the impossible," a "nonpower" or "inability" (*Animal* 28; also see *Beast* 2: 244). Early in Schreiner's novel, Lyndall declares that "When . . . I am strong, I will hate everything that has power, and help everything that is weak" (59–60) but also that "we will not be children always; we shall have the power, too, some day" (94). In a world of cruelty and injustice, the novel asks, should one aim to become "strong" and powerful in order to imbue power with justice? *The Story of an African Farm* ultimately abandons Lyndall's quest for this form of agential "power"; one can read this abandonment as pessimism, but it might better be understood as an embrace of that "possibility without power" or "non-power" that Derrida associates with nonhuman life, and that Schreiner at one point associates with what she calls "tenderness."[25] If Lyndall initially seeks rights and power, Derrida's analysis puts into question the efficacy of rights as the (or at least the only) basis for justice, instead proposing a different form of politics or redress based in "the finitude of life" and the "experience of compassion" (28). Schreiner's novel is valuable for the ways it imaginatively explores just such questions and possibilities.

John Kucich has called for a greater recognition of the ways Schreiner's novel seeks out "pain as a route to spiritual intensity" ("Psychoanalytic" 101); for Schreiner (as for Bentham and Derrida), I'd suggest, acknowledgment of and empathy for pain in fact inclines toward cross-species creaturely identification. Early on, Waldo endures a brutal beating from Bonaparte during which he is in effect animalized: "'Horses that kick must have their legs tied,' said Bonaparte, as he passed the other end of the rope round the boy's knees. 'And now, my dear Waldo,' taking the whip out of his pocket, 'I am going to beat you'" (Schreiner, *The Story* 91). Waldo accepts the beating with passive silence: "The boy looked up at him—not sullenly, not angrily. There was a wild, fitful terror in the eyes. Bonaparte made haste to go out and shut the door, and leave him alone in the darkness" (92). Kucich points out that this scene effects "a crisis of pre-oedipal abandonment, in which the ultimate parental surrogate, God, fails to rescue" Waldo ("Psychoanalytic" 96), and we could add that, for Waldo and Schreiner, Waldo's early recognition of the absence of God opens up a problem that is to some degree solved via a recognition of a divinity in life itself or in nonhuman creatures.

Waldo's beating by Bonaparte prompts Lyndall's comment that "we shall have the power, too, some day." In one sense this does in fact come to pass; Lyndall and Waldo grow up and they do achieve various forms of adult agency. The novel affords Waldo one opportunity, for example, to work through and perhaps reverse the trauma of his childhood beating when he is able to rescue a ox from being beaten to death by a sadistic driver. "From the black ox's nostril foam and blood were streaming on to the ground. It turned its head in its anguish and looked at me with its great starting eyes. It was praying for help in its agony and weakness, and they took their whips again. The creature bellowed out aloud. If there is a God, it was calling to its Maker for help. Then a stream of clear blood burst from both nostrils; it fell on to the ground, and the wagon slipped back" (226). Divinity, which seemed an absolute void or absence early in the novel, here in a sense reemerges (only?) in a scene of animal suffering and compassion. "If there is a God, it was calling to its Maker for help" is interestingly ambiguous in the way it leaves the space of divinity at one sense open but empty: *if* there is a God—and Waldo has determined that there is no God—then "the creature" was calling to it. A possibility of divinity emerges in the creaturely call to a provisional/absent God who cannot be appealed to via human language. One could read this scene as suggesting that a compassion capable of broaching the species barrier is in fact a solely human capacity (could the ox feel so for Waldo? could a mierkat?), yet, even if this is the case, such compassion embeds human sympathy in a transspecies exchange.

Waldo intervenes to halt the abuse, but Schreiner and Waldo do not represent the actual moment or action:

> The man walked up to it.
> "You are going to lie down, Devil, are you? We'll see you don't take it too easy."
> The thing was just dying. He opened his clasp-knife and stooped down over it. I do not know what I did then. But afterward I know I had him on the stones, and I was kneeling on him. The boys dragged me off. I wish they had not. I left him standing in the sand in the road, shaking himself, and I walked back to the town. I took nothing from that accursed wagon, so I had only two shillings. But it did not matter. (226)

Schreiner seems to evade the representation of this action as if to suggest that the adult Waldo is not so different from the child—his identity or sense of self not primarily invested in powerful agential action. He acts only to end suffering. Waldo's attack on the driver—recalling Agnes Grey's action in stopping young Tom from crushing the baby birds or any other such scene of the humane observer preventing cruelty to animals—could be read as a powerful act of agency; Schreiner, though, seems rather to want to characterize it as, in Anne-Lise François's terms, an "antiact" (75), one that occurs in an epistemological gap ("I do not know what I did") and that leads to a literal "emptyhandedness" (209), a "loss of the ability to take" (201). Waldo walks away from the wagon with nothing, having exerted the nonpower or tenderness of compassion for animal suffering; he seems to have achieved what Tobias Menely sees in the work of the poet William Cowper, a "sense of essential creatural substitutability, of shared subjugation" (149).

In the novel's conclusion, Schreiner pulls together many of the various strands of meaning I have been discussing throughout this book—relating to definitions and models of the human and animal, living and non-living—in her narration of Waldo's death. I've drawn on François's discussion of the ethics and aesthetics of renunciation and passivity as an apt hermeneutic for Schreiner's strange novel—and it is never more fitting than in the novel's final pages, when Waldo seems to slip away from the scene in a denouement that is extraordinarily passive for a novel's protagonist. John Kucich reads Schreiner as invested in a "politics of masochism" and "feminist self-wounding" ("Olive Schreiner" 82); in different but compatible ways, François's interpretive frame can allow us to see Waldo's death as a performance of passivity, tenderness, and receptive submission that embodies some of Schreiner's fundamental aesthetic and ethical goals. Waldo has earlier commented that in his brutally unrelenting labor "I was like an animal" turned into "only a body, not a soul" (223), and certainly Schreiner does preserve some sense of human distinction in the novel: Lyndall's comment that she and Waldo are "things that think" (177) defines a category that probably would not, in her view, accommodate chickens or tarantulas. Yet the novel also questions the all-important significance of human cognitive capacities and at least gestures (or, as we shall see, stretches) toward a different valuation of a nonhuman-centered way of creaturely living that human beings share equally with other creatures who may not think but who also move, perceive, occupy space, and eventually turn back into inorganic material.[26] If for Heidegger "only man dies" while the animal can merely "perish" (178), Waldo could be understood, in the end, to perish in this nonhuman sense.[27]

Two actions prove crucial to the novel's conclusion: stretching and enfolding. Stretching in the novel is sometimes associated with a perception of the infinite or numinous: "This thing we call existence; is it not a something which has its roots far down below in the dark, and its branches stretching out into the immensity above, which we among the branches cannot see? Not a chance jumble; a living thing, a *One*" (118). The stretching branches lead out of individually perceivable "finite" space into an "immensity" linked to the inexhaustible fecundity of organic growth (here embodied in a figure of a tree). Elsewhere, to stretch can become a figure for a certain gesture of cross-being, cross-species compassion, one that is importantly passive, tentative, provisional; a gesture of touching that makes no effort to grasp, take, or even necessarily to make contact.[28] When Lyndall stretches, it is a more purposeful gesture: "She stretched out her little hand to feel for his." For Waldo in his final hours, however, to stretch becomes a distinctive gesture of nonappropriative greeting offered to the nonhuman living, very different from the procedures of ordinary domestication or pet owning: "The fellow looked, and at last stretched out one hand to a little ice-plant that grew on the sod wall of the sty; not as though he would have picked it, but as it were in a friendly greeting. He loved it. One little leaf of the ice-plant stood upright, and the sun shone through it. He could see every little crystal cell like a drop of ice in the transparent green, and it thrilled him" (267). Waldo's final action on earth is another gesture of greeting in the form of stretching toward the little chickens he is observing:[29] "Waldo through his half-closed eyes looked at them. Thinking, fearing, craving, those tiny sparks of brother life, what were they, so real there in that old yard on that sunshiny afternoon? A few years—where would they be? Strange little brother spirits! He stretched his hand toward them, for his heart went out to them; but not one of the little creatures came nearer him, and he watched them gravely for a time; then he smiled, and began muttering to himself after his old fashion" (269). Waldo reaches toward these "tiny sparks of brother life"—the chickens are "tiny" like the mierkats or ants, their diminutive size suggesting lightness, slightness, ephemerality—but stops short of any contact thus performing another "antiact" in the form of a literally empty-handed move outward toward the nonhuman. These chickens' appeal seems to lie in part in their unknowability and difference within a context of proximity: he cannot know what their future will hold, and although he "stretched his hand" and "his heart went out to them," these physical and cognitive gestures fall in some sense short, at least insofar as the chickens—domesticated, not wild, but still other—remain apart from him. By stretching toward and greeting them, Waldo acknowledges the chickens while allowing them to remain other to him and apart from him; he allows them a creaturely space of human-animal encounter that falls short of full domestication.

The novel's ending gives not the last word but the final action to these chickens, who broach the distance they formerly kept from Waldo and now walk over his body.

The mother-hen was at work still among the stones, but the chickens had climbed about him, and were perching on him. One stood upon his shoulder, and rubbed its little head softly against his black curls; another tried to balance itself on the very edge of the old felt hat. One tiny fellow stood upon his hand, and tried to crow; another had nestled itself down comfortably on the old coat-sleeve, and gone to sleep there.

Em did not drive them away; but she covered the glass softly at his side. "He will wake soon," she said, "and be glad of it."

But the chickens were wiser. (270)

One critic comments that "the novel's utterly unsentimental last sentence . . . confirms at the last an absence of meaning—for the humans, at least" (Burdett 44). Schreiner concludes her (anti-) bildungsroman with an evacuation of human presence but one that is in fact accompanied by a proliferation of meaning. We understand that Waldo has now died, in what can be understood as an enactment of what François terms a "negative or renunciatory 'act' of desistance or leaving untouched" (34), or a ceasing to act, a leaving off, "an accepted satisfaction oddly indistinguishable from a willingness to let fade" (53). Waldo's death renders him inanimate—the chickens become willing to approach him because he has ceased to move—but more than this, it seems to turn him into a form of receptive surface or substance comparable to the "stones" among which the mother chicken was pecking and the ground more generally. In this sense, he has almost become earth, the ground on and in which the chickens perch, peck, and "nestle," on his way toward the state of Shelley's skylark, "just decaying and passing back into the dear old earth and grass" (*Letters* 74) or that "pollen, which the next wind will carry away" (184). Waldo's nonact and the novel's final assertion of the wisdom of the nonhuman—a wisdom that is a kind of anti- or nonwisdom in that it involves not cognition or reflection but something more like simple acceptance—together offer, in Derrida's words, a "radical means of thinking the finitude that we share with animals" (*Animal* 28).

Waldo's final act or antiact is then to "enfold" the chickens, one of which "had nestled itself down" into his sleeve, in a downward settling that recalls Waldo's own childhood lying down with and among the sheep in the veld. Schreiner declares that "[w]hen that day comes, that you sit down broken, without one human creature to whom you cling, with your loves the dead and the living-dead; when the very thirst for knowledge through long-continued thwarting has grown dull; when in the present there is no craving, and in the future no hope, then, oh, with a beneficent tenderness, Nature enfolds you" (268). Schreiner wrote to Havelock Ellis in 1885: "I wish I was a little child and God wrapt me up in his arms and took care of me" (*Letters* 64); here, Waldo has been enfolded and, as such, can enfold other beings. This seems a process perhaps less analogous to the one by which lesser beings in *Middlemarch* are "enwrap[ped]," than to what Lyndall described as the "realizing" of other lives. Schreiner pre-

sents it as an implied alternative to the coercive and instrumental forms of
"living with animals" practiced on the farm. Perhaps Waldo even attains
the wisdom of the chickens, the nonhuman wisdom of empty-handed desistance that Schreiner associates with the possibility of an "infinite compassion"—and of a novel form that might make room for the nonhuman
without fully incorporating or domesticating it. Waldo in his death seems
to become a new kind of realist character, animalized and dehumanized:
still a protagonist but a minor one, having abandoned much of the priority
and proprieties of the human.

∽

In this book, I have traced a history of the Victorian novel's gradual, partial, and ambivalent expansion of its form to greater recognition of animal
agency, consciousness, signification. In the period from Martin's Act in
1822 and the founding of the SPCA in 1824 through to the 1876 Cruelty
to Animals Act and the rise of the antivivisection movement in the 1870s
and 1880s, we see the realist novel at once responding to this sociocultural
rethinking of the human relationship to the nonhuman animal and con-
tributing to it by imagining and depicting new forms that such a relationship might take.

Derrida characterizes Defoe's novel *Robinson Crusoe*, the inaugural
text of English fictional realism, as "an immense zoology, both a taxonomy of the animals—a Noah's ark, a zoological park, a farm, a slaughterhouse, a hunting ground, a jungle of savage beasts" and "also a protection
society for domestic animals, a stockbreeding center, etc." (*Beast* 2: 49).
I have made a similar claim here for the Victorian English realist novel
broadly. The form operates as a form of domestication, a means of bringing
animals symbolically away from pure nature into culture; as an anthropocentric staging ground for human-animal encounters, for gestures of
humanization and domestication; but also—and increasingly in the later
part of the century—for less purely human-centered moments of encounter. And even in the earlier novels I examine, as in those by Dickens and
the Brontës, the animal is never fully or finally excluded: space is made,
albeit often limited, for animal life within its prose. The Victorian novel is
rarely only or exclusively human—it always contains a creaturely, transspecies presence and potential.

The experiments performed in Hardy's and Schreiner's novels finally
do also suggest, however, certain limitations of realist fiction as a form
for conducting a radical project of transspecies encounter. I asked in my

opening pages: how does one recognize a novelistic character? Can it be anything that is alive? Hardy and Schreiner certainly come closer to an affirmative answer to that question than the earlier novelists we've considered, but the answer remains equivocal. One might ask: does the late-Victorian realist novel finally do or offer justice to animals? Can literary realism truly accommodate animal personhood, let alone protagonicity, without turning into something else (such as children's or fantasy literature or perhaps the modernist novel)?

I have returned several times to Eliot's famous image, from *Middlemarch*, of the possible effects of "hearing the grass grow and the squirrel's heart beat" (124). The image sets a limit for Victorian realism—which aspires to greater and greater sympathy with more and more previously overlooked subjects but which hesitates at the boundary of the human, a boundary that it approaches, worries, and at times transgresses but never jettisons entirely. Eliot's concern seems to be that if one sympathizes too fully with—befriends too many—animals, one will not know where or when to stop. First dogs and cats and monkeys and cattle. Fine, perhaps, but then squirrels and—tarantulas? Crabs and sea anemone?

Charles Darwin's "heroic little monkey" is elevated from *a* monkey to *the* monkey, and becomes a particularized and recurring character—but such a promotion is by definition available to a limited number of creatures. Thomas Hardy laid out elevated walkways for his cats throughout his home; both he and Schreiner can be read as attempting to render the form of the novel, too, more hospitable for creatures that walk on all fours rather than upright, that create tracks rather than inscriptions. For all their efforts, however, both a human *home* and a *novel* remain, to a degree, anthropocentric forms, defined and constructed in reference to the capacities and habits of human beings. Hardy and Schreiner challenge Eliot's presumptions and widen her implied circle of conceivable sympathy—but realist fiction's commitment to discursive character, to the English language, and to print means that nonhuman life ultimately remains to some degree formally marginalized and minor within it, even as that life makes its presence increasingly felt as a necessary supplement. Compassion and fictional personhood within the realist novel are perhaps, even as they are expanded, finally finite rather than infinite.

ACKNOWLEDGMENTS

I'd like to thank Jane Desmond, directing editor of the University of Chicago Press's Animal Lives book series, and her colleagues Barbara J. King and Kim Marra for the guidance and enthusiasm they offered me; and more of the same to executive editor Doug Mitchell, editorial associate Kyle Adam Wagner, editorial project manager Carol McGillivray, production editor Christine Schwab, promotions manager Tyler McGaughey, and other members of the team. I feel very lucky to have become a University of Chicago Press author.

Some of the early work on this book took place when I spent an academic year as a Harrington faculty fellow at the University of Texas, Austin. Many people welcomed me and my family to Texas that year, but I'd especially like to thank Samuel Baker, Elizabeth Cullingford, and Lisa L. Moore.

I've been generously supported by many people and institutions at Indiana University, Bloomington. I received a research fellowship from the College Arts and Humanities Institute, a New Frontiers in the Arts and Humanities grant, and an Institute of Advanced Study Residential Fellowship for work on this project. The faculty and graduate students of Indiana's Victorian Studies Program and the journal *Victorian Studies* make teaching and working here feel like a year-round high-level Victorianist seminar. My chairs and colleagues in the English Department have helped to make Indiana a wonderfully supportive place to teach and research; a special shout-out to my current chair, Patty Ingham, for helping me get to the finish line. Thanks especially to my Indiana Victorianist colleagues and buddies (past and current): Rae Greiner, Lara Kriegel, Andrew Miller, and Monique Morgan. FBH 4eva.

Thanks to audiences and those who invited me to deliver early drafts of various pieces of this work at the CUNY Victorian Conference; the College of William and Mary Department of English; the University of Chicago's Eighteenth- and Nineteenth-Century Cultures Workshop; the Southern Illinois University–Carbondale's Department of English; Johns Hopkins University's Philological Society; Wesleyan University's Animals and Society Institute; the University of Wisconsin–Madison's Department of English; the Victorian Literature and Culture seminar at Harvard University's Mahindra Humanities Center; the Association of Literature and the Environment conference; the Society for Novel Studies conference; and several Modern Language Association, Society for the Study of Narrative Literature, and North American Victorian Studies Association conferences.

Andrew Miller, Anna Henchman, and Teresa Mangum read, in that order, my first attempts to put everything together as a manuscript and offered valuable advice, suggestions, and (most of all) encouragement. Thanks, too, to Teresa for encouraging me to send my book proposal to Chicago's Animal Lives series. I benefited from the superb editorial skills of my PhD student Mary Bowden in preparing the final manuscript. And I had the advantage of two readers for Chicago, Cannon Schmitt and another anonymous reader, who offered an ideal combination of generous enthusiasm and pointed suggestions for improvement.

Too many other friends and colleagues to name have offered support and advice of various kinds, but I'll mention Julie Bloom, George Boulukos, Judith Brown, Jennifer Fleissner, Daniel Itzkovitz, Jane Katz, John Plotz, Sandra Shapshay, and Steve Wagschal, as well as the members of an informal Second Book Group: Rachel Ablow, Daniel Hack, Richard Menke, and Rachel Teukolsky.

Small sections of the introduction and chapter 5 were originally published as "The Emotional Extravagance of Victorian Pet-Keeping" (39.2) and "Anthroprothesis; Or, Prosthetic Dogs" (35.2) in *Victorian Review*. An earlier version of part of chapter 2 was originally published as "Petted Things: *Wuthering Heights* and the Animal," in the *Yale Journal of Criticism* (18.1), copyright © Yale University and The Johns Hopkins University Press. Part of chapter 3 was published as "Dying Like a Dog in *Great Expectations*," in *Victorian Animal Dreams: Representations of Animals in Victorian Literature and Culture*, ed. Deborah Morse and Martin Danahay (Ashgate, 2007). Part of chapter 5 was published as "Pitying the Sheep in *Far from the Madding Crowd*," in *NOVEL: A Forum on Fiction* (42.3), copyright the Duke University Press. My thanks to the editors and publishers for allowing me to reuse this material.

Thanks to my parents, Thomas and Vera, my brother, Jake Kreilkamp, and most of all to my wife, Sarah Pearce, and my daughters, Celeste and Iris Kreilkamp, for support and for keeping me company throughout the process. And I'd be remiss, finally, not to thank the nonhuman creatures of our household: cats Pot Luck and Daisy, dog Felix, and chickens Princess Catkin (RIP: hawk), Barney (RIP: natural causes), Lemon Soufflé, Pepper, and Sunny.

J. Miller —

Animals, Literature
& the Victorians

JVC 21, 1,
2016

CHAPTER ONE

1. On the role played by animals in Victorian children's literature, see Tess Cosslett's *Talking Animals in British Children's Fiction, 1786–1914* and Jessica Straley's
Evolution and Imagination in Victorian Children's Literature. Straley observes that
her "analysis turns to fanciful children's books that foreground their very literariness
by inviting readers to engage with their most exaggerated unrealistic, nonsensical, and
intrinsically rhetorical elements" (23).

2. On pets as minor, see Monica Flegel, who says about her book, *Pets and Domesticity in Victorian Literature and Culture*, "A study such as this is necessarily idiosyncratic in its choice of texts to discuss, as pets so often occupy the margins of both text
and culture. . . . I am certainly committed to an exploration of what are usually referred
to as 'minor characters'" (11). I encountered Flegel's book as I was completing my own;
our arguments and readings occasionally overlap.

3. See also Nancy Armstrong, who argues that "not all fictional characters could
become the protagonists of a novel. In order to qualify, a character had to harbor an
acute dissatisfaction with his or her assigned position in the social world and feel com-
pelled to find a better one" (4).

4. Marianne DeKoven also poses the question in this form in her introduction to
the 2009 *PMLA* forum on animal studies.

5. The bibliography for work on the figure of the animal in philosophy and theory
expands continually. Jacques Derrida's work and Cary Wolfe's *Animal Rites: American
Culture, the Discourse of Species, and Posthumanist Theory*, as well as his edited col-
lection *Zoontologies: The Question of the Animal*, offered my first introduction to this
area of scholarship; since then, in addition to Wolfe's work, I benefited especially from
Kelly Oliver's *Animal Lessons: How They Teach Us to Be Human*, Matthew Calarco's
Zoographies: The Question of the Animal from Heidegger to Derrida, and Kari Weil's
Thinking Animals: Why Animal Studies Now?

6. Anthropologist Jonathan Z. Smith argues that "sacrifice is an exaggeration of domestication, a meditation on one cultural practice by means of another" ("Domestica-

tion" 200). In domestication, Smith argues, human beings transform and alter animals for human purposes; sacrifice is an intensification of this process.

7. On this, see Jane Bennett's point that "[t]oo often the philosóphical critique of anthropomorphism is bound up with a hubristic demand that only humans and God can bear any trace of creative agency" (*Vibrant* 120).

8. See, e.g., the recent collection *The Nonhuman Turn*, edited by Richard Grusin, or Wolfe, *What Is Posthumanism?*

9. I could be accused of occasionally conflating, in this book, the categories of animal and pet. One justification for this might be that any animal that is individuated and recognized in a novel is thereby domesticated, brought into the realm of the human and so granted a status somewhat resembling that of a pet. That most animals in Victorian culture were not granted such a status is, however, worth emphasizing.

10. Alex Woloch, in his *The One vs. the Many*, devotes a chapter (177–243) to the minor characters of *Great Expectations* but does not consider the novel's references to animals.

11. See Teresa Mangum on how and why dogs in Victorian culture "came so readily to be associated with late life, the passage of time, and death itself" ("Dog Years" 39).

12. See Michael Parrish Lee for an interesting argument about the symbolic roles of meat in H. G. Wells's work. Lee observes that "[t]he nineteenth-century novel is stuffed with meat—recall Catherine's refusal to eat her goose after Heathcliff's flogging in *Wuthering Heights* (1847), Pip's theft of pork pie for Magwitch in *Great Expectations* (1860–61), or Fred and Rosamond Vincy's quarrel over a grilled bone in *Middlemarch* (1871–72)—and if the subject has been largely passed over by critics in the field, we might attribute this neglect or resistance at least in part to the novel's own apparent tendency to separate bodily appetite from the more 'refined' pursuits of knowledge and human understanding that would seem to inhere in the act of reading" (249).

13. See, for example, Claude Lévi-Strauss: "Let us consider another case, that of cattle, the social position of which is metonymical (they form part of our technical and economic system) but different from that of dogs in that cattle are more overtly treated as 'objects' and dogs as 'subjects' (this is suggested, first, by the collective names we use to designate the former and, secondly, by the taboo on the eating of dogs in our culture)" (205).

14. See Flegel 56–95 on the Victorian emergence of the "crazy cat lady" trope.

15. See Colleen Glenney Boggs for a consideration of the relevance of animals to biopolitics in American literature. She argues that "[a]nimals are integral in two ways to a full understanding of biopolitics" (11)—both because the state regulates animal bodies as well as human ones and because biopolitics works crucially through policing the human-animal distinction.

16. Dominick LaCapra criticizes Agamben's conception of the "anthropological machine" as excessively "hyperbolic," while offering his own model of a comparable dynamic: "The putative decisive criterion" dividing humans and animals "often if not typically rests on a scapegoat mechanism whereby traits causing anxiety in humans are gathered up, expelled, and projected exclusively onto other animals" (155); "one might propose that the human is an animal that generates endless invidious distinctions, especially in the anxiety-ridden, self-serving quest to distinguish itself from

other animals" (158). Virginia Richter also draws on Agamben to define what she calls an "anthropological anxiety" that defines the human via "an attempt to separate the *anthropos* from the non-human, the animal, the mechanical" (8). Mario Ortiz Robles offers a useful discussion of what Agamben's concept brings to animal studies (14–15 and 146–47).

17. For a good argument about the ambivalent Victorian response to the claim of animal ancestry for human beings, see Straley's chapter "Amphibious Tendencies: Charles Kingsley, Herbert Spencer, and Evolutionary Education" (57–85). Also relevant is Cannon Schmitt's argument about Darwin's "invention" of a new kind of human subject (3).

18. See Kreilkamp, "The Ass Got a Verdict." Also see Susan Hamilton, "On the Cruelty to Animals Act," as well as Hilda Kean's book-length history of British animal-welfare policies, *Animal Rights: Political and Social Change in Britain since 1800*. In her essay "Animals and Ideology," Kathleen Kete considers "the role the animal/human divide plays in building a sense of social identity in modernizing Europe, in charting a shifting line between an 'us' and a 'them,' a line which unexpectedly runs through the Puritan, bourgeois, feminist, nationalist, and even Nazi revolutions" (20).

19. In a general discussion of the place of animals within contemporary cultural production, Susan McHugh comments—probably not thinking specifically of Eliot's squirrel!—that "[a]lthough no one to date seriously argues that squirrels write poetry, animals are being reconceptualized as key players in all sorts of cultural productions" (10).

20. On the problem of the limits of our sympathy for nonhumans and where to erect them, see Barbara Herrnstein Smith: "When the issue is our responsibility to others, questions about limits are inevitably complicated by questions about sorts, and the relation between them broaches a domain we might call ethical taxonomy. Should we, for example, have care for dogs, cats, cows, and horses but not birds, snakes, or butterflies? For leopards and walruses but not lobsters or oysters? For all these, but not wasps, ticks, or lice? Or for these, too, but not microbes or viruses?" (2). On the question of the proper limits of our love for animals and the problem of when such love becomes erotic, see McHugh on the "queer spectrum of interspecies intimacies" (117).

21. Also see Susan Fraiman's critique of what she characterizes as a pervasive masculinism and even "pussy panic" in not only Deleuze and Guattari but also much of the poststructuralist-inspired animal studies scholarship of the past decade or so (91). She offers particular attention to the work of Cary Wolfe: "The substitution of Derrida for [Carol] Adams, post-structuralism for ecofeminism is a move shaping *Animal Rites* as a whole and that, in general, subtends Wolfe's posthumanist approach to animal studies" (103).

22. As Flegel suggests, Dora uses Jip "to express her feelings" (34). Compare also the author of the 1881 article "Dogs of Literature," who concludes by declaring, "My aim has been to re-awake the associations, not of dog and hero, dog and gun, dog and horse, or dog and dog lover generally, but of dog and pen" (500).

CHAPTER TWO

1. On sovereignty and power over animals, see also Tobias Menely, especially his reading of Alexander Pope's "Windsor-Forest": "The hunt reenacts the sovereign's origi-

nal activity of founding the city by slaughtering wild beasts, of deciding, in essence, who is human and who is animal" (96).

2. On the animals of *Agnes Grey* and *The Tenant of Wildfell Hall*, see also Flegel 23–27.

3. Keridiana W. Chez makes a comparable claim: "Those who were identified as humane would feel appropriately sympathetic at the sight of another's suffering and appalled by its intentional infliction on a helpless being; the inhumane, in contrast, exhibited a diminished capacity to feel certain feelings" (7).

4. On the relation between the modern animal-rights or animal-liberation movement, often seen as finding its voice with the 1975 publication of Peter Singer's *Animal Liberation*, and the nineteenth-century antivivisection and anticruelty movements, Coral Lansbury writes that "the modern animal liberation movement, characterized by the works of Stephen Clark, Peter Singer, Tom Regan, and Mary Midgeley, . . . bears only occasional reference to the antivivisection movement of the nineteenth century. . . . The debate between Singer and Regan over the moral status of animals would have bemused the Victorians" (xi).

5. For a book-length history of vegetarianism in Britain, see Gregory.

6. On Hall's 1847 publications in *The Lancet* and their critics, see Manuel 97–100.

7. Harriet Ritvo writes that "at the beginning of the nineteenth century the English would have been surprised to hear themselves praised for special kindness to animals. . . . [But] as early as the 1830s, despite the circumambient evidence to the contrary, the English humane movement had begun to claim kindness to animals as a native trait and to associate cruelty to animals with foreigners, especially those from southern, Catholic countries" (*Animal* 125–27). Eighteenth-century sensibility discourse also contained a strong animal-sympathy emphasis, and the redefinition of Englishness as linked to kindness to animals does not begin punctually in the first decades of the nineteenth century. It does seem, however, that a noticeable shift occurs by the 1820s and 1830s in the mainstreaming of animal sympathy as a key component of national character. See Menely on the Romantic-era development of a discourse of sensibility that includes animals.

8. Ritvo and other historians emphasize the important distinctions between RSPCA narratives of the suffering of animals—usually dogs, cats, and horses abused in the streets—and the antivivisectionist denunciations of medical experiments. The latter genre was much less fully developed until the 1870s, since the early- and midcentury RSPCA made an implicit tactical decision to allow the suffering of animals at the hands of middle-class scientists. For my purposes, however, I am considering both types of narratives as part of a single larger genre of anticruelty discourse.

9. Keith Thomas writes, "As the factories multiplied, the nostalgia of the town-dweller was reflected in his little bit of garden, his pets, his holidays in Scotland or the Lake District" (14).

10. It should be noted, however, that Gompertz himself did not limit the category of protected animals. He went so far as to suggest that drinking milk should be avoided and that destroying tiny animals when drinking water was not an entirely innocent activity. Gompertz represents an early, radical road not taken for the English animal-

rights movement. He was eventually purged as head of the RSPCA and replaced by a less radical leader. See Turner 39.

11. On Victorians' mourning practices for their pets, Teresa Mangum writes, "Pet mourning practices may have encouraged the avoidance of responsibility toward 'animals' as a whole, but the obvious fact of many Victorians' attachment to pets and grief at their loss ought to be acknowledged" ("Animal Angst" 19).

12. An English doctor recollected attending lectures delivered in Paris by the French physiologist François Magendie: "In 1837 I attended . . . the class of Magendie. . . . The whole scene was revolting, not the cruelty only, but the 'tiger-monkey' spirit visible in the demoralized students. We left in disgust, and felt thankful such scenes would not be tolerated in England by public opinion" (qtd. in French 20). A small number of English scientists did, however, support limited forms of animal experimentation. Marshall Hall, in both 1831 and 1847, published controversial essays in England in which he "carefully outlined the circumstances and conditions under which he regarded experiments upon living animals to be justified" (21). On vivisection and animal experimentation in the period, see also White.

13. After publishing the article on which this chapter is based, I discovered an earlier essay I had initially missed that addresses comparable issues: Lisa Surridge, "Animals and Violence in *Wuthering Heights*." As she observes, "Numerous critics have identified Wuthering Heights and Thrushcross Grange with conflicting patterns of inheritance, labour, and architecture. But related to these structures of ownership and property is the control of working and pet animals" (166). Barbara Munson Goff asserts that "virtually all critics of *Wuthering Heights* have addressed themselves to the rhetoric of animality in the novel" (479), a claim that does not hold true for criticism published since the emergence of postcolonial theory shifted attention toward Brontë's racial and ethnic exoticization of Heathcliff. She adds that few critics have been willing to "grant animality more than a metaphorical status." Goff argues that "studying Brontë's work in the context of contemporary natural science confirms what had formerly been only an intuitive response to *Wuthering Heights*: that the novel is a hypothetical experiment in the breeding of human beings, conducted to suggest how the breed has been corrupted from its 'native state'" (480). Her focus on breeding and cultivation points her essay in a different direction than my own concern with animal suffering and cruelty. Goff also cites J. Hillis Miller's chapter on Brontë in which he argues that "the animal imagery used throughout *Wuthering Heights* is one of the chief ways in which the spiritual strength of the characters is measured" (167) and that "the characters in *Wuthering Heights* have *returned* to an animal state" (168). Although I am focusing on Brontë's depiction of Heathcliff as animallike, Miller points out that other characters are also linked to creatures: "Edgar Linton is a 'sucking leveret,' and Linton Heathcliff is a 'puling chicken.' Such figures are more than simple metaphors. They tell us that man in *Wuthering Heights* . . . is part of nature, and no different from other animals" (167).

14. Henry S. Salt addresses this problem in an 1890 late-Victorian text that Singer describes as "the best of the eighteenth- and nineteenth-century works on the rights of animals" (Salt viii) and a major influence on Gandhi and therefore on the history of

twentieth-century nonviolence and postcolonial politics: "Even the term 'animals,' as applied to the lower races, is incorrect, and not wholly unobjectionable, since it ignores the fact that *man* is an animal no less than they. My only excuse for using it in this volume is that there is absolutely no other brief term available" (18–19).

15. In *Animals' Rights*, Salt states: "It may be doubted, indeed, whether the condition of the household 'pet' is, in the long run, more enviable than that of the 'beast of burden.' Pets, like kings' favorites, are usually the recipients of an abundance of sentimental affection but of little real kindness; so much easier is it to give temporary caresses than substantial justice. . . . The injustice done to the pampered lap-dog is as conspicuous, in its way, as that done to the overworked horse" (42–43).

16. Marc Shell writes that "pethood derives its power from its ability to let pet owners experience a relationship ever-present in political ideology—that between the distinction of those beings who are our (familial) kin from those who are not, on the one hand, and the distinction of those beings who are our (human) kind from those who are not, on the other" (148).

17. See also Lucy Bending on pain, vivisection, and anesthesia in Victorian literature and culture. Bending, within a fuller analysis of Wilkie Collins's 1883 antivivisection novel *Heart and Science*, comments that "Emily Brontë, writing *Wuthering Heights* in 1847, at the same time as vivisection was coming very much to the fore in French medical schools, makes the links between cruelty, vivisection, and savagery very clear in her portrayal of Heathcliff" (128). Rachel Ablow observes that Victorian discussions of vivisection reveal "the fantasy that pain has the power to impel truth" (137).

18. Also see Richard Menke on the use of ether, chloroform, and chloral hydrate in 1840s experimental medicine (620).

19. See Jonathan Lamb for a fascinating analysis of the problem of cross-species sympathy. Lamb offers a valuable overview of the British philosophical tradition of considering the problem of sympathy in the work of Locke, Hume, and Smith, and concludes darkly that sympathy for animals—and animal sympathy for humans—may be little more than a comforting but dangerous illusion: "only by means of the grossest delusion is it possible to make such sentimental equations between the lives of humans and animals" (166).

20. Such scenes also place *Wuthering Heights* in the tradition established by eighteenth-century sensibility discourse. "When sensibility became central to ethical and all other psychological aspects of human nature," Ann Jessie Van Sant argues in regard to eighteenth-century novels of sensibility, "investigative and rhetorical or dramatic methods overlapped, inviting observers to 'read' scenes of suffering with sympathetic identification and objective scrutiny . . . the provocation of pain works both to create pity and to invite curiosity" (59).

21. Heathcliff's animalistic howl resembles that uttered by a vivisector in Marie-Espérance von Schwartz's 1887 German novella *Gemma or Virtue and Vice*. As he dies of madness, von Schwartz's villain hallucinates all the animals he has tortured "coming at me in mobs, in legions of all kinds, all breeds, those accursed beasts!" Finally, "thus ranting, he collapsed and uttered a howl that would have frightened and terrified even the wild beasts in the desert" (qtd. in Sternberger 68). The howl is at once the sig-

nature of the tortured animal and the nonlinguistic speech uttered by the inhuman torturer. (Sternberger notes that von Schwartz's book was explicitly identified as inspired
by Harriet Beecher Stowe's *Uncle Tom's Cabin* [1852], suggesting how antivivisectionism defined itself as a movement in reference to the earlier success of abolitionism.)

22. See Menke for analysis of George Eliot's fiction alongside George Lewes's writings on physiology, experimentation, and vivisection. Menke argues that as "Lewes
devotes his physiological research to studying the nerves and the mind, and Eliot represents the representation of moment-to-moment thought in her late fiction, their shared
task becomes the vivisection of consciousness" (619). Menke provides a very rich analysis of the 1870s discourse of vivisection and of the location of Eliot's fiction within it.

CHAPTER THREE

1. Trey Philpotts discusses this article and other Dickens writings on Smithfield
Market in "Mad Bulls and Dead Meat: Smithfield Market as Reality and Symbol": "the
abuse of bulls at Smithfield, which causes them to run amuck, injuring themselves and
others, . . . in *Bleak House* prefigures a larger concern with the abuse of human beings,
an abuse with its own ramifying effects, including, in the case of Jo, the smallpox he
contracts and passes to Esther Summerson" (33). Philpotts argues that Smithfield is for
Dickens a "liminal" as well as an "unrestrained and premodern" place (25).

2. See Anna Henchman on tallow candles, and other objects, in *Bleak House* as
"manufactured objects or commodities that reflect too closely the [animal] bodies from
which they originate."

3. For a somewhat different consideration of the instability of human/nonhuman
divisions in Dickens, see Tamara Ketabgian's analysis of the figure of the "animal machine" in *Hard Times* (47–70).

4. Colin Dayan has suggested that animals and slaves were each defined in relation
to one another in English law within the legal category of "chattel" (125).

5. For another argument about the role of animals in a Dickens novel, Mary Rosner
comments on the transformations that occur "as characters move back and forth between the civilized and uncivilized, the human and the bestial" in *Martin Chuzzlewit*:
"The imagery in this novel," she argues, "invites readers to recognize the animals in
man" (136).

6. On the question of how and whether it makes sense to understand animal communication as a kind of language or speech, see Hearne. Hearne's remarkable book
returns frequently, if always in passing, to Dickens and his work: see 25, 31, 60, 66, 69,
246, 262.

7. John Berger's famous essay "Why Look at Animals?" is dedicated to an analysis
of the meaning of the gaze that occurs between a human being and an animal in contemporary Western culture.

8. Peter Brooks discusses "the problem of identity, self-consciousness, naming, and
language" in *Great Expectations* (116–17).

9. On animals as the subject of personification, see especially Heather Keenleyside:
"Personification . . . is a figure that registers the sort of quasi-natural, quasi-figurative
creatures that all animate beings are" (7).

10. See Woloch on the minor character's tendency to appear and disappear abruptly: an unnamed minor character in Dickens's *The Pickwick Papers*, Woloch argues, possesses a singularity that is "conditioned by his sudden appearance and quick exit from the novel" (136).

11. Dickens's comparison of Magwitch while eating to a dog resembles this description of Mr. Barkis in *David Copperfield*: "I offered him a cake as a mark of attention, which he ate at one gulp, exactly like an elephant, and which made no more impression on his big face that it would have done on an elephant's" (114). The key difference would seem to lie in the distinction between the elephant's presumed impassivity and the dog's furtive, shamed hunger. Another analogy would be Jo in *Bleak House*, who "begins to gulp the coffee, and to gnaw the bread and butter; looking anxiously about him in all directions as he eats and drinks, like a scared animal" (719). As Allen Woodcourt tries to find a place for Jo, he considers, "It surely is a strange fact . . . that in the heart of a civilised world this creature in human form should be more difficult to dispose of than an unowned dog" (719). Dickens adds, "But it is none the less a fact because of its strangeness, and the difficulty remains."

12. See also Singer for an assessment and a rejection of the capacity for reciprocity as a valid criterion for the determination of which creatures deserve ethical stature ("Animal Liberation at Thirty" 24).

13. Dickens's implication that human beings might be grouped with animals as fellow "creatures" may well have been influenced by Darwin's *On the Origin of Species*, published a year before the first serial of *Great Expectations*. Gillian Beer writes that the effect of Darwin's work was to "range man alongside all other forms of life. The multi-vocal nature of metaphor allows . . . [Darwin] to express, without insisting on, kinship" (56). Beer, in turn, suggests that Darwin may have been "freed from some of the difficulties he experienced in expressing the nature of man to the rest of the natural order by his reading of Dickens, whose style insists on the recalcitrance of objects. . . . The theme of hidden yet all-pervasive kinship is one which their narratives share" (56). See also Morgentaler.

14. My thanks to Deborah Morse for pointing out to me the significance of this scene taking place on Christmas day.

15. On Pip's hunger and relation to food, see Watt.

16. The treatment with which Orlick threatens Pip, that of being killed and buried in an unmarked grave, carries a class-based implication as well, since to be buried without proper recognition in a pauper's grave was a much-feared fate in Victorian Britain. I am emphasizing a less-often recognized aspect of Orlick's threat, one relating not to the category of class so much as species, although the two cannot be entirely disentangled here; Orlick threatens to both animalize and pauperize Pip.

17. A dog possessing subjectivity, dignity, and a narrative voice is not, of course, in fact an impossibility within the history of the novel. Following the massive success of Anna Sewell's 1877 *Black Beauty*, other authors inspired by the anticruelty movement devised animal protagonists. Margaret Marshall Saunders's 1893 *Beautiful Joe*, the fictional autobiography of a dog whose former master had cut off its ears and tail, can, for example, be read as a kind of answer to Pip's fears. The narrative in effect remem-

bers and re-members a creature who had been, if not literally dismembered, certainly mutilated and abused.

CHAPTER FOUR

1. George Levine suggests that the "passive wait[ing]" of this swallower might be analogous to what Eliot describes in a different context as the "patient watching" of a scientific investigator, suggesting in turn an analogy between the patient swallower and the patient researcher who studies or captures the swallower (*Dying to Know* 7).

2. A classic statement on *Middlemarch*'s relation to contemporary science, particularly the work of Darwin, may be found in Beer 139–68. On the novel in relation to medicine and physiology, see Tambling, "*Middlemarch*," and Rothfield, *Vital Signs*.

3. I was led to this passage by Donna Haraway's discussion in *When Species Meet* (31).

4. Amy King describes the way Philip Henry Gosse was "particularly stirred by objects, such as zoophytes, whose status between animate and inanimate is indeterminate. . . . [I]n the tide pools Gosse finds creatures that are at 'the very confines' of the 'vital world'" (160–61).

5. See Shuttleworth. Shuttleworth cites Lewes's *The Foundation of a Creed*: "The structure of *Middlemarch* conforms to Lewes' definition of organic life: 'The part exists only as part of a whole; the whole exists only as a whole of its parts'" (147). The relation of the parts of this novel to a putative whole or wholes has, of course, been an abiding preoccupation of critics. See, for one example, Suzanne Graver discussing J. Hillis Miller: "At the same time, metaphors such as these, as Miller observes, are synecdoches. Like so much else in *Middlemarch*, they are parts that represent wholes, and they are also themselves wholes that represent smaller parts" (203).

6. Joanna Bourke writes, "Nineteenth-century matrimonial law . . . allowed for significant levels of injury. The marital bed proved to be the site of much terror" (421).

7. As Teresa Mangum suggested to me, *age* seems critical here. Victorian evolutionary biologists were concerned about the destructive effects of older males on a species when they reproduced. Being "absorbed" into an elderly man would have had a different valence than absorption into a virile, young male still capable of reproduction.

8. On the logic of the parasite in Eliot's and Lewes's work, Jeannette Samyn makes some points analogous to my own although focused on the relationship between Eliot's *The Mill on the Floss* and Lewes's *Sea-Side Studies*.

9. Flegel writes interestingly about Sir James's puppy in *Pets and Domesticity*: "Though voiceless and seemingly disposable, the dog occupies a highly complicated role in this exchange, with the Maltese representing both weak and spoiled femininity *and* man as pet, as someone who requires a woman to spoil him and put his interests first" (29).

10. Gwendolyn in George Eliot's *Daniel Deronda* is compared to an "imprisoned dumb creature"; the same paragraph shows her sharing some of this same murderous instinct: e.g., "If that idea which was maddening her had been a living thing, she would have wanted to throttle it without waiting to foresee what would come of the act" (590).

11. D. A. Miller comments that "it is no accident that the four protagonists in the community (Lydgate, Bulstrode, Dorothea, and Ladislaw) are made to leave town at the end of the novel: ritual sacrifices to the recovery of social routine. . . . The community levels their differences by subjecting them to the same fate of social exclusion" (87).

12. See Carol Christ on Eliot's broad interest in the urge to murder and its repression or guilty disavowal. One clear instance of this dynamic would be Gwendolyn's complex and guilty reaction to the death by drowning of her husband, Grandcourt, whom she has contemplated murdering. Gwendolyn's passive "failure to save" Grandcourt can be compared in some respects to Bulstrode's passive murder of Raffles.

13. Christ observes of this passage that "we can see that for Eliot sickness functions much as death to remove both the nurse and the patient from the possibility of aggressive confrontation" (134).

14. Eric Santner writes that the creaturely "names the threshold where life becomes a matter of politics and politics comes to inform the very matter and materiality of life" (12).

15. I am influenced in my reading here by Derrida's account of sovereignty as characterized by images of "devourment and voracity. . . . It's about mouth, teeth, tongue, and the violent rush to bite, engulf, swallow the other, to take the other into oneself too, to kill it or mourn it." (*Beast* 1: 47).

CHAPTER FIVE

1. For a discussion of Hardy's involvement with animal-rights and animal protection politics (and an argument of their implications for *Jude the Obscure*), see Morrison.

2. On pets and/as children in Victorian culture, see Flegel: "Continually confirming the purpose of the middle-class home, the domestic pet—and the dog in particular—could prove to be more than a child surrogate: a continually replaceable, and therefore seemingly permanent, child who would never grow up" (10).

3. In a comparable argument, Richard Kerridge writes that Hardy's "abundant relativity shows nature writers an alternative to the genre's most menacing traditions: Nietzschean admiration of nature's amoral power and conservative nostalgia for mythical feudal harmonies. Against these, Hardy offers the endless generation of meaning as the vivid life of a place, produced by its human, animal, and plant life" (138). Elisha Cohn offers the most compelling argument to date regarding Hardy's engagement with animal life and animality. She argues that in his novels he offers two different models for imagining animals and for understanding our obligation to them. In what she describes as a discourse of "lyrical becoming" (169), animals are allied with a broader natural world in a rapturous "becoming-animal" that offers a transcendence of individualized subjectivity. In a contrasting "ethical" (rather than "lyrical") discourse, animals become figured as passive "creatures"; in this "ethical" discourse, which Cohn argues takes over Hardy's work with *Jude* (but begins to appear in *Tess*), "wild animals . . . no longer embody an alternative to entrapment in social convention; instead, animal suffering is a symptom of its pervasive dominance" (176).

4. Romantic poetry, rather than the novel, remains the most obvious object for an ecological or ecocritical approach to literary analysis. For example, Dominic Head

argues that for eco-critics "there are grounds for pessimism about the dominance of the novel in twentieth-century literature, since this is a mode of discourse which speaks to an increasingly urbanized population whose concerns appear to have no immediate connection with the non-human environment" (237).

5. In *On Creaturely Life*, Santner writes of W. G. Sebald that "his entire oeuvre could be seen as the construction of *an archive of creaturely life*" (xii); he defines creaturely life as "the life utterly exposed, utterly abandoned to the state of exception" (180).

6. In *Raw Material: Producing Pathology in Victorian Culture*, Erin O'Connor has demonstrated how the development of artificial limbs in the nineteenth century proved an occasion for reflections on subjectivity and the definition of the human. Herbert Sussman and Gerhard Joseph have used Charles Dickens's friendship and correspondence with Charles Babbage to argue for understanding his uncanny reversals of things and people in a newly "protocyborgian" context. In *The Lives of Machines*, Ketabgian has profitably rethought Victorian industrial discourse as thoroughly enmeshed in a prosthetic logic according to which the mechanical is understood to be intertwined at many levels with the organic and the human (as well as the animal). Most recently, Christie Peterson has examined Charlotte Tonna's 1841 *Helen Fleetwood* in relation to "animals' complex role in negotiating the relationship between humans and technology" (109). Much of this work draws either directly or indirectly on Karl Marx's analysis of the ways industrial technology within capitalism displaces and subjects the human in a kind of destructive maximization of that technology's prosthetic potential. On this topic, see Scarry, *The Body in Pain* 251–55.

7. Chez, citing my work, argues that "[a]s prosthetic supplement, a living instrument attached to the human for self-enhancement, the dog could then provide or magnify an essential characteristic of humanity, the ability to feel or connect" (3).

8. Howard Babb observes of Fanny's dog that "[t]he description of the dog is consciously generalized, separating him from any particular breed and elevating him to something approaching a force of nature" (378).

9. Raymond Williams's *The Country and the City* is a classic reference point for such discussions of Hardy's pastoralism. Michael Squires writes that Hardy "wrote a novel about sheep and shepherds, the traditional pastoral subject; but he also wrote a novel at least partly in the traditional manner, by portraying rural life nostalgically and by stressing its beauty rather than its coarseness. The numerous pastoral scenes weave a solidly rural texture that has the smell of hay and the feel of fleece, and Hardy's knowledge of the agricultural world expresses itself in richly connotative prose that frequently crystallizes into poetry. Reminiscent and idealized, the result is a charming interpretive account of rural society. Yet the falsification and artificiality of traditional pastoral have been rigorously excluded from Hardy's account. In *Far from the Madding Crowd* (1874) there is no perpetual summer, no frolicking sheep, no piping shepherds who live without care. Instead, there are many realistic details of actual rural life: sheep die, storms threaten, shepherds have misfortunes both 'amorous and pastoral,' peasants work, and unhappiness and despair are spattered over the second half of the story" (299). Robert Langbaum has more recently argued that in Hardy's mature fiction he "seriously modifies" (247) and "always exceeds the limits of" pastoral (249).

10. I am reading *pity* for Hardy as implying a broader sense of sympathetic under-

standing than we usually associate with the term. On some of the limitations of pity as an affective stance toward animals, Richard Nash writes, "Pity, valuable as it is, always runs the risk of mere self-indulgence, of becoming the obverse reflection of the alienated Cartesian self" (59); within the discourse of pity, "the perspective of philosophic compassion is allowed to assert a primacy over the possibilities of a cross-species partnership that contribute[s] to primal, animal pleasures" (65).

11. Elaine Scarry writes, "The human creature is for him not now and then but habitually embodied: it has at every moment a physical circumference and boundary. Thus it is, in its work and its play, in the midst of great yearning and in the moment of great fatigue, forever rubbing up against and leaving traces of itself (its blood) on the world, as the world is forever rubbing up against and leaving traces of itself (its paint) on the human creature" ("Work and the Body" 90).

12. Gabriel's sensitive listening to his sheep recalls the shepherds in James Thomson's *The Seasons* who, as Menely argues in *The Animal Claim*, guide the sheep via attention to their cries: "The proper tending of animals requires the shepherd and husbandman to attend to their voices" (113). The good shepherd must be attentive to "a semiosphere that extends beyond the human" (122).

13. Hardy's allusion here to these odd sea creatures recalls the passage in *The Return of the Native* when Mrs. Yeobright observes, in a "nearly dried pool," "the maggoty shapes of innumerable obscure creatures . . . indistinctly seen, heaving and wallowing with enjoyment" (278). Hardy describes these as living in "a spot where independent worlds of ephemerons were passing their time in mad carousal." He gives us a brief glimpse into the teeming, "independent world" of "ephemerons" whose ephemerality, from the human point of view, can in no way exhaust their own meaning or the joy they experience in their own existence. On seaside studies, see Smith, *Darwin*, and King, "Reorienting." For a discussion, focused on Tennyson's "The Kraken," of the Victorian fascination with "polypi" and other "extremely basic organisms," see Maxwell 11.

14. See Bruce Johnson's classic essay on Hardy's representation of "the evolutionary oneness of all life" in *Tess*: Tess's "sympathy for animals," Johnson writes, "is a sign of the great and extremely subtle Darwinian bias in Hardy's mind when he created her" (276). See also Caroline Sumpter's argument about Hardy's engagement with contemporary debates about the evolutionary function of sympathy in "On Suffering and Sympathy." See Susan Lanzoni's examination of late-century debates about sympathy "by scholars in evolutionary and developmental psychology, ethics, and aesthetics" in the British journal *Mind* (267).

15. Derrida also discusses the tension between individualized creature and the pack, flock, or herd: "The 'rogue,' be it to do with elephant, tiger, lion, or hippopotamus (and more generally carnivorous animals), is the individual who does not even respect the laws of the animal community, of the pack, the horde, of its own kind" (*Beast* 1: 19).

16. Langbaum writes that in both *Far from the Madding Crowd* and *The Return of the Native* "characters appear for the first time as distant shapes on the heath, mysterious archetypes, taking on individualizing lineaments as they approach the observer" (245).

17. This sentence receives special attention from both Johnson (264) and Scarry ("On Vivacity" 10).

18. Interestingly, Charlotte Brontë also alludes to this parable in *Jane Eyre* when Rochester declares to Jane, "If the man who had but one little ewe lamb that was dear to him as a daughter, that ate of his bread and drank of his cup, and lay in his bosom, had by some mistake slaughtered it at the shambles, he would not have rued his bloody blunder more than I now rue mine" (314).

CHAPTER SIX

1. Claus Emmeche writes, "Under the influence of a new, realistic tendency in semiotics, inspired by among others the American philosopher Charles Sanders Peirce, we now view sign phenomena as occurring everywhere in nature, including those domains where humans have never set foot. This new field, called biosemiotics, concerns itself with signs in biological systems, ranging from communication among animals to the individual cell's genetic code as a sign system of its own" (*Garden* 126).

2. I'm thinking here, for example, of Roosth; also see Kawade.

3. Sarah Winter writes, "Darwin's theory of expression falls into place within Saussure's disciplinary chronology . . . by breaking with comparative philology's historical methods precisely in order to link animal and human cognition and communication as related forms within a synchronic biosemiotics of expression. By biosemiotics I mean not only a theory that reads biological systems in semiotic terms but also one that shows how such systems function at all levels through signaling and thus through producing nonlinguistic biological signs" (130); "Darwin imagined that language emerged gradually from expressions that were already semiotic in a biological sense, and that therefore already displayed evolutionary—what I am calling Darwinian—arbitrariness" (144).

4. Darwin writes in an 1838 notebook, "Lyell in his Principles talks of it as wonderful that Elephants understand contracts.—but W. Fox's dog that shut the door evidently did" (128); see his Notebook M: Metaphysics on Morals and Speculations on Expression.

5. Eduardo Kohn contrasts Peirce to Saussure as representing a path not fully taken for semiotic thinking, arguing that for Saussure "human language is the paragon and model for all sign systems," whereas "Peirce's definition of a sign, by contrast, is much more agonistic about what signs are and what kinds of beings use them; for him . . . not all the beings who use [signs] . . . are human" (29).

6. As Cosslett observes in *Talking Animals*, "It is never clear to whom Black Beauty is talking, and it is the unspecificity of the narratee that allows the reader to slide in and out of horse-consciousness" (69). Animal narrators in books like *Black Beauty* and its many nineteenth-century imitators "have the double authority of the affective genuineness of the speechless, and the rational speech of the autobiographer to the reader" (82).

7. Thomas Sebeok argues, "In one of his most memorable examples, Peirce recalls that the footprint Robinson Crusoe found in the sand was an index to him of some creature. In like fashion, a vast map of such records is printed overnight by animals of

all sorts, all over the countryside, leaving traces and tracks 'of immense variety, often of wonderful clarity'" (32).

8. In the same collection, Umberto Eco also takes Zadig as a forerunner of modern semiotics in his "Horns, Hooves, Insteps: Some Hypotheses on Three Types of Abduction."

9. See Menely's arguments regarding the "animal claim" articulated in the cries and vocalizations of animals; he argues in a discussion of a character's mourning of a wounded stag in *As You Like It*, for instance, that "[m]elancholy . . . may reflect the inadequacy of plaintive address or the impossibility of translation" (91) (i.e., of translation from animal cry to human language). Menely's arguments about animal vocalizations and/as signification—of an eighteenth-century literary tradition that understood the natural world to be "charged with semiotic meaning" (110)—are particularly relevant to this chapter. Alice A. Kuzniar also makes melancholy central to her arguments about human-animal relations in *Melancholia's Dog*.

10. On this, see Scarry, "Work and the Body."

CHAPTER SEVEN

1. This critic was presumably Andrew Lang, who wrote/complained that Schreiner wrote about "people . . . always tackling religious problems, or falling in love on new and heterodox lines, instead of shooting deer, and finding diamonds, or hunting up the archaeological remains of the Transvaal" (qtd. in Gilbert and Gubar 52). Gilbert and Gubar discuss Lang's criticisms in relation to Schreiner's preface.

2. A lion makes an interesting appearance, as a kind of representational temptation to exaggeration, in George Eliot's famous discussion of the aims of realism in chapter 17 of *Adam Bede*: "The pencil is conscious of a delightful facility in drawing a griffin—the longer the claws, and the larger the wings, the better; but that marvellous facility which we mistook for genius is apt to forsake us when we want to draw a real unexaggerated lion" (160).

3. Jed Esty does point out that Waldo "models his subjectivity on deep and inhuman forms of zoological, geographical, and metaphysical time" and briefly discusses his dissection of ducks and lambs but does not otherwise stress Waldo's link to nonhuman life (417–18).

4. Consider, too, Kohn's assertion that "the world beyond the human is not a meaningless one made meaningful by humans. Rather, meanings . . . emerge in a world of living thoughts beyond the human in ways that are not fully exhausted by our all-too-human attempts to define and control these" (73).

5. Also see LaCapra's discussion, in the context of a consideration of human-animal relations, of the possibility of an ethics associated with "a form of acknowledged or even affirmed vulnerability that does not exclude agency" (186).

6. See Oliver for a discussion of Derrida's "hyperbolic ethics," "motivated by concepts like the gift, hospitality, forgiveness, and democracy, concepts whose meaning and value are infinitely deferred to some (im)possible future" (135). In an interview with Elisabeth Roudinesco, Derrida usefully clarifies the difference between a "pure and unconditional hospitality" on the one hand and any practical "political or juridical con-

cept" on the other; in actual political life, Derrida explains, "it is indeed necessary to limit and to condition hospitality" (*For What Tomorrow* 59). In regard to human-animal relations, he suggests, a similar distinction applies: one must maintain an ideal of "unconditional hospitality" or nonviolence to nonhuman animals even as "according to the historical situation, it is necessary to invent the least bad solution" ("Eating Well" 76) and to find "the best compromise" (73). In Derrida's view, it is impossible absolutely to avoid harming the other.

7. Schreiner's claims about the evolutionary value of "selflessness" resonate with current research on the importance in human evolution of the development of a capacity for empathy as necessary for collaboration and successful group sociality. See, for example, Cheney and Seyfarth. Recent research on meerkats may undermine some of Schreiner's conclusions, however; see Norris.

8. On Waldo's overshadowing by Lyndall in critical history, Deborah L. Shapple observes that "[w]hereas critics have frequently discussed *The Story of an African Farm* as a feminist novel centered on the struggles of Lyndall, the novel's male protagonist has received less serious attention" (84).

9. For one instance of how attention to species and animality can enhance a feminist or gender-focused analysis of Schreiner, we could turn to a passage from her uncompleted introduction of Mary Wollstonecraft's *Vindication of the Rights of Woman* in which she discusses a native South African wife whose husband casts her out as garbage once she is old enough to be replaced by a younger woman: "'What is the use of her? Beat her. Do not give her too much food. Ah, throw her away like the dog when it is dead'" (qtd. in Burdett 57). The dog in this image could be read simply as one of many possible figures of denigration and dehumanization, but a better reading might position this scene in a richer context of Schreiner's varied representations of dogs and domestic animals. See also my discussion below of Lyndall's relationship with Doss.

10. This letter also contains a less appealing passage: "I cannot quite understand how the sense of unity shall extend to the most miserable, drunken Bushman with his sloping forehead and protruding jaw who limps past my house, and stop when I stand at the Zoo and see Sally looking at me from behind her bars with her great, passionate, fierce, reflective eyes!—my little sister growing on slowly to be me!" (214). Schreiner's unfavorable comparison of a "drunken Bushman" to a sympathetic simian recalls the infamous comments by Darwin, discussed in my introduction, about his preference for the "heroic little monkey" over a "savage . . . haunted by the grossest superstitions" (618). Schreiner's comments here open the possibility of viewing her desire to link human with nonhuman life as tied to a desire to disassociate European from African life, although elsewhere Schreiner demonstrates "[s]tartlingly advanced" antiracist thinking, which argues against such a general conclusion (McClintock 259).

11. Ruth First and Ann Scott sum up the influence of Spencer's *First Principles* on Schreiner: "she learned that 'all matter is alive,' that the social order reflected a deeper biological order, and that progress was not an accident but a necessity—indeed a law underlying the whole of organic creation" (59). Schreiner memorably describes the effect of Spencer's book on her as a teenage girl: "I always think that when Christianity burst on the dark Roman world it was what that book was to me" (*Letters* 36).

12. On the *plaasroman*, see Coetzee, *White Writing* 63; also see Burdett 18: "Schreiner locates her narrative almost exclusively on the farm of its title, and then ruthlessly works with the landscape's literal, historical, and moral meanings."

13. The idea of humanness as defined by uprightness and by a drawing up from the ground has wide currency in Enlightenment thought. See Oliver for an examination of Heidegger's discussion of man's "erecting into free-standingness" and Johann Herder's conclusion that "the posture of man is upright; in this he is unique on earth. . . . We cannot but note with a sense of wonder the peculiar organization of powers, deriving from the erect posture of man by which, and by which alone, he became what he is: man" (qtd. in Oliver 90–94).

14. See also Burdett on Waldo: "Frequently represented as lying or squatting close to the ground, he functions as a kind of metonym for the African landscape" (41).

15. Coetzee is, of course, particularly well situated (especially for my purposes) as a reader of this novel in his identity as a South African novelist who has written extensively on animals and issues of nonhuman ethics—although this line of his thinking had not yet fully emerged at the time of this essay's first publication in 1986; the essay addresses animals only indirectly as part of a broader argument about the novel's representation of nature.

16. McClintock observes, "The vast veld gave [Schreiner] metaphysical grounds for her longing for the infinite, but also concealed the very real history of colonial plunder that gave her privileged access to this immensity. There was nothing infinite about the Karoo; it was fenced by missionary intrusion, colonial land laws, the history of dispossession and colonial rout" (266). McClintock suggests that Schreiner's feeling of access to an "infinite" wildness is itself a mystified form of privilege; while I don't entirely disagree, I also would stress the ways the novel itself recognizes the power dynamics inherent in any experience of nature or wildness.

17. Here we might think about the relation of what might be considered two distinct models of posthumanist thought: first, one associated with the familiar poststructuralist deconstruction of the subject; second, a more recent attempt, associated with animal studies, to move beyond anthropocentric understandings of humanness and animality or nonhumanness. The relation between these two forms of posthumanism has been a recurring topic for, among others, Cary Wolfe; see his *What Is Posthumanism?* and *Animal Rites*, where he argues that "the humanist concept of subjectivity is inseparable from the discourse and *institution* of speciesism" (43). For our purposes here, it may be useful to consider that the Deleuze-Guattari model of "becoming-animal" has recently been repurposed as not just an exemplar of the poststructuralist "critique of the subject" but also as an important logic within postanthropocentric or animal-studies efforts to resituate the human within a broader species frame, and as such a bridging concept between the two approaches.

18. Gilbert and Gubar describe Tant' Sannie as "a huge, foreign woman whose search for a third husband seems to hint at a terrible female voracity" (56).

19. We could understand Tant' Sannie's bad dreams as figuring the revenge of the farm's creatures, however ineffectual, against her. A more explicit scene of a kind of nonhuman revenge can be found when the malign Bonaparte is terrified—and, at least momentarily, prevented from stealing Waldo's family possessions and papers—by what

he perceives as a ghost, but which is in fact an ostrich who has taken a dislike to the interloper: "He stuffed the papers into his pocket. As he did so, three slow and distinct taps were given on the crown of his head. . . . With terrific shrieks he fled, casting no glance behind" (Schreiner, *The Story* 68). Burdett explains how Schreiner's novel is positioned in relation to a South African economic history in which ostrich farming plays an important role: "[T]he first incubator for breeding ostriches was a British innovation. It helped in the expansion of an industry the export revenue for which tripled between 1869 and 1874 as farmers responded to the growing demand for ostrich feathers by the European fashion industry. . . . Set [in 1862] just prior to the boom in ostrich farming, the novel is also set on the cusp of South Africa's economic transformation into a world exporter of minerals" (41–42). This history complicates, of course, a reading of the ostrich as a native or indigenous creature of the farm: like Waldo, the bird is of foreign origin but is now adapted to the local context.

20. Christopher Hamlin provides a fascinating discussion of "the cremation controversy" that began in England "in 1874 and persisted for the rest of the century," a controversy that included a "preoccupation with imagining the courses of atoms as they move in and out of bodies" (14). As Hamlin explains, progressive believers in cremation, some of whom joined the Cremation Society, believed that human bodies should be cremated in order "to give the body's atoms, particularly its carbon, maximum mobility to move on to new and beneficent uses as soon as possible" (15).

21. Thomas Hardy was also fascinated by the possibility of human and animal bodies being "composted" into earth and then into new life-forms. In fact, he—like Schreiner—looked to Percy Shelley's "To a Skylark" for an image of this process; his poem "Shelley's Skylark," first published in the 1902 collection *Poems of the Past and the Present*, muses on the bird that inspired Shelley: "Lived its meek life; then, one day, fell / A little ball of feather and bone; / And how it perished, when piped farewell, / And where it wastes, are alike unknown. / Maybe it rests in the loam I view" (*Complete Poems* 101).

22. In contrast with Schreiner's depiction of the cows' indifference, her assertion of the tarantulas' *interest*, peering out "to see what was going on," could certainly be accused of anthropocentrism: if they are roused by the sound vibrations of Bonaparte's howling, should this really be understood as interest? In this regard Schreiner is inconsistent, freely shifting in and out of anthropomorphic language to describe nonhuman behavior, at times seeming to invoke very human frames of understanding as, perhaps, the best available means of acknowledging nonhuman intentionality or perception. Such inconsistency was in fact typical of the work of late-century scientists like Huxley and George Romanes. On the ways early twentieth-century ethologists defined themselves as anti-anthropocentric (in ways that some scientists are now, in turn, rejecting as too extreme) in reaction to the work of late-Victorian animal researchers like Romanes, see the introduction to *Thinking with Animals: New Perspectives on Anthropomorphism*, edited by Lorraine Daston and Gregg Mitman.

23. The images of Doss "following" Waldo and Lyndall recall a charming image from an 1899 letter in which Schreiner describes a visit to the rural South African farm of her husband's cousin (she married Samuel Cron Cronwright in 1894): "There is a little puppy here I love as I hardly ever loved a puppy before. . . . Cron's cousin would

give it to me but if there is war I can't go about with my little chain of puppies behind me" (*Letters* 383).

24. In this regard we could also consider Heidegger's association of human distinction with the hand as opposed to the paw; e.g., "No animal has a hand, and never does there arise a hand from a paw or a claw or a talon" (80).

25. In a letter to Karl Pearson, Schreiner repeats this sentiment in a form that emphasizes power less than tenderness: "That writing . . . on the first page, was written when I was 13, to remind me when I got rich and strong to be tender to everything that was weak and lonely as I was then" (qtd. in First and Scott 55).

26. Another way to think about this: earlier in the novel, Waldo experiences a profound revelation and "startled joy" when he discovers and reads a book by John Stuart Mill. Mill leads him to see that "he was not alone, not alone" because "there were men to whom not only kopjes and stones were calling out imperatively, 'What are we, and how came we here?'" (Schreiner, *The Story* 76). At this point, then, he moves into the symbolic order of literature and cosmopolitan (British) print culture and *beyond* an earlier, intuitive personal theology that finds its meaning primarily in the natural South African world of "kopjes and stones" (and sheep and dung beetles). I am arguing that the novel eventually brings Waldo back to that more indigenous and noncognitive or nonintellectual order of kopjes and stones and animals.

27. Oliver argues that "Heidegger opposes the very concept of existence—at the heart of his notion of Dasein—to life, which he identifies with animals" (41).

28. Schreiner's "stretching" has something in common with the "groping" that Henri Bergson associates with élan vital. On Bergson's élan vital as "drive without design, a searching that is a 'groping,'" see Bennett, *Vibrant* 79.

29. Waldo's acts of greeting recall his naïve but kind father Otto's own tendencies: "It was not his way to pass a living creature without a word of greeting" (Schreiner, *The Story* 53).

Ablow, Rachel. *Victorian Pain*. Princeton, NJ: Princeton University Press, 2017.

Ackroyd, Peter. *Dickens*. New York: HarperCollins, 1990.

Agamben, Giorgio. *The Open: Man and Animal*. Translated by Kevin Attell. Stanford, CA: Stanford University Press, 2003.

Armstrong, Nancy. *How Novels Think: The Limits of Individualism from 1719–1900*. New York: Columbia University Press, 2005.

Babb, Howard. "Setting and Theme in *Far from the Madding Crowd*." In *Far from the Madding Crowd* by Thomas Hardy, edited by Robert C. Schweik, 370–81. Norton Critical Edition. New York: Norton, 1986.

Beer, Gillian. *Darwin's Plots: Evolutionary Narrative in Darwin, George Eliot and Nineteenth-Century Fiction*. London: Routledge & Kegan Paul, 1983.

Bending, Lucy. *The Representation of Bodily Pain in Late Nineteenth-Century English Culture*. Oxford: Clarendon, 2000.

Bennett, Jane. "Systems and Things: On Vital Materialism and Object-Oriented Philosophy." In *The Nonhuman Turn*, edited by Richard Grusin, 223–39. Minneapolis: University of Minnesota Press, 2015.

———. *Vibrant Matter: A Political Ecology of Things*. Durham, NC: Duke University Press, 2010.

Berger, John. "Why Look at Animals?" In *About Looking*, 1–26. New York: Pantheon, 1980.

Boggs, Colleen Glenney. *Animalia Americana: Animal Representations and Biopolitical Subjectivity*. New York: Columbia University Press, 2013.

Bourke, Joanna. "Sexual Violence, Marital Guidance, and Victorian Bodies: An Aesthesiology." *Victorian Studies* 50.3 (2008): 419–36.

Brontë, Anne. *Agnes Grey*. Edited by Robert Inglesfield and Hilda Marsden. Oxford World's Classics. Oxford: Oxford University Press, 1991.

Brontë, Charlotte. *Jane Eyre*. Edited by Margaret Smith. Oxford World's Classics. Oxford: Oxford University Press, 1975.

Brontë, Charlotte, and Emily Brontë. *The Belgian Essays: A Critical Edition*. Edited and translated by Sue Lonoff. New Haven, CT: Yale University Press, 1996.

Brontë, Emily. *Wuthering Heights*. Edited by Ian Jack. Oxford World's Classics. Oxford: Oxford University Press, 1976.

Brooks, Peter. *Reading for the Plot: Design and Intention in Narrative*. Cambridge, MA: Harvard University Press, 1984.

Burdett, Carolyn. *Olive Schreiner and the Progress of Feminism: Evolution, Gender, Empire*. London: Palgrave Macmillan, 2001.

Butler, Judith. *Frames of War: When Is Life Grievable?* London: Verso, 2010.

———. *Precarious Life: The Powers of Mourning and Violence*. London: Verso, 2004.

Calarco, Matthew. *Zoographies: The Question of the Animal from Heidegger to Derrida*. New York: Columbia University Press, 2008.

Carroll, Lewis. *Alice in Wonderland*. Edited by Donald J. Gray. Norton Critical Editions. 3rd ed. New York: Norton, 2013.

Carson, Anne. "The Glass Essay." In *Glass, Irony, and God*, 1–38. New York: New Directions, 1995.

Cheney, Dorothy L., and Robert M. Seyfarth. *Baboon Metaphysics: The Evolution of a Social Mind.* Chicago: University of Chicago Press, 2007.

Chez, Keridiana W. *Victorian Dogs, Victorian Men: Affect and Animals in Nineteenth-Century Literature and Culture*. Columbus: Ohio State University Press, 2017.

Christ, Carol. "Aggression and Providential Death in George Eliot's Fiction." *NOVEL: A Forum on Fiction* 9.2 (1976): 130–40.

Cobbe, Frances Power. *Life of Frances Power Cobbe, by Herself*. Boston: Houghton-Mifflin, 1895.

———. *The Modern Rack: Papers on Vivisection*. London: Swan Sonnenschein, 1889.

Coetzee, J. M. *Disgrace*. New York: Penguin, 2000.

———. *White Writing: On the Culture of Letters in South Africa*. New Haven, CT: Yale University Press, 1988.

Cohn, Elisha. *Still Life: Suspended Development in the Victorian Novel*. Oxford: Oxford University Press, 2016.

Conan Doyle, Sir Arthur. "The Adventure of the Priory School." In *The New Annotated Sherlock Holmes*, edited by Leslie S. Klinger, vol. 2, 932–75. New York: Norton, 2005.

———. *The Hound of the Baskervilles*. Foreword and afterword by John Fowles. London: John Murray and Jonathan Cape, 1974.

Cosslett, Tess. *Talking Animals in British Children's Fiction, 1786–1914*. London: Routledge, 2006.

Darwin, Charles. *The Descent of Man, and Selection in Relation to Sex*. 2nd ed. London: John Murray, 1874. http://darwin-online.org.uk/content/frameset?itemID=F944&viewtype=text&pageseq=1.

———. Notebook B: Transmutation of species, 1837–38. CUL-DAR121. Transcribed by Kees Rookmaaker. Darwin Online, http://darwin-online.org.uk/.

———. Notebook M: Metaphysics on morals and speculations on expression, 1838. CUL-DAR125. Transcribed by Kees Rookmaaker, edited by Paul Barrett. Darwin Online, http://darwin-online.org.uk/.

———. *On the Origin of Species by Means of Natural Selection, or the Preservation of*

Favoured Races in the Struggle for Life. London: John Murray, 1859. http://darwin
-online.org.uk/content/frameset?itemID=F373&viewtype=side&pageseq=1.

———. *The Variation of Animals and Plants under Domestication.* 2nd ed. London:
John Murray, 1875. http://darwin-online.org.uk/content/frameset?itemID=F880.1&
viewtype=text&pageseq=1.

Daston, Lorraine, and Gregg Mitman, eds. *Thinking with Animals: New Perspectives
on Anthropomorphism.* New York: Columbia University Press, 2006.

Dayan, Colin. *The Law Is a White Dog: How Legal Rituals Make and Unmake Persons.*
Princeton, NJ: Princeton University Press, 2011.

DeKoven, Marianne. "Guest Column: Why Animals Now?" *PMLA* 124.2 (2009): 361–69.

Deleuze, Gilles, and Félix Guattari. *A Thousand Plateaus: Capitalism and Schizophre-
nia.* Translated by Brian Massumi. Minneapolis: University of Minnesota Press,
1987.

Derrida, Jacques. *The Animal That Therefore I Am.* Edited by Marie-Louise Mallet.
Translated by David Wills. New York: Fordham University Press, 2008.

———. "The Animal That Therefore I Am (More to Follow)." *Critical Inquiry* 28.2
(2002): 369–418.

———. *The Beast and the Sovereign, Volume I.* Translated by Geoffrey Bennington.
Chicago: University of Chicago Press, 2009.

———. *The Beast and the Sovereign, Volume II.* Translated by Geoffrey Bennington.
Chicago: University of Chicago Press, 2011.

———. "'Eating Well,' or the Calculation of the Subject." In *Points . . . : Interviews,
1974–1994,* edited by Elisabeth Weber, translated by Peggy Kamuf et al., 255–87.
Stanford, CA: Stanford University Press, 1995.

Derrida, Jacques, and Anne Dufourmantelle. *Of Hospitality.* Translated by Rachel
Bowlby. Stanford, CA: Stanford University Press, 2000.

Derrida, Jacques, and Elisabeth Roudinesco. *For What Tomorrow . . . : A Dialogue.*
Translated by Jeff Fort. Stanford, CA: Stanford University Press, 2004.

Dickens, Charles. *Bleak House.* Penguin Classics. New York: Penguin Books, 1996.

———. *David Copperfield.* Penguin Classics. New York: Penguin Books, 1996.

———. *Great Expectations.* Oxford World's Classics. Oxford: Oxford University Press,
1994.

———. "A Monument of French Folly." *Household Words,* March 8, 1851. http://www
.djo.org.uk/household-words/volume-ii/page-553.html.

———. *Oliver Twist.* Penguin Classics. New York: Penguin Books, 1966.

"Dogs of Literature." *Temple Bar: A London Magazine for Town and Country Readers,*
April 1881, 476–500.

Durant, John R. "The Ascent of Nature in Darwin's *Descent of Man.*" In *The Darwinian Heritage,* edited by David Kohn, 283–305. Princeton, NJ: Princeton University
Press, 2014.

Eagleton, Terry. *Myths of Power: A Marxist Study of the Brontës.* London: Macmillan,
1975.

Eco, Umberto. "Horns, Hooves, Insteps: Some Hypotheses on Three Types of Abduction." In *The Sign of Three: Dupin, Holmes, Peirce,* edited by Umberto Eco and
Thomas A. Sebeok, 198–220. Bloomington: Indiana University Press, 1988.

Eliot, George. *Adam Bede*. Edited by Carol A. Martin. New York: Oxford University Press, 2001.

———. *Daniel Deronda*. Penguin Classics. New York: Penguin, 1995.

———. *Middlemarch*. Edited by Bert G. Hornback. Norton Critical Edition. New York: Norton, 2000.

———. *Scenes of Clerical Life*. Penguin Classics. New York: Penguin, 1998.

Emmeche, Claus. *The Garden in the Machine: The Emerging Science of Artificial Life*. Translated by Steven Sampson. Princeton, NJ: Princeton University Press, 1994.

———. "A Semiotical Reflection on Biology, Living Signs and Artificial Life." *Biology & Philosophy* 6.3 (1991): 325–40.

Esty, Jed. "The Colonial Bildungsroman: *The Story of an African Farm* and the Ghost of Goethe." *Victorian Studies* 49.3 (2007): 407–30.

First, Ruth, and Ann Scott. *Olive Schreiner*. London: Women's Press, 1989.

Flegel, Monica. *Pets and Domesticity in Victorian Literature and Culture: Animality, Queer Relations, and the Victorian Family*. New York: Routledge, 2015.

Foucault, Michel. *Security, Territory, Population: Lectures at the College de France, 1977–78*. Edited by Michel Senellart. Translated by Graham Burchell. Houndmills: Palgrave Macmillan, 2007.

Fraiman, Susan. "Pussy Panic versus Liking Animals: Tracking Gender in Animal Studies." *Critical Inquiry* 39.1 (2012): 89–115.

François, Anne-Lise. *Open Secrets: The Literature of Uncounted Experience*. Stanford, CA: Stanford University Press, 2007.

Freedgood, Elaine. *The Ideas in Things: Fugitive Meaning in the Victorian Novel*. Chicago: University of Chicago Press, 2006.

French, Richard D. *Antivivisection and Medical Science in Victorian Society*. Princeton, NJ: Princeton University Press, 1975.

Freud, Sigmund. *Civilization and Its Discontents*. Introduction by Peter Gay. New York: Norton, 1989.

Fudge, Erica. *Animal*. London: Reaktion, 2002.

"Funeral-Fancying Dog." *Chambers's Edinburgh Journal*, Saturday, Marsh 28, 1846, 208.

Gallagher, Catherine. *The Body Economic: Life, Death and Sensation in Political Economy and the Victorian Novel*. Princeton, NJ: Princeton University Press, 2006.

Gallagher, Catherine, and Stephen Greenblatt. *Practicing New Historicism*. Chicago: University of Chicago Press, 2000.

Gaskell, Elizabeth. *The Life of Charlotte Brontë*. Edited by Alan Shelston. New York: Penguin, 1979.

Gilbert, Sandra M., and Susan Gubar. *No Man's Land: The Place of the Woman Writer in the Twentieth Century, Vol. 2: Sexchanges*. New Haven, CT: Yale University Press, 1989.

Ginzburg, Carlo. "Morelli, Freud, and Sherlock Holmes: Clues and Scientific Method." In *The Sign of Three: Dupin, Holmes, Peirce*, edited by Umberto Eco and Thomas A. Sebeok, 81–118. Bloomington: Indiana University Press, 1988.

Goff, Barbara Munson. "Between Natural Theology and Natural Selection: Breeding the Human Animal in *Wuthering Heights*." *Victorian Studies* 27.4 (1984): 477–508.

Gompertz, Lewis. *Moral Inquiries on the Situation of Man and of Brutes*. On the

Crime of Committing Cruelty on Brutes, and of Sacrificing Them to the Purposes of Man; with Further Reflections. London: printed by author, 1824.

Graver, Suzanne. *George Eliot and Community: A Study in Social Theory and Fictional Form*. Berkeley: University of California Press, 1984.

Gregory, James. *Of Victorians and Vegetarians: The Vegetarian Movement in Nineteenth-Century Britain*. New York: I. B. Tauris, 2007.

Greiner, Rae. *Sympathetic Realism in Nineteenth-Century British Fiction*. Baltimore: Johns Hopkins University Press, 2012.

Grusin, Richard. *The Nonhuman Turn*. Minneapolis: University of Minnesota Press, 2015.

Hall, Marshall. "On Experiments in Physiology, as a Question of Medical Ethics." *The Lancet* 49.1220 (1847): 58–60.

Hamilton, Susan. "On the Cruelty to Animals Act, 15 August 1876." *BRANCH: Britain, Representation and Nineteenth-Century History*. Edited by Dino Franco Felluga. Extension of *Romanticism and Victorianism on the Net*. http://www .branchcollective.org/?ps_articles=susan-hamilton-on-the-cruelty-to-animals-act -15-august-1876. Accessed December 8, 2017.

Hamlin, Christopher. "Good and Intimate Filth." In *Filth: Dirt, Disgust, and Modern Life*, edited by William A. Cohen and Ryan Johnson, 3–29. Minneapolis: University of Minnesota Press, 2004.

Haraway, Donna J. *The Companion Species Manifesto: Dogs, People, and Significant Otherness*. Chicago: Prickly Paradigm Press, 2003.

———. *When Species Meet*. Minneapolis: University of Minnesota Press, 2007.

Hardy, Thomas. *Complete Poems*. New York: Palgrave Macmillan, 2001.

———. *Far from the Madding Crowd*. Edited by Rosemarie Morgan with Shannon Russell. Penguin Classics. New York: Penguin, 2000.

———. *Jude the Obscure*. Edited by Norman Page. Norton Critical Edition. New York: Norton, 1978.

———. *The Life and Work of Thomas Hardy*. Edited by Michael Millgate. Houndmills: Macmillan, 1984.

———. *The Personal Notebooks of Thomas Hardy*. Edited by Richard H. Taylor. Houndmills: Macmillan, 1979.

———. *The Return of the Native*. Edited by Simon Gatrell. Oxford: Oxford University Press, 1990.

———. *Tess of the D'Urbervilles*. Edited by Tim Dolin. Introduction by Margaret R. Higonnet. Penguin Classics. New York: Penguin, 1998.

———. *The Trumpet-Major*. Edited by Richard Nemesvari. Oxford: Oxford University Press, 1991.

Harrison, Brian. "Animals and the State in Nineteenth-Century England." *English Historical Review* 88.349 (1973): 786–820.

Head, Dominic. "Ecocriticism and the Novel." In *The Green Studies Reader: From Romanticism to Ecocriticism*, edited by Laurence Coupe, 235–41. New York: Routledge, 2000.

Hearne, Vicki. *Adam's Task: Calling Animals by Name*. New York: HarperPerennial, 1994.

Heidegger, Martin. *Parmenides*. Translated by André Schuwer and Richard Rojcewicz. Bloomington: Indiana University Press, 1998.

Henchman, Anna. "Tallow Candles and Meaty Air in *Bleak House*." *19: Interdisciplinary Studies in the Long Nineteenth Century* 25, December 1, 2017. http://doi.org/10.16995/ntn.794.

Hiley, Nicholas. "George Gately: Cartoonist Whose Cool Cat Became an American Institution." *The Guardian*, October 6, 2001.

Hobbes, Thomas. *Leviathan*. Edited by John Charles Addison Gaskin. Oxford: Oxford University Press, 1998.

Huxley, Thomas. "On the Method of Zadig: Retrospective Prophecy as a Function of Science." In *Science and Culture and Other Essays*, 135–55. New York: Appleton and Co., 1882.

Ingold, Tim. "Introduction." In *What Is an Animal?*, edited by Tim Ingold, 1–16. London: Routledge, 1994.

Jaffe, Audrey. *Scenes of Sympathy: Identity and Representation in Victorian Fiction*. Ithaca, NY: Cornell University Press, 2000.

Jameson, Fredric. *The Antinomies of Realism*. London: Verso, 2013.

"Jesse's Scenes and Tales of Country Life." *Chambers's Edinburgh Journal*, May 11, 1844, 299–301.

Johnson, Bruce. "'The Perfection of Species' and Hardy's Tess." In *Nature and the Victorian Imagination*, edited by U. C. Knoepflmacher and G. B. Tennyson, 259–80. Berkeley: University of California Press, 1977.

Kaplan, Fred. *Dickens: A Biography*. Baltimore: Johns Hopkins University Press, 1998.

Kawade, Yoshimi. "On the Nature of the Subjectivity of Living Things." *Biosemiotics* 2.2 (2009): 205–20.

Kean, Hilda. *Animal Rights: Political and Social Change in Britain since 1800*. London: Reaktion, 1998.

Keenleyside, Heather. *Animals and Other People: Literary Forms and Living Beings in the Long Eighteenth Century*. Philadelphia: University of Pennsylvania Press, 2016.

Kerridge, Richard. "Ecological Hardy." In *Beyond Nature Writing: Expanding the Boundaries of Ecocriticism*, edited by Karla M. Armbruster and Kathleen R. Wallace, 126–42. Charlottesville: University of Virginia Press, 2001.

Ketabgian, Tamara. *The Lives of Machines: The Industrial Imaginary in Victorian Literature and Culture*. Ann Arbor: University of Michigan Press, 2011.

Kete, Kathleen. "Animals and Ideology: The Politics of Animal Protection in Europe." In *Representing Animals*, edited by Nigel Rothfels, 19–34. Bloomington: Indiana University Press, 2002.

———. *The Beast in the Boudoir: Petkeeping in Nineteenth-Century Paris*. Berkeley: University of California Press, 1994.

King, Amy. "Reorienting the Scientific Frontier: Victorian Tide Pools and Literary Realism." *Victorian Studies* 47.2 (2005): 153–63.

Kohn, Eduardo. *How Forests Think: Toward an Anthropology beyond the Human*. Berkeley: University of California Press, 2013.

Kreilkamp, Ivan. "The Ass Got a Verdict: Martin's Act and the Founding of the Society for the Prevention of Cruelty to Animals, 1822." *BRANCH: Britain, Representa-

tion and Nineteenth-Century History. Edited by Dino Franco Felluga. Extension
    of *Romanticism and Victorianism on the Net.* November 1, 2012. http://www
    .branchcollective.org/?ps_articles=ivan-kreilkamp-the-ass-got-a-verdict-martins-act
    -and-the-founding-of-the-society-for-the-prevention-of-cruelty-to-animals-1822.

———. "Can Fiction Show Us How Animals Think?" *New Yorker*, April 21, 2015.
    https://www.newyorker.com/books/page-turner/can-fiction-show-us-how-animals
    -think.

Kucich, John. "Olive Schreiner, Masochism, and Omnipotence: Strategies of a Preoedi-
    pal Politics." *NOVEL: A Forum on Fiction* 36.1 (2002): 79–109.

———. "Psychoanalytic Historicism: Shadow Discourse and the Gender Politics of Mas-
    ochism in Ellis, Schreiner, and Haggard." *PMLA* 126.1 (2011): 88–106.

Kuzniar, Alice A. *Melancholia's Dog: Reflections on Our Animal Kinship.* Chicago:
    University of Chicago Press, 2013.

LaCapra, Dominick. *History and Its Limits: Human, Animal, Violence.* Ithaca, NY:
    Cornell University Press, 2009.

Lamb, Jonathan. "Modern Metamorphoses and Disgraceful Tales." *Critical Inquiry* 28.1
    (2001): 133–66.

Langbaum, Robert. "Hardy: Versions of Pastoral." *Victorian Literature and Culture* 20
    (1992): 245–72.

Lansbury, Coral. *The Old Brown Dog: Women, Workers, and Vivisection in Edwardian
    England.* Madison: University of Wisconsin Press, 1985.

Lanzoni, Susan. "Sympathy in *Mind* (1876–1900)." *Journal of the History of Ideas* 70.2
    (2009): 265–87.

Lee, Michael Parrish. "Reading Meat in H. G. Wells." *Studies in the Novel* 42.3 (2010):
    249–68.

Levine, George. *Darwin and the Novelists: Patterns of Science in Victorian Fiction.*
    Cambridge, MA: Harvard University Press, 1988.

———. *Dying to Know: Scientific Epistemology and Narrative in Victorian England.*
    Chicago: University of Chicago Press, 2002.

———. "Hardy and Darwin: An Enchanting Hardy." In *A Companion to Thomas Hardy*,
    edited by Keith Wilson, 36–51. Malden, MA: Wiley-Blackwell, 2009.

Lévi-Strauss, Claude. *The Savage Mind.* Chicago: University of Chicago Press, 1962.

Lewes, George Henry. *Sea-Side Studies at Ilfracombe, Tenby, the Scilly Isles, & Jersey.*
    Edinburgh: William Blackwell & Sons, 1859.

Loudon, Jane Webb. *Domestic Pets: Their Habits and Management.* London: Grant
    and Griffith, 1851. https://play.google.com/books/reader?id=uDwDAAAAQAAJ&
    printsec=frontcover&output=reader&hl=en&pg=GBS.PR1.

Lupton, Julia Reinhard. "Creature Caliban." *Shakespeare Quarterly* 51.1 (2000): 1–23.

Lynch, Deidre Shauna. *Loving Literature: A Cultural History.* Chicago: University of
    Chicago Press, 2015.

Mallett, Phillip. "Hardy and the Biographers." In *The Ashgate Research Companion
    to Thomas Hardy*, edited by Rosemarie Morgan, 465–83. Burlington, VT: Ashgate,
    2010.

Mangum, Teresa. "Animal Angst: Victorians Memorialize Their Pets." In *Victorian
    Animal Dreams: Representations of Animals in Victorian Literature and Culture,*

edited by Deborah Denenholz Morse and Martin A. Danahay, 15–34. Burlington, VT: Ashgate, 2007.

———. "Dog Years, Human Fears." In Representing Animals, edited by Nigel Rothfels, 35–47. Bloomington: Indiana University Press, 2002.

Manuel, Diana. "Marshall Hall (1790–1857): Vivisection and the Development of Experimental Physiology." In Vivisection in Historical Perspective, edited by Nicolaas A. Rupke, 78–104. London: Croom Helm, 1987.

Margulis, Lynn, and Dorion Sagan. Acquiring Genomes: A Theory of the Origins of Species. New York: Basic Books, 2002.

Maxwell, Richard. "Unnumbered Polypi." Victorian Poetry 47.1 (2009): 7–23.

McClintock, Anne. Imperial Leather: Race, Gender and Sexuality in the Colonial Contest. New York: Routledge, 1995.

McHugh, Susan. Animal Stories: Narrating across Species Lines. Minneapolis: University of Minnesota Press, 2011.

Menely, Tobias. The Animal Claim: Sensibility and the Creaturely Voice. Chicago: University of Chicago Press, 2015.

Menke, Richard. "Fiction as Vivisection: G. H. Lewes and George Eliot." ELH 67.2 (2000): 617–53.

Meyer, Susan. Imperialism at Home: Race and Victorian Women's Fiction. Ithaca, NY: Cornell University Press, 1996.

Miller, D. A. "George Eliot: 'The Wisdom of Balancing Claims.'" In Middlemarch: New Casebooks, edited by John Peck, 84–94. Houndmills: Macmillan, 1992.

Miller, J. Hillis. The Disappearance of God: Five Nineteenth-Century Writers. Cambridge, MA: Belknap Press, 1975.

Millgate, Michael. Thomas Hardy: A Biography Revisited. Oxford: Oxford University Press, 2004.

Morgentaler, Goldie. "Meditating on the Low: A Darwinian Reading of Great Expectations." Studies in English Literature, 1500–1900 38.4 (1998): 707–21.

Morrison, Ronald D. "Humanity towards Man, Woman, and the Lower Animals: Thomas Hardy's Jude the Obscure and the Victorian Humane Movement." Nineteenth-Century Studies 12 (1998): 64–82.

Müller, Max. Lectures on the Science of Language: Delivered at the Royal Institution of Great Britain in April, May, & June, 1861. London: Longman, Green, Longman, Roberts, & Green, 1864. Hathitrust Digital Library: https://catalog.hathitrust.org/Record/007668375.

Nash, Richard. "Joy and Pity: Reading Animal Bodies in Late Eighteenth-Century Culture," The Eighteenth Century 52.1 (Spring 2011): 47–67.

Norris, Scott. "Murderous Meerkat Moms Contradict Caring Image, Study Finds." National Geographic News, March 15, 2006. http://news.nationalgeographic.com/news/2006/03/0315_060315_meerkats.html.

Nussbaum, Martha C. Frontiers of Justice: Disability, Nationality, Species Membership. Cambridge, MA: Harvard University Press, 2006.

Nussey, Ellen. "From Reminiscences of Charlotte Brontë [1871]." In Jane Eyre. Norton Critical Edition, 4th ed., edited by Deborah Lutz, 426–29. New York: W. W. Norton, 2016.

O'Connor, Erin. *Raw Material: Producing Pathology in Victorian Culture*. Durham, NC: Duke University Press, 2000.

Oliver, Kelly. *Animal Lessons: How They Teach Us to Be Human*. New York: Columbia University Press, 2009.

Pearson, Susan J. *The Rights of the Defenseless: Protecting Animals and Children in Gilded Age America*. Chicago: University of Chicago Press, 2011.

Peirce, C. S. "Man's Glassy Essence." In *The Essential Peirce: Selected Philosophical Writings, Volume I*, edited by Nathan Houser and Christian Kloesel, 334–51. Bloomington: Indiana University Press, 1992.

———. "Prolegomena to an Apology for Pragmaticism." *The Monist* 16.4 (October 1906): 492–546.

Peterson, Christie. "'The Level of the Beasts that Perish': Animalized Text in Charlotte Elizabeth Tonna's *Helen Fleetwood*." *Victorian Review* 37.1 (2011): 108–26.

Philpotts, Trey. "Mad Bulls and Dead Meat: Smithfield Market as Reality and Symbol." *Dickens Studies Annual* 41 (2010): 25–44.

Poovey, Mary. *Uneven Developments: The Ideological Work of Gender in Mid-Victorian England*. Chicago: University of Chicago Press,. 1988.

"Reply to Dr. Marshall Hall." *The Lancet* 49.1222 (1847): 135.

Richter, Virginia. *Literature after Darwin: Human Beasts in Western Fiction, 1859–1939*. London: Palgrave, 2011.

Ritvo, Harriet. *The Animal Estate: The English and Other Creatures in the Victorian Age*. Cambridge, MA: Harvard University Press, 1987.

———. *The Platypus and the Mermaid: And Other Figments of the Classifying Imagination*. Cambridge, MA: Harvard University Press, 1997.

Robles, Mario Ortiz. *Literature and Animal Studies*. Literature and Contemporary Thought Series. New York: Routledge, 2016.

Roosth, Sophia. "Screaming Yeast: Sonocytology, Cytoplasmic Milieus, and Cellular Subjectivities." *Critical Inquiry* 35.2 (2009): 332–50.

Rosner, Mary. "Reading the Beasts of *Martin Chuzzlewit*." *Dickens Quarterly* 4.3 (1987): 131–41.

Rothfels, Nigel, ed. *Representing Animals*. Bloomington: Indiana University Press, 2002.

Rothfield, Lawrence. *Vital Signs: Medical Realism in Nineteenth-Century Fiction*. Princeton, NJ: Princeton University Press, 1993.

Salt, Henry. *Animals' Rights: Considered in Relation to Social Progress*. Edited and with an introduction by Peter Singer. London: Society for Animals' Rights, 1980.

Samyn, Jeannette. "George Eliot, George Henry Lewes, and Parasitic Form." *Studies in English Literature* 58.4 (Autumn 2018), forthcoming.

Santner, Eric L. *On Creaturely Life: Rilke, Benjamin, Sebald*. Chicago: University of Chicago Press, 2006.

Saunders, [Margaret] Marshall. *Beautiful Joe: An Autobiography*. Introduction by Hezekiah Butterworth. Philadelphia: Griffith & Rowland, 1893.

Scarry, Elaine. *The Body in Pain: The Making and Unmaking of the World*. Oxford: Oxford University Press, 1985.

———. "On Vivacity: The Difference between Daydreaming and Imagining-under-Authorial-Instruction." *Representations* 52 (1995): 1–26.

———. "Work and the Body in Hardy and Other Nineteenth-Century Novelists." *Representations* 3 (1983): 90–123.

Schmitt, Cannon. *Darwin and the Memory of the Human: Evolution, Savages, and South America*. Cambridge: Cambridge University Press, 2009.

Schreiner, Olive. *From Man to Man*. London: Virago Press, 1982.

———. *Letters: Volume I: 1871–1899*. Edited by Richard Rive with Russell Martin. Oxford: Oxford University Press, 1988.

———. *The Story of an African Farm*. Oxford: Oxford University Press, 2009.

Schulz, Kathryn. "The Rabbit-Hole Rabbit Hole." *New Yorker*, June 4, 2015. http://www .newyorker.com/culture/cultural-comment/the-rabbit-hole-rabbit-hole.

Sebeok, Thomas A. *Signs: An Introduction to Semiotics*. Toronto: University of Toronto Press, 2001.

Sedgwick, Eve Kosofsky. *Between Men: English Literature and Male Homosocial Desire*. New York: Columbia University Press, 1985.

Sewell, Anna. *Black Beauty: The Autobiography of a Horse*. London: Jerrold & Sons, 1877.

Shapple, Deborah L. "Artful Tales of Origination in Olive Schreiner's *The Story of an African Farm*." *Nineteenth-Century Literature* 59.1 (2004): 78–114.

Shell, Marc. *Children of the Earth: Literature, Politics and Nationhood*. Oxford: Oxford University Press, 1993.

Showalter, Elaine. *A Literature of Their Own*. London: Virago, 1978.

Shuttleworth, Sally. *George Eliot and Nineteenth-Century Science: The Make-Believe of a Beginning*. Cambridge: Cambridge University Press, 1984.

Singer, Peter. *Animal Liberation*. New York: HarperCollins, 1975.

———. "Animal Liberation at Thirty." *New York Review of Books*, May 15, 2003, 23–26.

Smith, Barbara Herrnstein. "Animal Relatives, Difficult Relations." *differences: A Journal of Feminist Cultural Studies* 15.1 (2004): 1–23.

Smith, Jonathan. *Charles Darwin and Victorian Visual Culture*. Cambridge: Cambridge University Press, 2006.

Smith, Jonathan Z. "The Domestication of Sacrifice." In *Violent Origins: Walter Burkert, René Girard, and Jonathan Z. Smith on Ritual Killing and Cultural Formation*, edited by Robert G. Hamerton-Kelly, 191–205. Stanford, CA: Stanford University Press, 1987.

Spencer, Herbert. *First Principles*. New York: De Witt Revolving Fund, 1958.

Squires, Michael. "*Far from the Madding Crowd* as Modified Pastoral." *Nineteenth-Century Fiction* 25.3 (1970): 299–326.

Stallybrass, Peter, and Allon White. *The Politics and Poetics of Transgression*. Ithaca, NY: Cornell University Press, 1986.

Sternberger, Dolf. *Panorama of the Nineteenth Century*. Translated by Joachim Neugroschel. Introduction by Erich Heller. New York: Urizen: 1977.

Straley, Jessica. *Evolution and Imagination in Victorian Children's Literature*. Cambridge: Cambridge University Press, 2016.

Sumpter, Caroline. "On Suffering and Sympathy: *Jude the Obscure*, Evolution, and Ethics." *Victorian Studies* 53.4 (2011): 665–87.

Surridge, Lisa. "Animals and Violence in *Wuthering Heights*." *Brontë Society Transactions* 24.2 (1999): 161–73.

Sussman, Herbert, and Gerhard Joseph. "Prefiguring the Posthuman: Dickens and Prosthesis." *Victorian Literature and Culture* 32.2 (2004): 617–28.

Swabe, Joanna. *Animals, Disease and Human Society: Human-Animal Relations and the Rise of Veterinary Medicine.* London: Routledge, 1999.

Tambling, Jeremy. "*Middlemarch*, Realism and the Birth of the Clinic." *ELH* 57.4 (1990): 939–60.

Tamen, Miguel. *Friends of Interpretable Objects.* Cambridge, MA: Harvard University Press, 2004.

Thomas, Keith. *Man and the Natural World: Changing Attitudes in England 1500–1800.* London: Allen Lane, 1983.

Turner, James. *Reckoning with the Beast: Animals, Pain, and Humanity in the Victorian Mind.* Baltimore: Johns Hopkins University Press, 1980.

Van Ghent, Dorothy. "The Dickens World: A View from Todger's." *The Sewanee Review* 58.3 (Jul.–Sep. 1950): 419–38.

Van Sant, Ann Jessie. *Eighteenth-Century Sensibility and the Novel: The Senses in Social Context.* Cambridge: Cambridge University Press, 1993.

Warhol, Robyn. "'It Is of Little Use for Me to Tell You': George Eliot's Narrative Refusals." In *A Companion to George Eliot*, edited by Amanda Anderson and Harry E. Shaw, 46–61. Oxford: Wiley-Blackwell, 2013.

Watt, Ian. "Oral Dickens." In *Great Expectations* by Charles Dickens, edited by Edgar Rosenberg, 674–79. Norton Critical Edition. New York: Norton, 1999.

Webb, Stephen H. *Of God and Dogs: A Christian Theology of Compassion for Animals.* Oxford: Oxford University Press, 1998.

Weil, Kari. *Thinking Animals: Why Animal Studies Now?* New York: Columbia University Press, 2012.

White, Paul S. "The Experimental Animal in Victorian Britain." In *Thinking with Animals: New Perspectives on Anthropomorphism*, edited by Lorraine Daston and Gregg Mitman, 59–81. New York: Columbia University Press, 2005.

Williams, Raymond. *The Country and the City.* Oxford: Oxford University Press, 1973.

Winter, Sarah. "Darwin's Saussure: Biosemiotics and Race in *Expression*." *Representations* 107.1 (2009): 128–61.

Wolfe, Cary. *Animal Rites: American Culture, the Discourse of Species, and Posthumanist Theory.* Chicago: University of Chicago Press, 2003.

———. *What Is Posthumanism?* Minneapolis: University of Minnesota Press, 2009.

———, ed. *Zoontologies: The Question of the Animal.* Minneapolis: University of Minnesota Press, 2003.

Woloch, Alex. *The One vs. the Many: Minor Characters and the Space of the Protagonist in the Novel.* Princeton, NJ: Princeton University Press, 2003.

INDEX

＝＝＝＝＝

Page numbers in italics refer to illustrations.